D1124588

America's Other Voice

The Radio Liberty antenna farm at the Playa de Pals. (*Radio Liberty photograph.*)

Sig Mickelson

America's Other Voice

The Story of
Radio Free Europe
and
Radio Liberty

*For Ron Moore
with thanks for taking
such good care of our patient!

Sig Mickelson
Oct 19, 1983*

PRAEGER

PRAEGER SPECIAL STUDIES • PRAEGER SCIENTIFIC

Library of Congress Cataloging in Publication Data

Mickelson, Sig.
    America's other voice.

    Bibliography: p.
    Includes index.
    1. Radio Free Europe—History. 2. Radio Liberty
    (Munich, Germany)—History. I. Title.
HE8696.M52 1983   384.54' 53' 094   83-13659
ISBN 0-03-063224-2

Research for this book was sponsored by the Hoover Institution at Stanford University.

Published in 1983 by Praeger Publishers
CBS Educational and Professional Publishing
a Division of CBS Inc.
521 Fifth Avenue, New York, NY 10175 USA

© 1983 by Sig Mickelson

3456789 052 987654321

Printed in the United States of America
on acid-free paper

For Alan, Michael, Trevor, and Lars

Foreword

Anyone wishing to understand the complex and potentially explosive relations between the United States and the Communist bloc needs to understand the crisis-filled history, the accomplishments, and the enormous potential of Radio Free Europe and Radio Liberty. This book is the first and only full and frank treatment of the subject published to date. Sig Mickelson, following a long career as president of CBS News and later as president of RFE/RL, tells the story in broad perspective, lacing it with fascinating details and employing remarkable detachment and restraint. It is the story, as he says, "of intrigue, mystery, clandestine planning, sophisticated intelligence concepts and heavy-handed Communist attempts to demoralize or disrupt the flow of broadcasts." It is also the story of broadcast operations that can have enormous long-term impact if handled with wisdom and restraint.

As one who has twice been responsible for the Voice of America and the U.S. Information Service and served on the Board of RFE/RL (as well as editing a national news magazine and heading a major school of journalism), I believe Mickelson has performed an invaluable service in writing this book.

Early in the Cold War, distinguished public servants including James Forrestal, Allen Dulles, and Robert Joyce set up a plan to give outstanding émigrés from Eastern Europe a haven and something to do after they escaped from the Eastern-bloc countries. This led to the creation of the Free University in Europe and to Radio Free Europe. Partly as a matter of quick convenience, RFE was initially financed through CIA funds and some private donations. This was also a device to avoid having RFE directly identified with the U.S. government. Within a short time it was found that Radio Free Europe was playing a role far more important than that of providing useful activity for émigrés, by keeping citizens of Russia's satellites informed of what was going on in the outside world and, more importantly, what was going on in their own countries. Radio Free Europe's success soon led to the creation of Radio Liberty, directed at the Soviet Union itself.

Gradually, both Radios attained large and attentive audiences, generally larger than those of the Voice of America or the BBC. Both radios told of major developments in the outside world but did not concentrate on these or on official government pronouncements as does the Voice of America. In short, RFE and RL came to serve as a surrogate free press for the captive peoples.

One immediate purpose, in the apt phrase of Wallace Carroll, was that of "keeping the Russian bear so busy scratching its own fleas that it can cause less trouble to the rest of the world." A longer-term objective was that of keeping the captive peoples well-enough informed so that they could protest at least mildly when appropriate, so that they would retain long-term hope. In all of this it was important to avoid shrill exhortations and roundhouse denunciations of the Communist regimes and stridency in general—something that many members of Congress never fully recognized.

By the very nature of their set-ups, the Radios had internal troubles from time to time. These often resulted from the fact that some of the most brilliant émigrés felt so intensely about the governments in their homelands that stridency came naturally. (I even suspected that an occasional émigré, in the Voice as well as in the Free Radios, secretly desired nothing more than to instigate a war between the United States and the Communist regime in Russia.) In their early years RFE and RL had difficulty in controlling some of these voices. There also were broader difficulties reflecting the basic problem of mounting any sort of clandestine operation within a free society. Such problems finally led the Eisenhower Commission (on which I served) to recommend that U.S. Government support of RFE/RL be made quite open—but that they should have a degree of clear independence assured by a citizen board of directors and a European Advisory Committee. The recommendation was soon officially adopted, with funding and broad policy going to the Radios' board through a presidentially appointed Board of International Broadcasting. Under that admittedly cumbersome set-up, RFE and RL operated effectively for several years. Through its amazing system of monitoring the local press and radio in East Europe, interviewing émigrés and travelers, and otherwise collecting information, RFE/RL supplied the target audiences regularly with news they could not get through their own national channels.

In 1982, members of Congress, who sought "efficiency" and simply did not understand the subtleties involved, opted to abolish the citizen board and have the Radios work directly under the presidentially appointed board. This could work if that board proves wise enough to exercise restraint, concentrate on genuine news, and not feel obliged to parrot whatever hawkish views the administration in power at the moment might favor. Without such restraint, the credibility of RFE and RL could quickly be destroyed. Sig Mickelson's *America's Other Voice* should supply needed background and understanding to those grappling with the problem. It should help them comprehend an intricate and complex operation that requires sophisticated and deft handling.

EDWARD W. BARRETT

Contents

Acknowledgments

S O MANY PERSONS contributed cheerfully and at some inconvenience to themselves to reconstructing the story of America's little-known other voice that it would take much more space than is available to list them all. I am particularly grateful, though, to those few remaining persons who played significant parts in the creation of the two Radios in their little-known or understood earliest period, and to shepherding them through their formative stages: Larry Houston, Walter Pforzheimer, and Ray Cline, who were in a position to observe the birth of the Radios from their posts at the CIA; to Bob Lang and Gregory Thomas, the former Radio Free Europe's first director, the latter a long-time board member; to Tom Braden and Cord Meyer, who watched over the Radios from their CIA posts for more than two decades; and to Frank Lindsay, Jack Mitchell, and Allen Grover, who were among the very few who knew the real story of the origins of Radio Liberty. They knew the story because they were deeply and personally involved. Special thanks are due to Howland Sargeant who headed the Radio Liberty Committee for 21 years and was a rich source of background concerning that little-known institution. David Abshire made a major contribution, particularly through his graphic account of the negotiations leading to final passage of interim funding bills when the Radios were in deep jeopardy, and of the intensive efforts leading to the establishment of the Board for International Broadcasting.

It would take far too much space to list current and former RFE and RL employees who willingly answered questions about their roles and furnished in the process an invaluable record on audio tape for the Hoover Institution archives. Many of them are mentioned by name in the section headed *Notes on Sources*. Their number includes executives and lower-level workers alike; writers, reporters, announcers, technicians, researchers, program directors, and policy control personnel; American, Canadian, and British citizens, and refugees from the five East European countries and from Russia, the Ukraine, Belorussia, and the Tatar Bashkir Republic.

A list of acknowledgments would not be complete without recognizing the deep interest in the project demonstrated by the personnel at the Hoover Institution including associate director Dick Burress and publications distribution manager David Fleenor. Then, of course, there are Patrick Bernuth and his cohorts at Praeger, Lynne Nichols who typed the manuscript, and three exceedingly helpful secretaries at RFE/RL headquarters in Munich, Carolyn

Ruprecht, Ute Ettinger, and Alice Shankland, and one in New York, Justine Woollard. This could go on much longer. Surely some who have made major contributions have been slighted. My warm thanks to all of them and an apology for not naming them personally.

San Diego, California

SIG MICKELSON

Introduction

TENS OF MILLIONS OF PEOPLE around the world are familiar with America's official international short wave radio broadcasting organization, The Voice of America. Only a handful, however, have more than a smattering of information about America's other voice, Radio Free Europe and Radio Liberty. This volume is devoted to telling the story about that other voice.

Radio Free Europe and Radio Liberty are now generally considered only as important cogs in the United States' international broadcast machinery, somewhat suspect because of their CIA-related past, but cast in the same basic mold as the Voice of America. Only the more knowledgeable are aware that their mission is quite unlike that of the much better known VOA. Even fewer know much about their mysterious origins, how key international policy makers in the government and a number of influential private citizens maneuvered behind a thick screen of secrecy to bring the corporations into being. Nor do they remember many details of the international crisis that induced them to arrive at this novel solution. The fact is that RFE and RL are unprecedented instruments of public diplomacy, unlike anything in existence elsewhere in the world: they are wards of the government but not government agencies.

RFE and RL were organized as two entirely separate private corporations, chartered in New York and Delaware, respectively, and responsible to boards of directors made up of private citizens. Funding was furnished clandestinely through dummy foundations established for the purpose by the government's intelligence apparatus. One was incorporated in 1949 as the National Committee for a Free Europe and the other in 1951 as the American Committee for Freedom for the Peoples of the USSR, Inc. There was little communication between the two; in essence they represented separate cells of a secret society. Even their sources of policy guidance and funding were kept in separate and discrete units.

The two corporations were born out of a curious blend of charitable motives and a desperately felt need in government circles for developing new sources of intelligence concerning Communist intentions in Central and Western Europe and a better understanding of the methods that the Soviet Union was using to undermine democratic governments in the path of its westward expansion. The charitable motive arose out of the fact that hordes of penniless and hungry émigrés in the late 1940s were swarming into West Germany and other parts of Western Europe. Someone had to assume responsibility for feeding and clothing them and, in order to keep them from undergoing mass psychological breakdown, giving them something worthwhile to do. Western European governments, still recovering from the devastating war, lacked the resources or even the stability of government institutions to contribute, so the burden fell to the United States.

Some leading policy makers in the United States government, including notably the secretary of the newly created Department of Defense, James V. Forrestal, and the policy advisor to the Department of State, Robert Joyce, saw an opportunity to turn the problem to the nation's advantage. They recognized that furnishing charity and developing an invaluable intelligence resource were not necessarily incompatible: many of the refugees had been leaders in the societies from which they had emigrated, and their backgrounds could be used to obtain a better understanding of the techniques and devices that were being used by the Communists to undermine the democratic governments. Besides their serving as useful sources of intelligence, moreover, they could write articles or make statements that would have a powerful impact in their homelands, if a way could be found to deliver the material there.

Out of this set of conditions and this rationale came the forerunners of RFE and RL. Free Europe was organized first and it worked with refugees from Eastern Europe. Amcomlib, as it became known, followed and began its efforts with the emigration from the Soviet Union. Broadcasting, which ultimately became their sole function, was then considered as being only a possible fringe benefit, for full exploitation at such time as adequate facilities might become available.

How the parents of the Radios came into being as hybrid institutions, neither wholly governmental nor wholly private, is a fascinating side-bar to American history. It involves a number of actions that in retrospect seem inconsistent with traditional governmental decision making. An obscure and relatively minor intelligence group, the Office of Policy Coordination, which drew its budget from the CIA and its policy guidance from the Department of State but in fact paid little attention to either, was charged with the responsibility of overseeing the novel experiment. A group of distinguished New York lawyers and former officers in the wartime Office of Strategic Services took the initiative to organize and manage what was ostensibly a private American corporation, the National Committee for a Free Europe. Amcomlib was formed two years later, following essentially the same pattern, except that its first directors were journalists and academics rather than lawyers, and it was under less OSS influence. The creation of Amcomlib, however, added to the organizational mystery. Stimulus to organize, guidance, and funding came from a different compartment within the intelligence apparatus than Free Europe. Several years passed before oversight at the CIA for both Free Europe and Amcomlib was exercised by the same section.

It is my intention to trace the history of what started as the two separate organizations through their turbulent formative years, in which the relationships with émigrés changed from encouraging research, article writing, and speech making to broadcasting radio programs into Eastern Europe and the Soviet Union. This book relates Amcomlib's fruitless struggle to create a unified council of the emigration that would take responsibility for its full program; the Radios' complicated negotiations with West Germany, Spain, and Portugal for leases of property and licenses to operate from their soil; and Free Europe's traumatic convulsions following the Hungarian revolution in 1956, when it was accused of encouraging Hungarian freedom fighters to endanger their lives. Recounted, too, are the shocks that followed the revelation by *Ramparts* magazine in 1967 that Free Europe was in fact financed by the CIA; the deep trauma of the congressional hearings of 1971, 1972, and 1973 and the fallout from Senator Fulbright's efforts to discontinue the Radios; and the deliberations of the Eisenhower Commission. The merger of the two corporations in 1976 as RFE/RL, Inc., the Radios' uneasy life under Board for International Broadcasting oversight, and the ultimate dismantling of the private corporate board and the assumption of full authority for both management and oversight by members of the BIB are recounted in the final chapters.

The RFE/RL that exists in the 1980s is a far cry from the Free Europe and Amcomlib of the early 1950s. Broadcasting has become the sole function of the Radios. The émigré relations and publications divisions of Free Europe had long since been liquidated. Similarly, Amcomlib, by the middle 1960s known as the Radio Liberty Committee, has closed up its Institute for the Study of the USSR and eliminated all other nonbroadcasting functions.

In the middle 1980s RFE/RL broadcasts in 21 languages to the Soviet Union and Eastern Europe. Its programs are carried in six languages to Poland, Czechoslovakia, Hungary, Romania, and Bulgaria and in 15 languages to the USSR (Russian and 14 others). The operating headquarters and principal production center are in Munich. There are transmitters and antennas in Spain and Portugal and elsewhere in Germany. The program fare is largely news and information (it might be described as all-talk radio). There are also some music programs broadcast into Eastern Europe, particularly to Romania and Hungary, where there is no jamming and the reception is relatively clear.

There are 45 shortwave transmitters in use, using some 9 million watts of power. They broadcast 24 hours a day in Russian, 19 hours daily in Polish, Czech and Slovak, and Hungarian; 12 hours daily in Romanian: 8 in Bulgarian; and lesser totals in the major languages spoken in the Soviet Union, in addition to Russian.

There are some 1700 employees who gather the information, write and deliver the programs, operate and maintain the studios and transmitters, work in the news department's newsroom and the contributory bureaus and production centers in places such as Paris, Brussels, London, New York, Washington, Bonn, and Rome. Of these employees, about 1000 are stationed in West Germany, and there are roughly 400 in Spain and Portugal manning the two largest transmitter bases; the remainder is scattered throughout the production centers in Paris, London, and New York and the news bureaus. The annual budget averages a little more than $100 million. Sophisticated audience research departments keep a close check on listenership in the target countries and on program preferences. They operate with surprising effectiveness, even though they cannot interview directly in the target areas. Ingenuity and the application of sophisticated measurement techniques compensate for their inability to operate on the scene where the broadcasts are heard.

The history of the Radios is necessarily one of intrigue, mystery, clandestine planning, sophisticated intelligence concepts, massive campaigns to build cover, heavy-handed Communist attempts to demoralize or disrupt the flow of broadcasts or cause them to cease altogether, noisy and sometimes bitter congressional debate, and public suspicion. Because of their carefully concealed origins within the intelligence community and the desire of both State and Defense to remain behind the scenes, little is available in public documents about the early period. Much of what is written here had to be reconstructed from personal interviews with the many participants who are still available fortunately to relate the details of their participation. Published books and even magazine articles regarding the Radios are of little assistance in piecing the story together. Only two books on the subject have been published, both about RFE and both in the late 1950s and early 1960s. Neither even recognized the CIA as a factor in Free Europe's founding, financing, or direction. RL remains to this date largely a mystery; its history, although it is almost as old as RFE, has remained largely obscure. With the publication of the present volume, it is hoped that those mysteries and obscurities will be a thing of the past.

1
A Quiet Night in Munich

THE NIGHT OF SATURDAY, February 21, 1981, in Munich was typical of midwinter in Bavaria. The temperature hovered just under freezing. A leaden sky promised snow but only a few flakes had fallen during the day.

At 9 P.M. the sprawling office complex housing RFE/RL's production center and general administration was operating at reduced weekend levels.* Only 41 employees were in the building, in contrast with the 400 or more who would be there on Monday morning to begin their regular work week. The principal activity was preparing for the regular hourly news broadcasts to the five East European countries—Poland, Czechoslovakia, Hungary, Romania, and Bulgaria—and to the Soviet Union. The central news division was functioning with a skeleton crew of four who were hunched over their keyboards and visual display terminals.

Ingeborg Eberl was on duty at the telephone switchboard in the basement of B wing and Lothar Seidel of the Protective Services Department was stationed in the main lobby where he was in a position to operate the buzzer that unlocked the front door and at the same time keep an eye on the long central corridor of the building. Contract guard Christopher Pagget was on duty in the kiosk at the entrance to the south parking facility at the front of the building.

At 8:58 P.M. Pagget began one of his irregularly scheduled inspection tours of the building, a sprawling three-floor frame construction designed in the shape of a wide hand with seven stubby fingers, its palm backed up against a chain-link fence marking the boundary of the heavily wooded English Gar-

---

*RFE/RL, Inc. is the corporate name of the American company that operates Radio Free Europe, broadcasting to Eastern Europe, and Radio Liberty, which broadcasts to the Soviet Union.

den. The seven fingers, from A wing at the north to G wing at the south, pointed toward the Isar River, less than half a mile to the east. Between the building and the Isar was a tennis club and a row of multistory apartment houses.

Pagget's function was to walk the entire circumference, approximately 1000 yards, and to insert a key in time clocks at various locations on the building walls. He checked windows, flashed his light into the surrounding trees and hedges, and kept an eye out for anything unusual. At 9:08 P.M. he turned the key in the clock in the open space between wings B and C at the point where wing B intersects with the main 335-yard-long central corridor.

Having made sure that everything was in order, he continued his tour and returned to the south parking lot kiosk at 9:16, a few minutes earlier than on most similar inspection tours. Eberl was sitting alone at the switchboard in the basement of wing B. The basement is shallow so that the floor level is no more than four or five feet below ground level. There were no calls coming in, so she turned on her television receiver and watched a popular Bavarian television program, "The Blue Buck."

Directly above her, on the first floor of wing B, three members of the Czechoslovak news staff were preparing for the 10 P.M. news broadcast. They included Allan J. Antalis and Rudolf Skukalik, who edited, wrote, and broadcast the news, and clerk-typist Marie Pulda. Their news booth, where they would air the program at 10 P.M., was immediately adjacent to their working headquarters.

Technicians Nestor Bahrjanyj and Heinrich Lutz were busily at work in Master Control on the second floor of the main corridor between wings A and B. Much of the programming had been prerecorded on audio tape, so their main function was keeping the tape machines loaded, but they also had to be prepared to feed the 10 P.M. news broadcasts live to the five transmitter sites— three in Germany, at Holzkirchen, Biblis, and Lampertheim, the one at the Playa de Pals in Spain, and the one at Gloria in Portugal.

At 9:46 the private-line telephone in the Czechoslovak newsroom rang. Skukalik picked it up, said "Hello," and waited for a moment before he said "Hello" a second time. A deafening, ear-shattering boom broke the silence. Timbers buckled and crashed, panes of glass fell and splintered, pieces of masonry were hurled through space, the roof rose a few inches and collapsed back on the frame, office equipment did a wild dance and crashed to the buckled floor.

Eberl was stunned by the sudden thunderclap of sound. She had no time to move as pieces of glass and concrete flew past her and walls cracked around her. The frame of the large window beside her was hung around her neck like a horse collar. Still in a near stupor, she got to her feet and made her way through the debris for the door, bleeding profusely from cuts across the bridge of her nose and one elbow. The corridor leading to the reception area was relatively free of broken timbers and masonry, but swinging glass doors were blocked, so she had to move piles of the wreckage in order to clear the doors and free herself. She could hear loud screams from above her, but her primary concern then was the thick pall of dust in the air; she was determined not to escape a bomb blast only to die of suffocation.

The full force of the blast hit the Czechoslovak newsroom directly above the telephone switchboard room. Skukalik was knocked down and pinned to the floor by a jumbled mass of desks, office equipment, and parts of the ceiling. Pulda and Antalis were both seriously, although not critically, injured, mostly by the glass that had been rocketed out of the windows by the tremendous force of the blast. Regardless of their injuries, however, they started down the corridor toward the reception room. In the master control booth both technicians had been knocked to the floor by the force of the blast. The clock was knocked off the wall and stopped at 9:46:27. The south wall of the master control room on the side facing toward wing B was moved three or four inches. But the transmission equipment was in working order: tape machines were running and the signals were going out to the transmitter stations. The technicians calmly loaded extra tapes into their machines, called Holzkirchen and asked personnel there to relay the information about the blast to the other transmitter stations, and made plans to stay no matter what might happen.

Guard Seidel, in the main reception room, was shaken by the blast but unhurt. He checked the phones, found them out of order, and ran into the street to find a usable phone in order to call police and fire departments. He had traveled only a short distance before he met Jutta Bengs, the supervisor of housekeeping maintenance. Bengs, who lived in one of the apartment units facing toward the RFE/RL building, had already called the police and was hurrying to the building to do what she could to help. Seidel turned with her and rushed to the front entrance. Both started a meticulous search of the building for victims.

By that time the police, fire engines, and ambulances had begun to arrive. Pulda and Antalis were placed in ambulances and rushed off to a nearby hospital. Since her injuries were judged slight, Eberl was placed in a private motor car for the trip. There was still concern that more ambulances would be needed for the seriously injured. Skukalik was eventually freed from his trap and carried to an ambulance.

Maintaining communications constituted a major problem. The transmitter bases had been notified in time to feed standby programming into their tape units, but the only continuing link available from headquarters was the one through Master Control to Holzkirchen. Holzkirchen would have to relay messages to the transmitter bases. The path to Master Control was so strewn with rubble it was almost impossible to negotiate.

The Poles had been alert enough to include news of the bombing in their

10 P.M. news. But the telephone switching center had been completely shattered. A jumbled mass of wires, cables, and equipment racks was all that remained. (It was the room Eberl faced as she sat at the telephone switchboard.) There was a pay phone in the reception lobby, but no one had the two ten-pfennig pieces necessary to get a line. Someone remembered that contract guard Pagget had a collection of ten-pfennig pieces in the south parking lot kiosk. Radio president Glenn Ferguson, who had arrived by that time, gave Pagget a fifty-dollar bill for the entire collection, which filled a medium-large-size cigar box.

At about 11 P.M., more than an hour after the blast, the police ordered the building evacuated, which meant that the Master Control operators had to leave their tape units and their voice circuit to Holzkirchen. But the units continued to roll unmanned until the tapes were played out. By that time, the transmitter bases were nearly ready to take up the slack with standby material, so the total number of minutes lost on all services was limited to less than an hour. Eight services were broadcasting at the time— five to Eastern Europe, along with the Russian, Ukrainian, and Turkmen services.

Munich and Bavarian police immediately began an intensive effort to determine the cause of the blast and the people responsible. There was never a question that the damage was done by a bomb. It had been either set beside or affixed to the building at almost the precise location of the time clock that Pagget had punched at 9:08. It was clear that it had been deposited between 9:08 and 9:46. Possibly, the call received by Skukalik at 9:46 had been placed by one of the bombers in the hope that he could obtain quick proof of the success of his venture.

It would have been possible for the bomber or bombers to remain in a car parked facing the tennis courts across the street from the RFE/RL building while Pagget made his 8:58 inspection tour. As soon as Pagget rounded the corner of the wing A at the north end of the building, at about 9:12, it would have been possible to carry the bomb through a thick hedge, deposit it, return to the vehicle, and leave. Such a maneuver would not have been visible from the south parking lot, even if Pagget were to have returned in time. The vegetation between the south parking lot and the point of the explosion was so heavy that it was unlikely that he could have seen figures moving through the darkness.

Police first estimated the size of the bomb at 10 kilos, or about 22 pounds. They later raised the estimate to 15 kilos (33 pounds), or even to as much as 25 kilos (about 55 pounds). The explosive material was found to be the type unavailable anywhere in Western Europe except, perhaps, to military personnel. Terrorist groups in the West had never, according to Bavarian police, used similar explosives, nor would they have had access to them.

The finger of suspicion quickly pointed to the East. There was one report that a vehicle with Czech license plates had been seen in the vicinity of English Garden a number of times, but the rumor was never confirmed. The fact that the Czech service was the main target rather than Master Control, which would have put the whole operation off the air for days, added credence to the theory that Czech agents were involved. But it is more probable that the bomb had been placed where it was because cover was better there. At any rate, German police and American investigators are almost certain that the bombing plot was hatched in the East and that Czechs most probably were responsible for carrying it out.

Only someone from the East had ample provocation for the act. The Soviet Union and its Eastern allies had not only been motivated to destroy both Radio Free Europe and Radio Liberation (as it was then called) from the time the Radios had begun to broadcast, but they had engaged, almost from the beginning, in campaigns of intimidation, terrorism, and in some cases assassination. The chief of the Radio Liberation Azerbaijani desk, Abo Fatalibey, was murdered, presumably by Soviet assassins, in November 1954. Two months earlier, the body of Leonid Karas, a writer on the Belorussian desk, was discovered in the Isar River, the victim of a suspicious drowning. Security personnel are sure that Soviet secret agents were responsible.

Cord Meyer, the CIA executive who was the principal overseer of the two Radios on behalf of the agency from 1954 to the early 1970s, confirms that terror and intimidation were rampant in the 1950s. In 1959 a poison called atropine had been placed in the salt cellars of the RFE canteen by a Czech diplomat from Austria. There were only mild stomach disorders among the broadcasters, so the motive may have been only to frighten staff members and cause defections. But it is more likely that a major disaster was averted by a chemical miscalculation on the part of the diplomat.

The most bizarre incident occurred in September 1977. Georgi Markov, a Bulgarian freelancer for RFE, was walking across the Waterloo Bridge in London on his way to an appointment when he was struck in the thigh by the tip of an umbrella. Four days later, he died mysteriously. It took several months before a coroner's report decided that Markov had been "unlawfully killed by ricin poisoning when a metallic pellet was inserted in the back of his thigh." Ricin, a highly lethal chemical, was identified as the culprit by the British government's top-secret chemical and germ-warfare research center. Evidence unearthed by the BBC for an article in its magazine *The Listener* charged that the Bulgarian secret police were responsible for Markov's death, as well as for the death ten days earlier of Vladimir Kostov, another Bulgarian exile who had done broadcasts for RFE. Markov was judged to be a prime target because before defecting he had been a confidant of dictator Todor Zhivkov and was privy to a vast amount of embarrassing information about the Bulgarian leadership.

Radio Free Europe has been broadcasting steadily since 1950 and Radio Liberty since 1953. Hundreds of exiles from the target countries, described by the regimes from which they came as "renegades," "dogs," "Nazis," "agents of the CIA," and "turncoats," have kept the stations on the air night and day, through revolutions in Portugal, a shift from Francoist rule to monarchy in Spain, the passing of leadership in Germany from the CDU to the SPD and back to the CDU, and from Democrats to Republicans and back three times in the United States.

Assassinations, bombings, sabotage, carefully orchestrated redefections, arm-twisting in international organizations, subtle and not-so-subtle pressures on the countries that are hosts to the Radios' facilities, and threats and intimidations against individual employees have all been used to drive the two stations off the air. They must be perceived behind the Iron Curtain as menaces with power and influence far exceeding their budgets, personnel components, and signal strength. The magnitude of the response suggests that Radio Free Europe and Radio Liberty are institutions to fear, that the stability of Communist regimes is not impervious to the flow across their borders of objective information from the outside, that uncensored news and ideas may be fearsome to Communist dictatorships.

Be that as it may, relatively little is known in the United States or in Western Europe about the target of these attacks. Radio Free Europe, which is by far the more widely known of the two, is frequently confused with the Voice of America, and Radio Liberty remains almost a total mystery. There is only sketchy and not totally accurate information available concerning the complex conditions prevailing in the earliest postwar years that persuaded private citizens and government officials to join hands in a quasi-government, quasi-private effort of a type never before attempted in this country—one that still has no authentic counterpart anywhere else in the world.

The story of the Radios is a fascinating one, a tale of mystery and intrigue, one of attempts at building and maintaining cover, of congressional adversaries and recurring internal crises caused by highly emotional émigrés with disparate ideologies and aims. But more important, it is the story of information-disseminating agencies becoming increasingly more sophisticated, professional, and objective, responding to the temper of the times.

For the first two decades of their existence the Radios were wards of the CIA. Since 1971, they have been openly funded by congressional appropriation. But information about them still lies scattered about like pieces of a jigsaw puzzle. What follows is an attempt to fit those pieces together and create a pattern that will enable citizens of the West to be as well informed as leaders in the East and to understand why the government of the United States embarked on this remarkable adventure and how it went about implementing plans.

2
Our Friends
in the South

RADIO FREE EUROPE (RFE) and Radio Liberty (RL)* owe their creation to the rapid and deep incursions made into Central and Western Europe by the Soviet Union in the years immediately following World War II. They are products of an effort on the part of the United States to understand the reasons for the Soviet successes, to formulate programs to slow the Communists down or to halt them, and in the process to find useful outlets for the talents of the thousands of refugees from communism being cared for by the U.S. government. They were conceived by senior officials of the Department of State, the Department of Defense, and the intelligence community. Their purpose was to enable the United States to deal more effectively with forces that threatened to shake the foundations of an uneasy peace and open the door to further westward moves by a determined and expansion-minded Soviet Union.

Soviet expansionism, which by 1947 had already fastened a tight grip on Poland, Hungary, and Bulgaria and was speedily establishing an unassailable position in East Germany, was also threatening to crush democracy in Italy and France. Massive Communist parties were organizing to take control in both countries through the electoral process. The responses from the United States, except for the notably successful Marshall Plan, were feeble at best. The most vulnerable element in the response was its weak, disjointed intelli-

*In January 1964, with the change of the corporation's name from American Committee for Liberation, Inc., to Radio Liberty Committee, Inc., the name of the station was accordingly changed from Radio Liberation to Radio Liberty. Throughout this book, the acronym RL is used for either name.

gence effort. An effective wartime intelligence mechanism had been shattered almost before the gunfire ended, with the dissolution of the Office of Strategic Services ordered in September 1945 by President Truman. The OSS had proved to be remarkably effective and had built up in a few short years a cadre of experienced and dedicated experts. The functions of the OSS were parceled out following the dissolution to the State and War Departments. Some of its personnel stayed on for some time, but within a year only about one-third of the wartime complement remained. The remainder drifted back into peacetime occupations, many to New York law firms, but many did not lose the zest they had acquired during the war for intelligence activities.

Government leaders in the front lines of international relations were groping for some way to rebuild the dismantled machinery, but too frequently what appeared to be a reasonable suggestion collided with personal ambitions, territorial protectionism, or genuine disagreement on how it should be harnessed.

By 1946 it was obvious that something had to be done to strengthen the nation's intelligence capabilities. In an effort to centralize some functions the Central Intelligence Group was created. Although it had the title, the group was not given the authority to demand cooperation from the military services and the State Department. Within less than a year it was obvious that stronger medicine was required. In 1947 a new National Security Act was written. Its principal purpose was to unify the military services into a single Department of Defense, but in the process a new National Security Council (NSC) was established, receiving final responsibility for coordinating intelligence. The portion of the act dealing with the NSC's responsibilities for intelligence was written by a young Washington lawyer, Lawrence Houston, who had been counsel to the old OSS. Houston called on two other former OSS executives to assist him: Allen W. Dulles and John Warner.

The section of the act regarding the NSC clearly bore the OSS imprint. The government still, however, was not willing to face up to reality. While a strong intelligence chief was called for, one who could stand up to cabinet officers and the new Joint Chiefs of Staff, what they got as the new director of central intelligence was a low-ranking navy rear admiral, Roscoe C. Hillenkoetter. It was only days prior to his appointment as director that he had received his first admiral's stars. As a new boy on the block it was obvious he was not going to be able to carry much weight with officers many years his senior. A government document describes him as "lacking in leverage to be effective."[1] His record, moreover, suggests that more than a lack of seniority curtailed his effectiveness: he simply lacked the strength of will to bring the disparate parts of his diffuse agency under firm control.

While the nation was trying to put its intelligence house in order, the Soviet Union was accelerating its efforts to extend its grip into Western Europe. The United States was shaken in late 1947 and early 1948 by a variety of

Soviet efforts to destabilize the West. Communist-inspired strikes in Italy and France were brief but paralyzing while they lasted. A coup in Czechoslovakia in February 1948 brought down the democratic government and replaced it with a Communist dictatorship. National elections scheduled for Italy in March 1948 threatened to produce similar results, this time through the ballot box. French elections would come a year later but the threat there was equally fearsome. In the last French election Communists had polled more than 28 percent of the votes.

The gloomy mood in Washington almost turned into panic in early March when a cable arrived from General Lucius D. Clay, the U.S. commander in Berlin. The cable suggested that war was imminent. It later turned out that the general's panicky message was based on faulty evidence or was at the least a faulty reading of available intelligence. It is now assumed that the signs Clay had actually based his assessment on were the first indications that the Soviets were planning to impose a blockade on West Berlin—a step they took three months later. The waves of near panic that swept through official Washington following receipt of Clay's cable called attention to a shocking weakness in the nation's intelligence operations.

One of the most glaring weaknesses was the total absence of any effective covert intelligence capability. The NSC had taken preliminary steps to rectify the matter in December 1947. It had given the new Central Intelligence Agency responsibility for covert psychological operations. With the Italian election coming up in three months and a Communist victory a distinct possibility, the need for a no-holds-barred effort was obvious. Only two weeks after the CIA was given the authority to go ahead it was instructed to create a Special Procedures Group (SPG) to carry out the mandate and to plunge into the Italian election campaign. Money to finance the campaign was plentiful and no questions were to be asked about tactics.

Both the Defense and State Departments would have liked control over covert psychological operations, but neither wanted to assume operational responsibilities. Each was fearful of the embarrassment that might result from exposure, so the CIA won by default. There were other, logical reasons for assigning the responsibility to the CIA. Approximately one-third of the CIA personnel was composed of veterans of the OSS, who were the only experienced intelligence personnel the nation had. By handing over to the CIA those delicate functions that did not necessarily follow all the niceties of ethical conduct, there would be no need for State or Defense to go to Congress to defend appropriations, in the process possibly exposing secrets that might raise eyebrows and give the enemy valuable clues. Finally, the CIA already had an overseas logistical capability.

Operations in Italy were a smashing success. As a result of a prodigious effort lavishly financed, including substantial undercover grants to the Christian Democratic party, the Communists were turned back and the Christian

Democrats took control of the government—a control they were not to relinquish for three decades.

The Italian election was the most dramatic and demanding effort during the winter of 1948, but the SPG was active in a number of less visible ways. In preparation for future activities it acquired three important physical assets that were to play an important part in Free Europe and RFE operations at a later date: a printing plant for clandestine publishing efforts, a shortwave radio transmitter that would project a signal across the Iron Curtain, and the first units in what was intended to be a fleet of balloons to carry printed materials into East European areas seized by the Communists.

Another vexatious problem was concurrently creating concern in government circles: what to do about the thousands of impoverished and dispirited refugees from East Europe and the Soviet Union languishing in refugee camps and milling about in West European cities and Washington and New York. Senior government executives speculated whether there might be a way to accomplish two purposes simultaneously: keep them busy and at the same time use their experiences for intelligence purposes. Creating an ostensibly civilian organization to work with them seemed a plausible answer.

The gestation period for the Free Europe Committee, the parent of RFE, and the American Committee for Freedom for the peoples of the USSR, Inc., parent of RL, can be dated back to May 1948, when memories of the success of covert operations in staving off communism in Italy were still fresh. George Kennan, the director of the policy planning staff of the State Department, who was directly concerned with the refugee problem and worried about the weakness of the nation's intelligence apparatus, advocated the creation of a covert political action capability designed to complement covert psychological operations somewhere in the governmental structure. He was deeply impressed by the results achieved in Italy and foresaw similar crises arising in the future. His intention was to create a mechanism for direct intervention in the electoral processes of foreign governments—expansion on the tactics used in Italy. He did not believe that the nation should be forced to rely on public relations efforts launched through the media. He wanted a directorate for both overt and covert political warfare. It would be under the control of the Department of State, specifically the policy planning staff, but it would not be formally associated with the department. State was still skittish about dealing openly with foreign governments on the one hand and carrying out covert destabilizing efforts on the other.

The NSC accepted the Kennan recommendation to the extent that, one month later, in June 1948, it created the Office of Special Projects (OSP) which was assigned to the CIA to replace the SPG. Kennan's suggestion that control be vested in the State Department was respected to the extent that the director of the new unit would be designated by the secretary of state and policy guidance would be furnished to the director by both State and Defense.

Budget and personnel would be the responsibility of the director of central intelligence, but he would have little or no authority over activities.*

At this point two men who were to play dominant roles in both Free Europe and the American Committee for Liberation, move center stage: Allen Dulles and Frank Wisner.

Dulles, a Princeton graduate, was a New York lawyer who had compiled a dazzling record as OSS station chief in Switzerland during the war. He almost epitomized the popular notion of the master spy: charming, gregarious, shrewd, a genuine bon vivant. Following the invasion of Germany he was transferred there as chief of OSS operations. After the dissolution of the agency he remained on for several months to participate in the dismantling process, then rejoined the New York law firm of Sullivan and Cromwell, of which his elder brother, John Foster Dulles, was senior partner. But he never fully gave up his interest in intelligence activities. In 1947 he helped draft the portions of the National Security Act that dealt with intelligence. In 1948 he was one of the three experts who wrote the NSC directive leading to the creation of the SPG. Each of the chiefs of the nation's intelligence activities during this period consulted him frequently, and he kept his hand in on European activities by making frequent trips to the continent on behalf of the law firm's clients.

The second key player, Frank Wisner, was also an alumnus of Princeton, with a law degree from the University of Virginia; he was almost revered by his coworkers. Wisner had served during most of the war with the OSS in Romania and the Balkans, where he was credited with instigating and carrying off a number of tricky operations. Late in the war he was transferred to Germany, where he served as deputy to Dulles.

Following his OSS service, Wisner, like Dulles, returned to the practice of law in New York with the firm of Carter, Ledyard and Milburn, but he quickly became restless at a desk dealing with the innumerable details involved in corporate law. He was invited back to Washington in 1947 as deputy to the assistant secretary of state for occupied territories; he promptly accepted the invitation. In his new assignment he made it a point to make frequent visits to the areas in Western Europe where most of the refugees were concentrated. Germany, where he had served with Dulles, was the main target of his trips. Conversations with exiles enabled him to become intimately acquainted with their problems and their hopes for the future. At the same time he was not totally oblivious to their potential value to the United States as sources of in-

---

*Kennan, by virtue of the fact that he succeeded in goading the administration into implementing the plan, deserves a major share of the credit. Walter Pforzheimer, who was deputy general counsel of the CIA at this time, points, however, to the significant contributions made by James V. Forrestal, the first secretary of defense, and Robert Joyce, Kennan's predecessor as chief of policy planning at State, in developing the basic plan.

formation concerning Communist tactics employed in the takeover of East European countries and the possibility that they might form the nucleus of forces that could eventually move back into the Communist-controlled countries from which they came.

Secretary of State George Marshall assigned to Kennan responsibility to designate someone to assume the directorship of the new OSP. Dulles, who had been involved in writing the document leading to its creation, saw only one possible choice as its head: Frank Wisner. His view prevailed. The designation of the new unit was changed to the Office of Policy Coordination (OPC) and Wisner was named its first director.

As a result of the ambiguity in establishing lines of authority and relationships to State, Defense, and the CIA, Wisner saw an opportunity to stake out a more or less independent position for himself. He regarded Admiral Hillenkoetter with contempt and proceeded to distance himself from the agency. Wisner was nominally obligated to obtain policy guidance from State and Defense, but he rarely did so. As a result, the OPC soon became a freewheeling, semiautonomous unit of the U.S. government that within reasonable limitations was writing its own ticket.

The OPC was not without resources from the very beginning. It quickly acquired the assets of its predecesor, the SPG. These included about $2 million of unexpended funds, an experienced staff of old OSS hands, and physical equipment that had been stockpiled by the SPG, including the printing press, the shortwave radio transmitter, and the fleet of communications balloons designed to carry printed leaflets to the East.

One of the lessons learned as a result of the clandestine efforts to deprive the Communists of victory in the Italian election was that it is difficult to mount a campaign against a dynamic political force without an understanding of the appeals used to make its program sufficiently attractive to win massive support. The United States had no machinery established to obtain and evaluate reasons for Soviet success in winning sufficient support to impose its will. The effort in Italy was successful, but Czechoslovakia had fallen and France was still threatened. Without detailed examination and analysis of the appeals used by the enemy it would have been exceedingly difficult to design a counter-offensive.

A source of the necessary background was readily available. In camps in West Germany and in clusters in Paris, London, New York, and Washington there were thousands of displaced persons, refugees from the Soviet Union and the East European nations that had fallen under Soviet domination. Many of them had fled just ahead of Soviet advances. Some had escaped after Communist takeovers. They had seen at close range how the Soviets operated; they had observed the tactics used by the Communists in building sufficient support to topple established governments. Many had been leaders of the nations that had been crushed by the Soviet advance. Among their members were former cabinet members, members of parliaments, editors, writers, academics, and a smattering of broadcast journalists. The U.S. government had accepted the responsibility for feeding and clothing them, but it had no agency with either the background or the authority to use their talents and experience. In the meantime, they were ragged and underfed, disillusioned by idleness and beginning to suffer pangs of despair.

The Department of State was deeply concerned about the refugees, partly because it was obvious that they had to be fed, clothed, and housed and assigned to useful work to restore self-respect, but also because of the possible contribution the exiles could make toward restoring democratic European governments once the Iron Curtain was rolled back. At the same time, recognizing that diplomacy's principal function is to deal with governments in power, State Department leaders were embarrassed when representatives of the governments of East European countries sat in Foggy Bottom reception rooms next to shabbily dressed exiled leaders from the same country, both waiting for appointments. They were quite willing for Wisner and his OPC to relieve them of the responsibility. The paramount question was, what kind of a plan could be set in motion that would organize the exiles, put them to work at useful occupations, and keep them available for intelligence purposes? The answer was not long in coming.

With the creation of the OPC and the appointment of Wisner to head it, the stage was set for the creation of the National Committee for a Free Europe, the parent of RFE. Wisner agreed with the State Department analysis of the refugee problem, but he saw another possible benefit. In addition to recognizing the exiles as a prime intelligence source, Wisner was one of those who confidently believed the Soviet grip on Eastern Europe could be loosened and the Soviets driven back within their borders. In order to speed the accomplishment of this objective, he needed personnel and facilities to destabilize the Communist regimes. In order to carry out the destabilizing process, he needed writers, speakers, propagandists, printing presses, and radio transmitters to carry the message back into Eastern Europe. Obtaining adequate funding would be a problem, but the $2 million nest-egg he had acquired from the SPG was a start, and the growing fear of Soviet power compounded in late 1948 by the imposition of the Soviet blockade of West Berlin helped loosen the purse strings. Since the OPC would be funded by the CIA, which in turn received its support from the Defense Department budget, the OPC would be free to operate without economy-minded congressmen looking over their shoulders.

Kennan is credited in published reports with being the first specifically to propose the establishment of a private corporation to deal with the refugee problem. The published version of Free Europe's creation relates that Kennan, in his capacity as long-range advisor to the secretary of state, Dean Acheson, talked informally in late 1948 and early 1949 with a number of State

Department colleagues about the possibility of encouraging the formation of a group outside government to deal with the refugees. Among them were the secretary and former Ambassador Joseph C. Grew.* According to published accounts, Acheson suggested that Grew take the lead in recruiting a group of prestigious U.S. citizens, with Grew himself as chairman, to deal with the refugee problem, ostensibly outside government. The purpose would be to find some useful outlet for their talents and to see that they were fed, clothed, and housed. No mention is made in the published versions of Wisner, Allen Dulles, the OPC, or the OPC's efforts over several months in working with refugees; nor is mention made of the government's deep interest in strengthening its covert psychological warfare apparatus. Sources of financing for the proposed organization are never mentioned.

As the official story goes, the ball was now in Grew's court. He went to New York to see an old Department of State colleague who was also (perhaps not incidentally) a former OSS senior officer, DeWitt C. Poole, to discuss the creation of a private organization that would work with the exiles, aid them in organizing, publish articles they would write, distribute those articles as widely as possible in their homelands, and provide them with some opportunity to broadcast to their countrymen at home. Poole's selection rounded out the "Princeton Connection": Kennan, Dulles, Wisner, and Poole, all Princeton graduates, were clearly the four persons most responsible for creating what became later Radio Free Europe.

Grew and Poole set out to create a New York State corporation that would accomplish these objectives. But it is evident they had significant help in so doing. Less than a month after the February Acheson/Grew meeting, on March 14 Poole leased space for offices in New York's Empire State Building.† On May 11 a certificate of incorporation for the Committee for a Free Europe, Inc., was filed with the secretary of state of New York. On May 17 the incorporators, including Poole, met to sign the articles of incorporation. At the same meeting directors and officers were elected, corporate headquarters established, and a press conference scheduled to announce the accomplishments. Legal documents essential to incorporation had been drawn by lawyers from Sullivan and Cromwell, two of whom are also listed as incorporators. Allen Dulles, still practicing law at Sullivan and Cromwell, was one of the small group "recruited" by Poole to serve on the board of directors of the newly

---

*Grew had acquired a distinguished record as a foreign service officer (he had served as ambassador to Japan at the time of the attack on Pearl Harbor) and was regarded as a valuable sounding board among senior statesmen.

†It is interesting that the lease remained in Poole's name until November 15 when the board voted to transfer it to the National Committee.

formed private corporation. He was, in fact, elected Free Europe's first president.*

The first announcement to the public concerning the creation of the Committee for a Free Europe came on June 1. On that date Grew, who was not actually elected chairman until two weeks later, conducted a press conference at which he formally reported that the committee had been chartered. He listed three objectives. The first was "to find suitable occupations for those democratic exiles who have come to us from Eastern Europe." The second was "to put the voices of these exiled leaders on the air, addressed to their own peoples back in Eastern Europe, in their own languages, in their familiar tones." The third objective, Grew told the press, would be to enable the exiled leaders to see democracy at work and to experience democracy in action; then, said Grew, "they can testify to what the trial of freedom and democracy in the United States has brought." In addition to broadcasting to their homelands, Grew promised that "we shall also help them, if we can, to get their messages back by printed word."[2]

On June 2 the corporate name was changed to the National Committee for a Free Europe (NCFE). Three committees composed of board members were appointed by the president, Allen Dulles. Their titles suggest a range of potential activities, paralleling Grew's announcement. One was described as the committee on intellectual activity; the second, the committee on radio and the press; and the third, the committee on American contacts. The committee on radio and press started immediately to look into processes by which the written and voiced product of exiled leaders could be delivered to Eastern Europe.

At the June 16 meeting of the board Dulles resigned the presidency to be succeeded by Poole, and Joseph Grew's name appears on the board roster for the first time as he was voted a board seat and elected chairman. An executive committee was to be chaired by Dulles and supported by Poole and another member who would later take a dominant position in organizing NCFE's radio operations, Frank Altschul. By July 29 the board was ready to convert its ad hoc committees into standing committees. Altschul was named chairman of the committee on radio and the press. Radio still seemed to be only an incidental function of Free Europe, as shown by its being lumped with

---

*Dulles probably was not totally surprised by his election to the presidency. He, along with Poole and two other OSS veterans, Frederic Dolbeare and Spencer Phenix, met informally several times during 1948 to discuss the possibility of forming a civilian group to deal with the refugee problem and its possible relationship to a strengthened national intelligence capability. On one occasion they invited the wartime OSS station chief for the Iberian Peninsula, H. Gregory Thomas, to meet with them. They inquired whether Thomas might help obtain rights to broadcast to East Europe from Spain or Portugal.

the press.* The focus of the committee's attention at this stage was on encouraging refugees to engage in research and the preparation of scholarly papers.
Advice, however, was being sought from broadcast consultants with a view
toward establishing a plan of action for the use of radio facilities. There was a
prevalent feeling, even though the now defunct SPG had acquired a shortwave transmitter almost two years earlier, that time on the air could be obtained more easily and inexpensively either by purchase or grant of air time
from existing stations. But the plans were still vague.

The new corporation almost immediately began to spend money in substantial amounts. It expanded its headquarters space in the Empire State
Building several times in a few months, requested communications consultants to prepare technical recommendations, and started to employ staff,
some of them with OSS backgrounds.

All of these commitments were made without any visible means of financial support and within only weeks of the day when Kennan had gone to see
Grew. It would be years before the methods used to channel funds to Free
Europe and the future American Committee for Liberation would be
divulged. Some members of Congress, however, had to be in on the secret
from the beginning. A limited number of members of the subcommittees of
the Appropriation, Foreign relations, and Defense Committees of the House
and Senate, it was felt, had to be informed. Representatives of the CIA, which
funded the OPC, in supporting budget requests, were completely candid with
these limited few. But somewhat fewer than 20 members of both houses were
privy to the secret. Representatives of some of the nation's most influential
media giants were also involved early on as members of the corporation, including magazine publishers Henry Luce and DeWitt Wallace, but not a word
of the government involvement appeared in print or on the air.

The secret of the corporation's origin and financing was still well kept.
The June 1 press conference at which Grew announced the formation of the
committee and enunciated its objectives had been innocuous enough. Aiding
refugees did not seem at all unusual. Hundreds of other American organizations were engaged n a wide variety of charitable enterprises, and the organization of an obscure new corporation to aid in caring for European refugees
did not seem very exciting news. Many similar organizations had launched
their projects in a blaze of publicity, existed for a few years or months and
then sunk into oblivion. There was no clear evidence that Free Europe was
any different.

---

*It may have been regarded incidental by the board, but evidence suggests it held
a high-priority position at the OPC. Engineering studies pointing to the Iberian Peninsula as the most likely site for transmitter bases had been completed, Thomas had
been asked by the informal Dulles group whether he might be willing to negotiate for
specific property, and Edward W. Barrett, the wartime director of the VOA, had been
consulted.

The board showed some signs of concern later in June when it named a committee on advertising with Howard Chapin, general advertising director of General Foods, serving the committee in an advisory capacity. By the end of July it took another step that foreshadowed massive national fund drives in the future. The minutes of its July 27 board meeting show that a

> . . . finance committee is being formed to give attention to fund raising . . . ; attention is being given to the feasibility of forming in various cities around the country, small committees or groups which will assist in making known the objectives and work of the national committee and aid in the raising of funds.[3]

It is plainly evident that "aid in the raising of funds" is subordinate, almost an afterthought, to what appears the key objective: "to assist in making known the objectives and work of the national committee."

The OPC's participation in funding was deeply concealed. Creating Free Europe as an independent corporation that was funded clandestinely through a little-known government agency devoted to covert activities solved a number of problems. Its budget was so deeply imbedded in CIA and Defense Department appropriations that it was virtually free of congressional scrutiny, except for the handful who were in on the secret. The Department of State, while in a position to offer guidance, was relieved of the responsibility for dealing with refugees, but those refugees would still be available as sources of critically important intelligence concerning Communist methods of subversion. The OPC would have access to an invaluable source of intelligence and, potentially, manpower that would be formed into cadres for destabilizing the governments established by the Soviets in Eastern Europe and, it was hoped, even move back into their homelands to restore democratic governments. The committee would appear to be an activity created and supported by private U.S. citizens, thus protecting both the State and Defense Departments from any embarrassment that might result from identification with covert actions or clandestine activity.

The OPC's dominant role would have been clear to anyone who had access to classified memoranda. Budget requests from Free Europe executives were submitted to "F.W.," "one of our friends in the South." Memos regarding organizational disputes or controversies also went to "our friends in the South," and the first set of initials on the documents was almost invariably "F.W." It does not require skill in cryptography to interpret the name behind the initials.

The Free Europe board's primary task now was to set its operating committees in motion. Two of the committees—which were aimed at making American contacts and achieving cooperation from the intellectual community—required no physical facilities, only organizational efforts. There would be a need for access to research facilities and some mechanism for booking lectures and less formal public appearances, but this was a relatively uncomplicated matter.

Radio broadcasting was a far more complex prospect. Sophisticated electronic facilities were required: studios for program production, recording gear, transmission circuits, transmitters, and antennas. Moreover, exiles who were competent at research, writing, and lecturing might not necessarily be talented broadcasters. Training programs would probably be essential. Board members in the summer of 1949, fresh from having created Free Europe, had not yet thought the problem through to its conclusion. They were hopeful that existing broadcasting facilities might be made available for the purchase or grant of air time. The possibility that some exiles might not be able to communicate effectively was not considered. Altschul and his radio and publications committee, however, were aware that it was not too late to start planning. And they were hopeful that facilities could be made available through their "friends in the South" to lead the committee by the hand through the elementary stages.

NOTES

1. U.S. Senate, *Final Report of the Select Committee to Study Government Operations with Respect to Intelligence Activities*, Book IV (Washington, D.C.: Government Printing Office, 1976), p. 11. The report also observes that Admiral Hillenkoetter "did not have the instincts or the dynamism for dealing with senior policy makers in State and Defense."

2. NCFE, "President's Report for the Year," 1950, p. 5.

3. Minutes are available in the corporate minutes books at RFE/RL, Inc., headquarters in Washington, D.C.

3
You Can't Dream Big Enough

FREE EUROPE BOARD MEMBERS had only the vaguest notions in the first few weeks of the corporation's existence about implementing their radio broadcasting plans. The radio and press committee appointed at the July 1949 board meeting was headed by Frank Altschul, an investment banker, not a broadcaster—it was a weakness Altschul was quite willing to admit; at the same time he was eager to learn. Joseph Grew had announced at the June 1 press conference that exile leaders were to be given an opportunity to speak to their former homelands, but he did not say how that would be effected. He did not mention the shortwave radio transmitter purchased by the SPG in 1948—he may not have even known of it.

It was time now for Altschul as the chairman of the committee to start developing specific plans for presentation to the executive committee. For this purpose he was able to rely on Peter Mero, a former OSS officer with a strong technical communications background. Mero had been consulting with the CIA since leaving government service and was now under contract as a consultant to the committee. He had his own company in Chicago, Consolidated Electric, and was engaged in product development relating to shortwave broadcasting. He was a logical choice as advisor to the fledgling operation even if, in fact, he was not actually assigned to Free Europe by Wisner.

Shortly after Altschul's formal appointment to the chairmanship of the committee, he called Mero in Chicago to ask for recommendations concerning an individual who might spend approximately six months advising the committee and organizing a broadcasting program from the bottom up. Mero replied that he had an idea and would get back to Altschul. He called Battle

Creek, Michigan, and asked for a young product advertising director at the Post Cereal Company, Robert E. Lang, who had been a colleague of his in the OSS through much of the war.

Lang had stayed with the OSS for a year after the war and had then joined Fred Waring as manager of Waring Enterprises, which, in addition to hotels and resorts, included a popular big band. The Waring Band was a regular broadcaster, and through his management activities Lang had gotten at least a taste of network broadcasting. As a product advertising director at Battle Creek for a company that did a substantial volume of radio advertising, he had further increased his background in the medium. He had never been an actual broadcasting executive or worked directly in radio except in connection with OSS communications during the war. His OSS experience, though, fitted him for functioning in the type of environment that characterized the Free Europe committee. The proposal was to serve as a full-time consultant in New York for a period of six months. Lang accepted the invitation and left Battle Creek to learn what the committee had in mind. When he met the members of the national committee at their headquarters in New York, he was surprised that most of them were colleagues of his from the OSS: Allen Dulles, DeWitt Poole, Charles Spofford, Adolf Berle, John Hughes, Spencer Phenix, Frederick Dolbeare, H. Gregory Thomas, and Frank Altschul. Altschul was to be his immediate superior.

Lang's assignment seemed relatively simple at the outset. No programming more sophisticated than putting the exiles on the air to talk to their homelands was contemplated. It was assumed that air time could be made available on existing radio stations reaching into Eastern Europe either by time purchases or by grant of facilities. Lang's job was to check out stations and negotiate for time; it was a job for which he was well suited by experience.

The committee's view of international radio broadcasting, however, was a simplistic one. Lang first went to see Walter Lemon, owner and operator of a shortwave station based in New York and Boston. Lemon had no time available and was not about to release any for the purpose in mind, and his station did not reach into the target area anyway. Obviously, a European trip was called for to check particularly on three highly successful medium-wave stations that operated commercially: Radio Luxemburg, Radio Monte Carlo, and Europe Number One, which was based in the Saarland. Lang was asked in early December 1949 to make a European trip to check out these three possibilities and any others that might offer the type of service Free Europe would require.

Perhaps the Free Europe board did not fully trust him or perhaps other considerations were involved; at any rate, the board asked H. Struve Hensel, a member of the Carter, Ledyard law firm in New York and a former colleague of Wisner, to accompany him. Hensel was also a former colleague of John J.

McCloy, the U.S. high commissioner for Germany. Hensel and McCloy had both joined the Cravath, deGersdorff, Swaine and Wood law firm in New York as associates in 1925 and had worked together there for a number of years. During the war years they were both in government jobs in Washington, McCloy as assistant secretary of war and Hensel first as a legal counsel for the Navy Department and later as its assistant secretary.

Hensel's participation would ensure the hearing before McCloy that would probably open other doors. It also would furnish an opportunity to discuss alternative plans and the acquisition of additional property in West Germany for transmitter and antenna sites, if that should prove necessary. McCloy assigned one of his aides, Forrest McCluney, to work with Hensel and Lang and to carry on with any negotiations required after the two returned to New York.

The response from the three European stations was no more favorable than the one from Lemon. Even if their signals were capable of sporadically reaching the target area, they were not about to sell time for political speeches by refugees. Their business outlook was governed by the profit motive, and in order to maximize revenues they intended to broadcast attractive entertainment programs. The Lang-Hensel proposal hardly met their program standards. Hensel's written report, delivered to the board in April 1950, sums up his reaction: "These facilities are impractical," he wrote.

In Berlin, though, Lang had found something that interested him: Radio in the American Sector (RIAS), a full-time station operated by the U.S. government, broadcast a complete schedule of news, information, music, drama, comedy, and variety into East Germany. Lang quickly came to the conclusion that the answer was to establish a full-blown station or several stations and program a full schedule.

While Lang was arriving at this conclusion, the former commanding general of the U.S. occupation forces in Europe, General Lucius Clay, was commending RIAS to board members. Clay had returned to the United States in June 1949 at the completion of his tour of duty. In Berlin he had been an avid RIAS supporter. In December 1949, while Lang and Hensel were touring Europe, he received an invitation to serve on the Free Europe board, an invitation he promptly accepted. His vigorous support for RIAS in addition to Lang's enthusiasm and the discouraging news from the Lang-Hensel trip, helped build a favorable climate in the Free Europe board for creating a similar enterprise. The proposal to establish a station or stations in the image of RIAS brought the board face to face with a new set of problems, far more complicated than contracting for air time for speeches by exiles. It meant building a complete broadcasting facility, from microphones and studios to transmitters and antennas, with all the support services required to make it work.

In order to build audience, it was evident that RFE would have to be competitive: it would have to fight local-regime radio for audience, be sufficiently attractive to its potential listeners to demand a large enough share of audience to justify its existence. This meant that there had to be attractive, skillfully produced programs, as well as a balanced program fare and complete program schedules. A program fare consisting only of talks by exiles, no matter how eloquent or persuasive, would not do.

In a status report he submitted to the board several months later, in May 1950, Altschul wrote that "our friends in the South" had come to a similar conclusion, presumably independently and without reference to Clay's and Lang's enthusiasms. The objective of the "friends" was more limited, however, than that of the board; they were thinking primarily of psychological warfare and how their own facilities could be converted into a mighty propaganda weapon.

> The objective of the National Committee for Free Europe and Radio as originally understood in New York [Altschul wrote] was to provide a channel over which distinguished exiled political and intellectual leaders could speak to their compatriots abroad. Subsequently, it became apparent that in the view of our friends in the South a far broader objective was contemplated. The Voice of America, because it is an arm of government, is not in a position to engage in hard-hitting psychological warfare. A committee of private citizens, on the other hand, would suffer from no such disability. Accordingly, if such a committee succeeded in establishing adequate facilities and was provided with a flow of lively topical information, it could enter a field prohibited to the Voice.[1]

In emphasizing "hard-hitting psychological warfare," the "friends in the South" were probably responding in part to an NSC directive that had been issued a month earlier, on April 14.[2] The directive, designated NSC 68, called for a nonmilitary counteroffensive against the USSR, including covert economic, political, and psychological warfare to stir up unrest and revolt in satellite countries. RFE would certainly be qualified "once it got on the air with its own facilities, to participate in a psychological offensive against the satellite countries."

Two essential elements in addition to the "adequate technical facilities" would be required in order to enable RFE to participate effectively in the campaign. One would be an engaging program schedule designed to lure audiences to their receivers; the other would be "the flow of lively topical information." No thought had previously been given to a news or information schedule, and no steps had been taken to acquire the raw material necessary for building the information program. Lang described his conception of the program philosophy in this fashion: "We needed to create a long-distance CBS to compete on equal terms against a local NBC. If they had comedy, we'd have comedy. If they had music, we'd have music. If they had commentary, we'd have commentary. If they had news, we'd have news."

The board now had to contemplate using refugee talents and American production skills to reach large audiences in East European countries. They had to plan to build an organization that broke new ground, one that had no precedents anywhere in the world. The British Broadcasting Corporation (BBC), the Voice of America (VOA), and other Western broadcasters used exiles to broadcast to their homelands, but the scripting was done by central staff, not by the exile personnel who read the scripts on the air. The objective was to interpret the policies, institutions, and aspirations of the sponsoring countries for better understanding by residents of the countries to which they broadcast. The exiles translated what had been written for them and made texts available to exiled broadcasters. What Free Europe began to visualize was something entirely different.

Altschul and his group expected exiled Poles to write and speak to Poland, Czechs and Slovaks to Czechoslovakia, Hungarians to Hungary, Romanians to Romania, Bulgarians to Bulgaria, and later on Albanians to Albania*—not in lectures, but in carefully produced programs. They would speak of matters of direct interest to citizens of the target areas and, insofar as it was possible, about events and developments in those countries, providing information that was otherwise barred to those citizens because of heavy-handed censorship policies. This informational programming would be interspersed with serious and popular music, drama, and cultural readings. In effect, RFE would provide local radio stations broadcasting from outside East European national borders.

While VOA and BBC broadcast an hour or two or even three hours daily, RFE, to create the illusion of being local, would have to broadcast all day and well into the night. The RFE staff would have to fight for audience with local regime radio on their own home grounds even if they had to broadcast from bases hundreds of miles away. What they wanted to create was local radio for Warsaw and Lodz, Prague and Brno, Budapest and Bucharest, Sofia and Plovdiv.

It was an ambitious concept, but the Free Europe Committee, presumably with support from "our friends in the South," replied favorably. Plans had to be drawn to create an organization that could deliver along these lines. This would require planning much more elaborate facilities than originally contemplated. An effort would have to be undertaken to discover sources that would contribute the "flow of lively topical information" from the target countries. This was no small task considering the fact that no reporters could

---

*It seems evident that Wisner had a special interest in Albania, hardly justified by its population of no more than 1.5 million and its geographical position well outside the mainstream of Eastern Europe. Albania was one of the countries in Wisner's sphere of operations during the war. RFE eventually scheduled broadcasts to Albania but suspended them after only a few months.

be stationed in the target countries and little except carefully controlled information flowed through normal channels out of the closed societies.

In addition, Lang and his few associates would have to train producers, directors, writers, and actors for entertainment programs as well as for news and talks and recruit American professionals to act as teachers. This was a much more difficult task than simply booking talks or broadcasting world news as seen through the eyes of a London or Washington staff or a staff stationed in Germany. It called for the recruitment of skilled and resourceful talent and an administration that could weld all of its diverse units together. But the stakes were high. Music and drama would constitute the entertainment fare that would bring large audiences to Free Europe channels—the sideshow that would bring the customers into the main tent. No one doubted that once listeners were attracted, there would be an almost insatiable thirst for information in those closed societies where all media of communication were tightly controlled by government. From the point of view of "our friends in the South," RFE would then be making a significant contribution to "hard-hitting psychological warfare."

It was critically important that Lang and the committee recruit competent, professional program talent. Chapin, the newly recruited advertising advisor to the committee, became at this point a key player in the game. One of General Foods' principal advertising agencies was Young and Rubicam, the agency with the largest and most skillful radio writing and production staff on Madison Avenue. Lang desperately needed the nucleus for a programming staff to start creating recorded programs and to begin training exiles as broadcasters while he attended to the multitude of requirements on the European scene. Chapin helped him recruit program personnel at Young and Rubicam, who then took primary responsibility for building a production team, training exiles, and starting to produce programs.

The exiles, who had found their way to the New York area in the meantime, were being organized into program departments, one for each of the five European nations to which RFE intended to broadcast: Poland, Czechoslovakia, Hungary, Romania, and Bulgaria. American producers were assigned to work with the exile staffs, teaching broadcast techniques and producing and directing programs. Contracts signed with recording studios filled the gap until RFE's own studios were built at New York headquarters. The early objective was to produce a backlog of tapes that could later be broadcast once transmitter facilities were ready to begin an on-the-air broadcast schedule.

Highest priority at RFE's headquarters in the Empire State Building was given to getting on the air, at least with a temporary signal. There was no carefully drawn master plan. Everything was done on an ad hoc, emergency basis. "Dream," Poole once told Lang. "You can't dream big enough." This characterized RFE's earlier operations; and the dreams were backed up by money in sufficient amounts to bring them to reality. "Money," Lang says, "was no object. We had all we needed." Although his optimism led him to exaggerate (money was to be in short supply for a time in the fall of the same year), generally, the committee was able to furnish the sums required, provided they were reasonable and were backed up by full justification. Budgets were carefully checked by "our friends," but essentially Lang was right about the availability of funds.

As the first six months of 1950 came to a close, substantial progress had been made. A programming philosophy had been developed, the nucleus of a program staff had been hired, and the first experimental programs were in production. Some were even being stockpiled for possible broadcasting once facilities were available. Finally, Lang had the makings of the management staff in place. During June, McCluney took up his post in Munich as European director. With his arrival the first steps were undertaken toward creating a European program headquarters. The objective now was to get on the air. For that step, a functioning transmitter was required.

This first transmitter appeared much earlier than anyone had anticipated. In fact, Lang was barely back from his December 1949 European trip with Hensel when Free Europe was offered the gift of a small portable transmitter. Lang's version is that two of his former associates in the OSS, Roger Bennett and Claude "Bucky" Harris, offered the Free Europe committee a 7½ kilowatt shortwave transmitter for almost immediate delivery. The more formal version of the offer, included in a summary document in the corporation's files dated October 16, 1950, adds a few details. A paragraph reads:

> In February 1950, Mr. Lang received a letter from Mr. DeWitt C. Poole, president of the National Committee for Free Europe, which stated that he was in receipt of the gift of a seven and one-half kilowatt RCA shortwave army surplus transmitter. This letter commissioned Mr. Lang to accept the gift on behalf of the committee, to see it safely to its site south of Frankfurt, Germany and to direct and operate it at that location.*

The "site south of Frankfurt" was a former Luftwaffe air base at Lampertheim, a few kilometers north of Mannheim. The property had been acquired by the Army Signal Corps at the conclusion of the war and was turned over to Free Europe in time to accommodate the transmitter that Lang went to Bremerhaven to accept. The 7½ kilowatts of power produced barely a whisper compared to the 250-kilowatt giants that would be in operation at the

---

*It is likely that the transmitter in question is the same one stockpiled by the SPG in early 1948. Bennett and Harris had been involved in the Special Services Unit at OSS, which was later folded into the CIA. A Roger Bennett is also listed as an employee of Continental Electric Company of Chicago, the company owned by Peter Mero, who was advising RFE on communications facilities and had been an ongoing consultant for the CIA.

end of the decade, but it gave RFE a chance to get on the air. With the relatively less crowded spectrum that prevailed in 1950, there was at least a hope that it could reach some listeners in Eastern Europe. Lang's story is that the two former OSS communications experts also helped build a portable rhombic antenna that could readily be adjusted to sending signals with minimal effort into each of the target countries.*

The transmitter, now christened "Barbara," was loaded onto a flatbed truck in Bremerhaven and transported to Frankfurt. In early May, accompanied by additional trucks carrying the portable antenna system, it started down the highway from Frankfurt toward Mannheim. Near the village of Lampertheim the convoy turned left into the woods, found the clearing, and proceeded to prepare for the first RFE broadcast to Eastern Europe.

On July 4, 1950, only 13 months after the founding of the Free Europe Committee and seven months after creating RFE, the new international broadcast station fed its first 30 minutes into Barbara's electronic tubes and on through the antenna system to Czechoslovakia. The hastily organized Czechoslovak staff working in the New York headquarters had produced a program consisting of news, information, and political analysis. In subsequent days, the rhombic antenna was reoriented so that it was possible to begin broadcasting to Romania on July 14, to Hungary and Poland on August 4, and to Bulgaria on August 11.

So Barbara achieved a position in history even though its signal was pitifully weak and its rhombic antenna dwarfed not only in antenna-gain but in size by the giant curtain antennas that were later to be strung from poles as high as the Washington Monument. But RFE was on the air and now attention could be turned to the permanent installations to come and to transmitters powerful enough to ensure that its targets could be reached.

The New York staff, operating from headquarters in the Empire State Building, was turning out recorded programs. Programming cadres built around émigrés from the five countries were fine-tuning their organizations and fitting their talents into place. American producers and directors were working with them, teaching them how to write for the microphone, how to use music, and how to produce dramatic and satirical programs. Preliminary steps had been taken to create a central news-gathering and -processing staff. Plans were being made to build studios in New York, thereby reducing the reliance on commercial producing and recording agencies. Lang, moreover, had decided that life in Battle Creek, creating and placing advertising for breakfast cereals held less allure for him than playing with his fascinating new

---

*A rhombic antenna consists of wires strung over a wide expanse in the shape of a parallelogram. When a signal from the transmitter is fed into it, the antenna concentrates the power output and aims the signal toward the target area. The signal can be "steered" by variations in the power output.

toy, which not only presented a challenge with infinite pitfalls, but also promised to have a profound effect on international political developments.

The plans hatched by Dulles, Wisner, and Kennan, with assists from Grew, Poole, and Altschul, had come to partial fruition in a remarkably short time, but the shape the organization was assuming was not exactly what its initiators had planned for it: broadcasting to Eastern Europe, which had originally been no more than a secondary goal, had suddenly become dominant. Vastly larger and more effective facilities than little Barbara could offer would be required to reach the target areas with sufficient clarity to command an audience.

It was evident long before Barbara's first broadcast that a major production facility in Europe would in fact be a necessity to supplement the center in New York. It was awkward to produce programs in New York and either ship or transmit them across the Atlantic by the noisy, low-quality shortwave radio circuits then in use. RFE could not deliver timely information or high-quality signals without serious delays unless it had European facilities. Furthermore, a much larger pool of exile talent was available in Europe. East European newspapers, even though heavily censored, could be obtained there. East European broadcasts could be monitored. Some refugees were still drifting across the borders into Germany, thus furnishing access to a self-renewing stream of personnel. It was also felt that there was a psychological advantage in maintaining a program center close to the target area. Émigrés so close to their homelands, it was felt, would more likely continue to maintain understanding and sympathy with the areas for which they were preparing programs.

As Lang had pointed out, it was RFE's intention to recruit the youngest and most recent exiles. They would have the most intimate knowledge of current conditions. Germany was the logical country in which to intercept them and thus the obvious place to search for a site. It was still an occupied country, which simplified the process of obtaining the required leases and licenses, and it had the largest concentration of refugees. The OPC had been working there ever since its founding and Wisner knew the country intimately. John McCloy could be of assistance in clearing the way for negotiations. When McCluney took up his new duties as European director in June 1950, RFE was ready to move toward selecting a site, negotiating leases, and preparing to build a headquarters structure. It was not until November 14, 1950, however, that the minutes reported that "consideration is being given to establishing a very small Munich programming set-up."

Munich is the largest German city in U.S. zone (excepting Frankfurt), the closest to the Eastern borders, and it was already in 1950 a haven for exiles. The OPC was working there with exile groups, both Soviet and East European. It was a logical choice as a headquarters city, being far enough away from Frankfurt to avoid the strong identification with the United States there surely would have been, had it been close to the high commissioner's headquarters.

Permission to operate from the U.S. occupation zone in Germany required no special effort. The U.S. High Commission could arrange for that. Leases would be necessary, however, from the city of Munich to establish the headquarters building there, and from the land of Bavaria for the rights to operate any facility outside the city.

With McCloy's support and the power and influence of the U.S. government behind the effort, it took only a short time before Munich city officials and the government of the land of Bavaria had agreed to making available a site on the edge of the English Garden, Munich's largest park, for a headquarters building. This site would be leased to Free Europe and the building constructed with Free Europe funds, and the site would revert to the city on the termination of RFE activities. It was a choice piece of property, within less than two miles of the city center but still in a natural setting. Munich city authorities, while responsive to the U.S. request, had some second thoughts about releasing such a desirable piece of land, but in 1950 when the negotiations got underway, they were still seriously weighing the merits of rebuilding the bomb-pocked and rubble-strewn city or alternatively starting fresh at an entirely new site outside the city limits of Munich at that time.

McCluney was charged with the responsibility for negotiating leases, commissioning architects' drawings, soliciting bids, signing contracts, supervising construction, and hiring personnel to manage facilities once they were in place. It was decided that the building should be constructed in modules if possible, so that production units could be moved in as soon as space was ready. Building design was complicated by the fact that few expected RFE to last beyond a few years. It was still the established wisdom that East European Communist regimes would soon fall—partly as the result of Free Europe Committee activity—and that there would be no further need for an RFE. In order to prepare for this contingency, plans called for constructing a convertible building, one that could be swiftly shifted to a variety of possible uses. This requirement did not make the most efficient use of space, but it did not slow construction.

By January 16, 1951, Lang was ready to appear before the board of directors of Free Europe to present preliminary architects' drawings. The structure he described was one that could be ready for limited operations in the remarkably short period of 60 days, if weather was not too unfavorable. The decision of the board was positive. Lang was instructed to proceed with the greatest possible dispatch, "even if costs should be somewhat increased thereby."

The next move was McCluney's. It was his assignment to make good on Lang's promises. Sixty days turned out to be a little optimistic, but by June, only five months after the board had voted approval, wings number one and two of the building were ready for occupancy. Wings number three and four were completed by the following February, and five and six by August 1952. By November 1952, the swiftly growing structure included six operating wings, 22 studios, six control rooms, and a master control in addition to space for editorial, technical, and maintenance services. Facilities were now in place for producing a complete and varied program schedule as contemplated during the winter of 1950.

Transmitters and antennas, however, offered more persistent problems. In a memorandum to the board on November 2, 1950, Peter Mero pointed out that international broadcasting bands were deteriorating rapidly "due to a most substantial increase in Soviet radio activities." Only greater transmitter power, higher antenna-gain, and the use of as many frequencies as could be obtained, Mero said, would furnish any guarantee that an acceptable signal could be heard through the increasingly crowded spectrum.[3]

RFE, however, started to build relatively low-power permanent facilities in Germany while preparing to negotiate for property rights in North Africa, Portugal, or the Azores for the construction of the massive facility that Mero believed necessary. As a justification for selecting from among those alternatives, Mero pointed out that "no other location seemed politically available in the fall of 1949."

Barbara's 7½ kilowatts of power were obviously only a token, so negotiations had to begin for more impressive facilities. McCluney succeeded in obtaining a lease for a suitable piece of land at Holzkirchen, about 20 miles southeast of Munich, in the spring of 1950. In June of the same year a 135-kilowatt medium-wave transmitter was ordered from Brown and Boveri in Switzerland. Eleven months later, in May 1951, it was on the air broadcasting to Czechoslovakia and Hungary. Barbara remained at Lampertheim, but the committee decided to shift its transmitter operations to a nearby piece of property at Biblis, which would then become its principal German shortwave operating base. By November 1950, Biblis boasted of three 10-kilowatt transmitters and one with 50 kilowatts of power.

While installations were proceeding in Germany, it became increasingly evident that, as Mero had argued, the secondary line of facilities Mero had recommended had to be established at a greater distance from the target area. Efforts to locate and obtain rights to a suitable location in this secondary line were hastened by fears generated by the Korean War, which broke out on June 25, 1950. It was considered possible that West Germany would be overrun by the Soviet Union, thus jeopardizing all facilities in that country. Free Europe officials even looked into evacuation plans for employees and considered the possibility that as many facilities as possible should be made portable for a quick removal to safer ground. The Iberian Peninsula and

North Africa were the most likely back-up sites. They would offer the highest and most consistent signal quality and the safest havens from possible Soviet attack.

As 1950 came to a close, Free Europe was frustrated in its efforts to obtain government approval to begin the search and negotiations in what appeared to be the most desirable locations. The Department of State was dragging its heels on giving the assent that would be heeded before the required permissions could be sought. Mero, who was trying to expedite an answer, reported on November 14 that "the Department apparently wishes to delay diplomatic representation on behalf of Radio Free Europe . . . until such time as similar plans for the Voice of America had crystallized." Thus, although RFE had developed a programming philosophy, started building a stronger staff and was operating some limited facilities, it was still in need of a major facilities breakthrough. That breakthrough depended on the breaking down of State Department reluctance; following the receipt of permission, hard negotiations could be started with the country selected as offering the most likely site to obtain the necessary privileges and licenses.

NOTES

1. Altschul papers. Lehman Collection, Columbia University Library, New York.

2. U.S. Senate, *Final Report of the Select Committee to Study Government Operations with Respect to Intelligence Activities,* Book IV (Washington, D.C.: Government Printing Office, 1976), p. 32.

3. A copy of the memorandum can be found in the Archives of the Hoover Institution.

4
We Enter This Fight with Bare Fists

I T WAS NOT NECESSARY for RFE to give much thought to program production problems and content before the spring of 1950. When Lang and Hensel went to Germany in December 1949, the RFE plan was still to build a program schedule by buying air time from existing facilities for talks by exiles. It was late winter before the committee had been fully convinced by the negative reports from Hensel and Lang that some alternative approach was necessary. In mid-February the committee was assured that the 7½-kilowatt transmitter was available for RFE use. Several weeks passed before it could be transported to a suitable site and prepared to begin broadcasting. As winter turned to spring and the opening air date approached, program content became a major concern.

Members of the Free Europe board had been so preoccupied with other more pressing matters that little thought had been given to what might be said on the air. There were three factors, however, that influenced their attitudes toward their mission. The first was the psychological warfare heritage both of the agencies of government that stimulated its founding and furnished financial support and of the board members who created it. The second was the idealistic, emotional, and sometimes even belligerent cast of the refugees who were presumably to bear the brunt of the program responsibility. The third was NSC 68, which called for a nonmilitary offensive against the Soviet Union to stir up revolt in the satellite countries. These factors would influence program planning and the actual character of the output during the first few months. They would give it an image of bare fists and brass knuckles. The intention was to hit hard and not be worried about the niceties of broadcast ethics. The more they could embarrass East European governments and the leadership of the Soviet Union, the better.

This all sounded very simple: just turn the exiles loose and leave them on their own. There were fundamental philosophical and organizational problems, however, that demanded board attention if RFE were to be anything but a loose conglomerate of disjointed exile groups working under the supervision of recently recruited Americans who had been given neither firm guidelines nor a clear sense of direction about what they were trying to create. It was not even clear that the American supervisors did in fact have any authority over program output.

It was Altschul, the Free Europe board member responsible for RFE, who persisted during the spring and early summer of 1950 in trying to bring the Free Europe board to come to grips with a number of issues he felt demanded immediate attention. He felt that some introspection was required and that Free Europe should bite the bullet on the question of the degree of responsibility that should be granted to the exiles:

> To what extent is Radio Free Europe the voice of the émigré groups, rather than the voice of American citizens using émigré groups to their maximum advantage in a psychological warfare offensive? To what extent are émigré intellectuals and political leaders to be afforded an opportuntity to speak over the channels of Radio Free Europe. . . . and under what degree of supervision?[1]

By mid-May, Barbara had been transported to the open field at Lampertheim and had begun broadcasting test signals. Within weeks it would be ready to undertake a regular schedule of broadcasts to the East. But the national committee remained indecisive. It was quickly approaching its inaugural air date without resolving underlying issues regarding its role in programming, staff organization, policy control and the sources of the "lively information" that would interest audiences in the East, and, if effective, eventually embarrass their governments.

Altschul felt that little could be done without solving a paralyzing conflict in the national committee's management structure. In his report to the board submitted on May 8, he pointed out that although Lang was accepting appointment as director of RFE with full responsibility for organizing and building a broadcast operation, he had little or no authority over the exiles, who were to constitute the bulk of the program staff. They reported to the exile relations division. Only Poole, the Free Europe president, had authority over both divisions. The exiles, who were being hired for the growing language desks and who would produce programs once RFE went on the air, were being, in Altschul's words, "recruited through the head office of NCFE." Altschul and Lang had responsibility over real estate and hardware but little else.

Altschul was not only worried about the awkward if not unworkable management structure they were building, but also concerned about the image that RFE would create among its listeners if full responsibility for editorial output were to reside with the exiles. He felt that the national councils, into which the exiles were organized, were behaving like quasi-governments in exile. "These councils," he wrote, "represent the past, . . . in a measure, an unpalatable past, of the people we wish to influence. It would be self-defeating, to attempt to expand the gospel of Twentieth Century liberalism through the recognized voice of Nineteenth Century reaction."[2]

What Altschul most wanted was full divisional status for RFE. He wanted RFE to take full responsibility for all radio functions, including hiring, information gathering, program production, and policy formulation. He wanted Lang appointed vice president-in-charge, with clearly defined goals and responsibilities. He himself would be willing to oversee RFE performance on behalf of the board. Poole, however, was reluctant to relinquish his own prerogatives. There followed a period of intensive in-fighting, genteel name calling, a blizzard of memoranda, and countless lunches, dinners, phone calls, and personal meetings involving Free Europe and OPC personnel, including Wisner. Altschul threatened to resign as both the overseer of RFE operations and as Free Europe treasurer unless some decisive action was taken. As with such disputes, this one resulted in compromise. An RFE committee with Altschul as chairman and Spencer Phenix and Frederic Dolbeare as members, was created and assigned responsibility for RFE. Altschul went along with the compromise even though he was convinced that a committee was an ineffective and inefficient way to approach problems as complex as those RFE would be required to face.*

Limited as it was, the reorganization at this stage enabled RFE to move forward gradually toward building a broadcast arm that would operate under managerial discipline. It could begin to balance the role of the émigré against that of the U.S. leadership in designing content and writing policy for the organization.[3] It could make a start toward building coordinated and varied program schedules. It could begin to integrate possible program schedules with broadcast facilities as they became available. And it could begin to consider the role of RFE in implementing American national policy.

Altschul was still not satisfied with the flow of information that was to constitute the substance of the early program efforts. He complained that information simply was not available. The board had counted on the OPC and

---

*The battle evidently left scars that failed to heal. Poole left the presidency in February 1951, less than six months after the controversy came to a head. In March 1952 he resigned from the board. Altschul, too, left within a year after the argument. He resigned the treasurer's job in August 1951 and resigned from the board in January 1952.

the National Councils of Exiles to be fruitful sources.* Neither turned out to be of much use, however. The board had made arrangements with the International Federation of Free Journalists† and the magazine *The New Leader* to furnish items for RFE use. They had even gone to Foy Kohler, then director of the VOA, requesting permission to station an RFE representative in the VOA offices to collect and deliver items to RFE's New York headquarters.

"As of today, [June 1950]," Altschul wrote, "none of these sources nor all of them taken together, give us anything like the volume of information that is necessary for a hard-hitting daily program in all six languages." He was particularly critical of the OPC: "At the outset we had been promised by our 'friends down South' an adequate flow of topical information . . . and we had been assured that this would be supplemented by a considerable volume of similar material to be obtained through the medium of the National Councils. To date none of these expectations has been realized." He was not optimistic for the future. In his June 12, 1950, memo he lamented, "It is quite uncertain whether enough will be at hand unless a far greater flow is obtained as originally planned from 'our friends in the South.' . . . [The] result to date has been pitifully inadequate, and we are now told that what we had been led to expect simply does not exist in sufficient volume." He concluded, "With the best will in the world, we can neither make an omelet without eggs nor a brick without straw."[4]

Altschul was not finished criticizing "our friends in the South." He was as disappointed with the quality of material received from "our friends" as with the quantity.

> We receive, with some regularity a daily selection of what purported to be significant news items with the condition that they must be used word for word in the form sent, unless changes are cleared by telephone. Only the fewest of these items are of any use at all. . . . [By] way of increasing this appallingly limited flow, our friends have recently been sending us translations from foreign newspapers . . . which have no value whatsoever. They are taken from papers anywhere from two to five months old.[5]

What pained Altschul most was that these broadcast items were supposed to be "the spice of the program . . . to convince our listeners that we were in constant touch with developments in their own lands." He again

---

*Four of the exile groups, those representing Czechoslovakia, Hungary, Romania, and Bulgaria, had formed national councils, but the Poles had failed to organize because of bitter internal disputes. Thomas W. Braden, who later acquired the responsibility for CIA oversight, does not think RFE missed much in not getting National Council support. All they had to contribute, Braden says, was petty gossip.

†Another organization, that received subsidies from the CIA, it was learned later.

pointed the accusatory finger directly at "our friends in the South": "The ultimate responsibility for furnishing us with the means of discharging our mission falls clearly upon them. . . ."

It was apparent that RFE was mistaken in relying on outside sources for news that would attract an East European audience. One logical move was to contract with one of the international press agencies to furnish teletype service. But a press agency contract was not the final answer to obtaining "an adequate flow of timely topical information." The wire services would not deliver much of the type of information that would "confuse and confound the enemy." That, it had become apparent, could be delivered only by building an internal news-gathering staff in RFE. The appointment of Harry Sperling in late September was the first decisive move toward filling the news-gathering vacuum. Sperling set out at once to employ professional journalists and to contract for press agency services.*

Contracts were soon signed with United Press, the American agency; Reuters, the British service; and Deutsche Press Agentur (DPA) from West Germany. Building RFE's own news-gathering machinery, however, took more time. Gradually, staff personnel were employed and assigned to "information-gathering centers" in major European cities where refugees who had recently crossed the borders or travelers from the East could be interviewed.†

The ethics committee of the American Society of Newspaper Editors would hardly have approved of the "information" produced. It was heavily loaded with gossip, but at that point in RFE's development, it responded to the standards set down by government sponsors and the organization's own board. Under Sperling's prodding, RFE personnel began to explore another potentially invaluable source of background information: the press, periodicals, and radio broadcasts of the East European countries and the Soviet Union. Manpower and facilities were both too limited in late 1950 to exploit this resource, but it was not long before monitoring East European radio and subscribing to newspapers and magazines became standard operating procedure. Most important for the future of the organization, the gathering and

---

*Paul Henze who was deputy director of RFE's policy control department in Munich in the 1950s and later served in the nation's intelligence service, regards Sperling as one of the four persons most responsible for creating a successful RFE. The others were Lang, William Rafael, and William Griffith, later policy director in Munich, who joined Free Europe as assistant to DeWitt Poole.

†The term "information" rather than *news* was used in the first few years of RFE's existence because the objective of the "information" gatherers was more closely related to obtaining embarrassing items of gossip than to presenting hard news that would meet Western journalistic standards.

editing of news and information was beginning to become an essential ingredient in broadcast production.[6]

Policy controls would certainly be required in the selection, editing, and presentation of a commodity as sensitive as news, but OPC personnel apparently had not given much thought to this facet of the operation, nor had they suggested the creation of machinery to deal with it. Altschul complained about the lack of policy guidance: "At present we receive only an occasional, unidentified 'flimsy.' Of these we have had little more than a dozen in all, and none of them has contained very much that was helpful." He pointed out that personnel had had to decide matters of policy themselves and to struggle along without clear-cut directives. It seemed that "the friends in the South" were unconcerned with policy formulation and oversight.[7]

There was obviously a wide open chance for irreparable mischief if no action were to be taken. Turning highly emotional refugees loose to plead their own cases, with no policy guidance or management control other than a mandate to carry on psychological warfare in an effort to "confuse and confound the enemy," could lead to nothing but chaos. At this stage no one seemed to recognize that in the long haul establishing credibility was an essential preliminary to exercising influence. Perhaps no one cared, however, since everyone expected restoration of democratic governments and the withdrawal of the Soviets in a couple of years.

The émigrés who were being recruited to make up the language staffs wanted above all to upset the existing Communist leaderships and return home to new democracies. They were both idealistic and emotional. Most of them had been brutally wrenched from their homes either by wartime or postwar Communist takeover. They had been sufficiently angered to be willing to give up the lives they knew—in many cases their families and relatives—to an unknown future.

The belligerent attitude of the exiles was not necessarily at odds with Altschul's efforts to install some policy guidance apparatus, however. Altschul was not a news purist: he was interested in uniformity and consistency, not restraint and objectivity. He wanted guidance at the top and carefully drawn guidelines to keep programs focused on a single goal. RFE would then be better prepared to carry out the mandate of the OPC and the NSC. And that mandate still called for using all the tricks of psychological warfare to destabilize the enemy.

So in the first few months Free Europe was outspokenly belligerent. Statements made by early Free Europe executives and circulated memoranda are revealing in their candor and cold-blooded appraisal of various techniques:

It is the work of gray-black propaganda [Poole wrote in November 1950] to take up the individual Bolshevik rulers and the quislings and tear them apart, exposing their motivations, laying bare their private lives, pointing at their meannesses, pillorying their evil deeds, holding them up to ridicule and contumely.[8]

In Poole's view, RFE's broadcasting efforts should be carried forward along two main lines: the first, "exile voices"; the second, "gray-black propaganda." "The purpose of exile voices," he wrote, "is to keep burning the thought of an alternative to the Bolshevik designs for Eastern Europe. The purpose of gray-black propaganda is to unsettle and confound these designs." The psychological warfare background of so many of the Free Europe directors is reflected in another sentence: "It [gray-black propaganda] seeks by all the tricks of psychological warfare to sow in their [East European rulers'] minds and hearts dismay, doubt and defeatism and to foment among them mutual suspicion and distrust."[9] Poole was not alone in taking the hard line. Commenting on this memorandum, Altschul wrote on the day after the board meeting, "Our methods of doing all this are regularly growing in ingenuity and variety."[10]

In a speech delivered in May 1951, Altschul described RFE as "A citizen's adventure in the field of psychological warfare. . . . [Its] mission is to keep hope alive among our friends behind the Iron Curtain and to sow dissension among our enemies. . . . [We] are unhampered by the niceties of intercourse. We enter this fight with bare fists."[11] Allowing for some hyperbole, since Altschul was probably on this occasion speaking on behalf of Free Europe's money-raising arm, the Crusade for Freedom, it still reflects the attitudes demonstrated by Free Europe leadership. The speech described methods used by RFE program personnel in carrying out their mandate from the board. "We identify Communist collaborators by name. We give their addresses and an account of their misdeeds."

By some time in 1951, RFE's tone was becoming less shrill, its pronouncements less strident, its information broadcasts a little more objective. The gradual change from bare-knuckled advocacy to thoughtful restraint and emphasis on the factual took several years and at least one major crisis before it was firmly installed. In January 1951, C. D. Jackson, publisher of *Fortune* magazine, replaced Poole as Free Europe's president. While the Luce publishing empire was hardly noted for objectivity, it did have a justified reputation for aggressive journalism. Jackson, who had also been in psychological warfare during the war, brought experience in both fields to the job. And he was regarded by his associates as a supreme activist and irrepressible salesman.

The assignment of Walter "Beetle" Smith to the directorship of the CIA on October 1, 1950, was perhaps even more important. Wisner continued to hold the responsibility for RFE, but the OPC was now brought under General Smith's tough administrative control. Within three months Allen Dulles was in Washington as Wisner's immediate superior, and agency relations were regularized rather than continuing to function on an ad hoc basis. An international organizations division was soon set up within Wisner's OPC; Thomas W. Braden was given responsibility for managing the division. Most of the responsibility for contact with RFE fell to Braden's assistant, William P. Durkee, until 1954, when the position was assumed by Cord Meyer, who was to remain in the job for almost two decades. Durkee became Free Europe's president in 1967.

Meyer, who joined the CIA in 1951, maintains that the movement toward a more low-key, objective approach avoiding the excesses of the earlier days had started well before his assignment to radio oversight in 1954. "By that time," he said, "it was agreed that credibility was foremost." He says he does not think the shrill and strident approach lasted much beyond the first year or so of RFE operations, or until about the time that "Beetle" Smith had completed reorganization of the CIA.

NOTES

1. Altschul papers. Lehman Collection, Columbia University Library, New York.

2. Altschul papers. Analysis of potential policy weaknesses, dated August 15, 1950.

3. Memorandum re the organization of Radio Free Europe, dated June 12, 1950, in the files of the Lehman Collection. It was not until well into 1952 that the issue was finally settled and it was agreed that the leadership and policy guidance should be the responsibility of the Americans. Representatives of the language groups, however, continued to raise the question and as recently as the late 1970s some of them were still quoting the statement made by C. D. Jackson at the dedication of the Radio Free Europe building in Munich in 1951, when Jackson is reported to have said, "I'm turning over to you the keys to this building which is yours to operate as you see fit."

4. *Ibid.*

5. Altschul papers. Altschul letter to DeWitt Poole, dated May 23, 1950.

6. Altschul papers. Altschul memorandum to DeWitt Poole, dated August 15, 1950.

7. *Ibid.*

8. Altschul papers. Memorandum by DeWitt entitled "Radio Free Europe" and marked "strictly private." It is indicated on the manuscript that the memo was approved by the NCFE board of directors on November 15, 1950.

9. *Ibid.*

10. Altschul papers. Memorandum by Altschul entitled "Observations on the Memorandum by DeWitt C. Poole entitled 'Radio Free Europe,' " dated November 16, 1950.

11. The manuscript of this speech is to be found in the Altschul Collection, but it is undated and there is no reference to the place where it was delivered or to the group to which Altschul talked. There is a reference, however, to the 135-kilowatt transmitter at Holzkirchen that went "on the air two days ago." This would place the manuscript's date of preparation in early May 1951.

5

Contract Approved. Salazar

BARBARA'S FIRST BROADCAST from Lampertheim on July 4, 1950, was a symbolic triumph but hardly a significant step toward meeting the broad objectives set down by the Free Europe board and the "friends in the South." Vastly more signal strength was required and many more frequencies. The time had come in the autumn of 1950 for implementing the "second-line" facilities that Mero had recommended.

The increasingly crowded radio spectrum called for quick and decisive action in order to deliver acceptable signals to target areas. The growing scope of the Korean War increased concerns as to whether West Germany and RFE installations there would be safe from threats of a Soviet attack. The Free Europe board at a late July meeting had even considered writing stand-by evacuation plans for personnel stationed in Germany and suggestions had been made that only portable equipment be ordered, so that it could easily be moved back to safer bases. Some action toward building the much discussed "second line" was believed imperative, but neither Free Europe nor the "friends in the South" were in a position to start active negotiations for other possible transmitter sites until the Department of State gave final approval. Negotiations with governments of other countries were a State Department prerogative.

Mero complained to board members of lengthy delays that he discovered had been caused by efforts of the State Department to give its own Voice of America first option on desirable locations. The communications consultancy firm of A. D. Ring and Associates had been advising State on sites for VOA facilities and was subsequently employed by Free Europe to furnish RFE similar services. The Ring company had already drawn propagation maps indicating the areas most likely to furnish the most effective signal path to the RFE target areas.*

The long delays imposed by the State Department finally gave way to approval in mid-December. On December 21 Spencer Phenix reported at a special meeting of the board that State had finally given approval for negotiations in the preferred areas. Three weeks later the minutes of another special meeting reported that arrangements had been completed for board member H. Gregory Thomas to go to Spain and Portugal on behalf of the corporation "to explore the possibility of establishing a second line of radio facilities in one of those countries." The State Department had sent a message to the U.S. ambassador in Lisbon, informing him that Thomas was on the way.

Thomas, the owner of the company that distributed Chanel perfumes in North America, had been the senior staff member of the OSS for the Iberian Peninsula during the war. His office was in the U.S. embassy in Lisbon and his title was economic counselor. This was the man selected by the Free Europe Committee to be its latterday Argonaut, who would travel widely in search of a new Golden Fleece—in this case a license to broadcast from some point on the Iberian Peninsula.

A gourmet, raconteur, and member in high standing of a worldwide wine-tasting club, specializing in the wines of Bordeaux†, Thomas had been educated in Italy and Spain, and was a superb linguist. He says with a smile that the OSS sought him out early in the war because he had successfully carried out a mission, shortly after the war broke out, to bring scarce perfume oils back to the United States from European sources. In order to do so Thomas had had to cross the Italian-Swiss border and the Swiss-French border and move from France into Spain—no mean feat on a continent at war. In the course of his duties in Spain and Portugal during the war he had struck up an acquaintance with Antonio de Oliveira Salazar, the president and dictator of Portugal. More important, he had made warm friends of a number of prominent Portuguese citizens, including Ricardo do Spirito Santo, Portugal's leading banker and a confidant of the president.

---

*The most effective range for a shortwave signal is approximately 1500 miles. On leaving the sending antenna, the signal rises to the ionosphere and is reflected back to earth. The distance between antenna and target can be adjusted by raising or lowering the angle of fire (the higher the trajectory, the shorter the distance, and vice versa), but the 1500-mile range is considered optimum. Propagation engineers are also inclined to favor a south–west to north–east path in order to avoid electronic interference from the Aurora Borealis. These considerations pointed to the Iberian peninsula as the ideal location for RFE transmitter and antenna bases.

†Le Commanderie de Bordeaux.

Shortly after approval was received, Thomas was off to Lisbon, disregarding the permission that had been granted for checking on Spain. His first call was on his banker friend, who offered to help him to get an appointment to see the president. Portugal was already a member of NATO and historically had been close to England. Salazar was not likely to refuse an appointment. A favorable response might create an opportunity for gaining additional stature among his Western democratic allies. He was desperately interested in enhancing Portugal's prestige and becoming a full-fledged member of the club of Western nations. But, he felt, in order to avoid any controversy later, support for an agreement would have to come to him voluntarily from bureaucrats in his government before he could give final approval. He offered, however, to help Thomas get started and told his guest that he would ask Manuel Bivar, the director of engineering for the Portuguese broadcasting company, Emissora Nacional de Portugal, to help him.

Salazar was as good as his word. Shortly after Thomas left, Bivar picked up the phone in his office to be told that the president was calling. Salazar explained Thomas's mission to Bivar and asked him to cooperate in finding a suitable locale. This was a relatively simple problem for Bivar. He had scoured the country looking for similar choice locations for Portuguese radio and had discovered at least two excellent sites that measured up to all the requirements.

Meanwhile, Thomas had been busy doing the necessary spadework to be able to go to Salazar with a specific proposition. Spirito Santo suggested he see a prominent Portuguese attorney, Tito Arantes, who was also the head of Salazar's political party. Arantes called Thomas's attention to a Portuguese law that specified that only Portuguese companies could obtain licenses to broadcast from Portuguese soil. Thomas would have to work through a Portuguese company, a minority of whose stock Free Europe and its committee members could own; the majority control had to be Portuguese.

Salazar approved of this approach and suggested that Thomas get in touch with Tomas Pinto Basto, a member of another prominent Portuguese family involved in shipbuilding, shipping, tourism, and banking. Pinto Basto was more than cordial; he was enthusiastic about the idea—so much so that more than three decades later he was still the principal Portuguese representative on the board of the company that had sprung from those talks. With the assistance of Arantes, Thomas and Pinto Basto created Radio Retransmission de Portuguaise S.A., or RARETSA (later shortened to RARET). With the instrumentality in place and a sufficient number of Portuguese citizens willing to serve on RARET's board, the time had come to start actively seeking an appropriate site for the operating base.

Bivar recommended a site he had explored on the south or left bank of the Tagus River. The right bank was rough and hilly, but the left bank flat and in some spots marshy, ideal terrain for shortwave transmission. He had already selected a favorite spot, a cork plantation belonging to George Montreal, the count of Montreal. Montreal was also a friend of Spirito Santo and Pinto Basto, both of whom knew that the property was for sale. Thomas, Bivar, Pinto Basto, and George Caesar, an American who had been assigned by the Free Europe Committee to manage the facility if Thomas succeeded in obtaining a license, set out in a Chevrolet sedan to inspect the prospective transmitter base.

The trip was not an easy one. The ride up the north, or right, bank of the Tagus was slow. They had to ferry across the river and then set out through the flatlands and rice paddies toward the cork plantation near the village of Gloria. A dirt road ran as far as approximately four miles from Gloria but from then on it was only a trail, barely passable for a car. This was all to the good. There was no obsession with secrecy, but it was the consensus that the base would function most effectively if it were inconspicuous.

The citizens of Gloria, all three or four hundred of them, were poor, intensely proud, and totally insular. Few saw any reason to travel down the approximately four miles to the nearest village and so had never seen any need for building roads. Their main source of cash income was the cork plantation. Since cork harvests are nine years apart, these people had to survive from day to day on the few crops they grew—some potatoes and rice, a few orange trees—and on a limited number of sheep and hogs, barely enough to maintain a minimum subsistence level. The only contact with the outside world came when they took some of their produce to the adjoining village, bringing them a little cash. To Free Europe Gloria was a choice site. Even after a road had been built, it would be at the end of the line, dead end.

Thomas and his party eased their Chevrolet along the trail until they reached the edge of the plantation. They noted that very little would have to be done to the property to prepare for erecting transmitter housing and antenna towers. Living quarters would be required for technicians who would operate the equipment and administrators who would manage the facility. A road would be built in order to bring in equipment and supplies. Electric transmission lines would be required to bring in power. Ferries and inadequate bridges would make the transport of heavy equipment difficult, but the problem was judged not insuperable. Temporary housing would be required for the first construction workers on the scene, but an already existing shed on the property might suffice. Thomas and Bivar were satisfied and they began negotiations with Montreal for purchase, contingent upon RARET's obtaining official registration from the Portuguese government and the rights to the use of radio frequencies. Once registration was obtained, RARET would buy the property with funds obtained from Free Europe.

All this happened in March. Thomas had been there since January. Nothing further could be done before RARET was officially sanctioned under Portuguese law. He had assurances that the president would sign as soon as the paperwork arrived on his desk, but before reaching there it would have to be approved by several layers of bureaucrats. By early April, Thomas decided it was time to take some risks in order to get the matter settled. The Munich building project was underway. New York was stockpiling programs. Staffs were being recruited and trained. The need for a major second-line operating base was becoming desperate. And equally desperate was the need for frequencies on which to broadcast.

During one of their two-person meetings on a garden bench on the palace grounds, Thomas told Salazar that he would have to return to the United States; Salazar still assured Thomas that the registration of RARET would be approved. During Thomas's few days remaining prior to departure, however, no message came from the president's office. Thomas was discouraged almost to the point of believing his mission was a total failure, but he decided there was only one course open to him—board the flight he had booked and hope for the best.

During a refueling stop in the Azores, when the plane was about to begin taxiing to the runway for its final leg to New York, a Portuguese colonel came aboard and handed Thomas an envelope. Thomas unfolded the paper inside and saw only two words and a signature: "Contract approved. Salazar." Thomas had successfully completed a complicated international diplomatic negotiation outside normal diplomatic channels. An American corporation, clandestinely backed by the U.S. government, would broadcast provocative programs from Portuguese soil to the client nations of the Soviet Union in Eastern Europe using frequencies assigned to Portugal by the International Telecommunications Union.

Salazar was as good as his word. On April 10, 1951, almost before Thomas reached New York's new Idlewild Airport, RARET was officially registered by the government of Portugal. That meant it could negotiate a purchase contract for the Gloria property, and this it promptly proceeded to do. The purchase agreement was duly signed. By that time plans for construction on the property had been drawn and approved. The first major task was to build a road so that heavy equipment could be brought in. Some clearing of the cork plantation was also required.

Clearing the cork took a little time and effort, but it yielded cash results. A fund that was set up with the proceeds of the cork sales proved later to be a valuable source of cash for various charitable purposes. It enabled RFE to perform community services in the Gloria area that otherwise would have been impossible. In that respect the fund served as a valuable public relations tool as well as a humanitarian resource.

Long before official governmental approval was obtained, Free Europe had been impatient to start some kind of activity from the base. Lang had reported to a February 15 board meeting that if agreement were reached on time, they could be on the air with a minimum signal by May 1. There was a

60-day delay, but the little 7½-kilowatt transmitter that had beamed the first RFE broadcasts into Eastern Europe was again pressed into service. It was decided that Barbara should be moved from Lampertheim, where it was inactive, and delivered to the new Gloria base in time to broadcast again to Eastern Europe on July 4, 1951, the anniversary of RFE's first broadcast.

Henry Lolliot, the man in charge at Lampertheim, was given the assignment of getting Barbara to Gloria on time. He was up to the challenge. Lolliot decided that the surest way to make the deadline was to load Barbara on a flatbed truck and transport it over the highways. Three other trucks were in the caravan that set off from the German base. Lolliot himself drove the truck bearing Barbara.

On July 4, 1951, less than three months after Thomas had received his terse cable from Salazar, and exactly one year to the day after the first RFE broadcast to Czechoslovakia from Lampertheim, Barbara was speaking again to Czechoslovakia. Sufficient space in the cork grove had been cleared to set the antenna poles in place and to string the rhombic antenna. Czechoslovakia was the first target, but others soon followed.

Barbara's ouput, though, was only temporary. A permanent installation had to be built and completed speedily if the Free Europe board of directors' timetable was to be met. On September 1 construction on the main transmitter building began. Later that month antennas were being installed. On October 16, only six weeks later, the transmitter hall in the main operations building was completed. On Christmas day, 1951, the first 50-kilowatt transmitter, more than six times more powerful than Barbara, was in regular operation. This fell within considerably less than a year of Thomas's arrival in Lisbon. On January 14, 1952, the second 50-kilowatt transmitter was ready. On February 5 the third, and on February 27 the fourth was ready.

In Lisbon, with Pinto Basto's help, RARET had found an office and studio building. On March 5, Czechoslovak and Hungarian program staffs were in place producing backup programming. The uncertain nature of communication lines between Munich and Gloria made it imperative that a backup program staff be available to fill any gaps. Engineers did not trust the transmission system from Munich to Gloria to deliver 100-percent performance, and they were concerned about possible jamming. Later, as equipment improved, it was possible to reduce the Lisbon program staff and eventually to eliminate it completely.

When construction had moved along well enough to begin installation, electronics specialists had to be recruited. The resourceful Manuel Bivar suggested employing a number of recent graduates of Portugal's technical university. They could get hands-on experience and RARET would have graduate engineers working on the project.

No one knew how the Gloria residents would take this invasion of their area. At first they reacted with shock as the strange people from the outside world swarmed over what had been a peaceful cork grove. There was some resentment. Stones were thrown on occasion at RARET cars. Understanding and even friendship quickly replaced hostility, however, as some of the men began to be employed for cash-paying work. After installation had been completed, management started a conscious program of training Gloria personnel to function as part of the labor force.*

On November 12, 1952, with the transmitter base operating at full capacity, representatives of the Portugese government, RARET, and the Free Europe Committee dedicated a monument at the entrance to the base to the success of the project. In the center of a square reflecting pool, directly in front of the main transmitter building, they had erected a concrete base on which they placed a replica of the Freedom Bell, which had now become a symbol of the Free Europe Committee.† On either side of the base were inscribed statements by the two contracting parties pointing out their motives in building Gloria and detailing hopes for its success. The Free Europe Committee's plaque read:

> This vital link in the freedom network of Radio Free Europe built by the National Committee for a Free Europe through the generosity of the people of the United States of America with the understanding support of the Government of Portugal is dedicated under God to the service of truth. "May the truth prevail."

Salazar's statement on the other side seemed less enthusiastic, even apologetic. It read:

> A great number of European countries, threatened in their lives and liberty, can from now on depend on the United States for aid and rely on each other for the defense of their patrimony of civilization. It would seem difficult in such circumstances for us to be absent. Signed, Salazar.

Today, the visitor to Gloria is struck by the fact that the side of the monument facing the entry to the grounds is blank. Following the 1974 revolution that ousted the last remnants of the Salazar government, workers at Gloria asked that the former president's message be erased. RFE executives consid-

---

*This program would stand RFE in good stead when revolution came in 1974. Gloria stood firmly with RFE even though Communist sympathizers among the revolutionaries would have been overjoyed at being able to throttle the efforts of a radio complex beaming unwelcome programs into the Communist states of Eastern Europe.

†The original Freedom Bell, commissioned by the Crusade for Freedom, a money-raising adjunct to Free Europe, had been dedicated a few months earlier in West Berlin. That part of the story is related in Chapter 6.

ered the recommendation and came to the conclusion that they had no recourse but to accede.

With the official dedication of the Gloria base, RFE's facilities were all in place: the headquarters building in Munich, the medium-wave transmitter base and communications center at Holzkirchen, a technical monitoring base at Schleissheim, and another transmitter base at Biblis near Lampertheim in Germany. While negotiations were in progress for Gloria, Free Europe had arranged with the government of the land of Hesse to turn over the property at Lampertheim that had been used for Barbara's broadcast to a new U.S.-supported exile organization called the American Committee for the Liberation of the Peoples of Russia, whose radio arm was called Radio Liberation. Biblis was acquired as a substitute. The principal concern now had to be directed to what RFE needed most: to continue developing and perfecting its programming staff and talent.

6
Building the Cover

I T WAS CLEAR from the very outset that it would not be long before inquisitive people would start asking questions about the financial support of the Free Europe Committee, particularly considering the free hand shown in incurring financial obligations. The fact the nation was in the throes of a near hysterical wave of anticommunism in the early 1950s probably shielded the committee from embarrassing questions. But it was inevitable that questions would come.

It was obvious that Free Europe would have more credibility among its East European audience if it appeared to have massive financial and moral support from the freedom-loving American people. A government operation could not project quite the same image of genuine public appeal. Furthermore, owning up to support from the CIA or the OPC would make the whole effort seem a part of clandestine international spy activities. In short, it was imperative that the Free Europe Committee create at least a perception that its support came from the general public, and any monies actually received from the general public would be a welcome bonus. A plan was conceived to create a national organization that would mobilize support for Free Europe with a great outpouring of national patriotism. The primary purpose was to encourage the public to feel a sense of participation in the activity.

The first tangible evidence that thought was being given to a nationwide fund-raising campaign appears in the minutes of the Free Europe board meeting of July 29, 1949, just ten weeks after articles of incorporation were filed. The minutes reveal that "a finance committee is being organized to give attention to fund raising[,] . . . to the feasibility of forming in various important cities around the country small groups or committees which will assist in making known the objectives and work of the national committee and aid in raising funds." It is noteworthy that "making known objectives" came ahead of "raising funds" in the committee's order or priority.

There is no further reference in the minutes to fund-raising plans until January 19, 1950, when a resolution was passed calling on officers to "organize and conduct a nation-wide fund raising campaign." General Lucius Clay, who had been elected a director the previous month, Allen Dulles, DeWitt Poole, and Arthur Page were appointed to the committee, and $180,000 was appropriated to mount the campaign. Shortly later, Poole called an old acquaintance, Harry Bullis, chairman of one of the nation's largest milling and diversified food companies, General Mills, Inc., in Minneapolis. He sought Bullis's support in arranging to interview one of the members of the staff of the General Mills public relations department, Abbott Washburn.* The criteria leading to the invitation extended to Washburn were much the same as those that prevailed in the selection of Robert Lang to head radio operations. Washburn had been in the OSS during the war, knew many of the Free Europe Committee's members, and had significant public relations experience. Bullis encouraged Washburn to go to New York to meet committee members.

Washburn was initially interested but not enthusiastic. He agreed to go, but he wanted to take along an associate, Nate Crabtree. An account executive in the Minneapolis office of Batten, Barton, Durstine and Osborn, Crabtree's principal responsibility was the General Mills account. He had worked closely with Washburn and the two had developed mututal respect and a warm friendship. Crabtree was interested and the Free Europe Committee agreed to the condition, so Washburn and Crabtree took off for New York. Both were more than a little surprised when they walked into the comfortable Free Europe headquarters in the Empire State Building. They had expected something more like a barren loft suitable for a struggling young organization with severely limited resources.

Poole and his associates explained what they had in mind: a gigantic, nationwide drive to obtain support for the activities of the Free Europe Committee.

"How soon?" asked Washburn.

"Immediately," replied Poole.

Washburn and Crabtree started back for Minneapolis, already spinning off ideas on the approaches they might develop, the devices they might use, the theme they might promote in order to create in a few short weeks a firestorm of response throughout the country.

The following Saturday morning they met in Crabtree's office in the Northwestern National Bank Building in Minneapolis. Their first objective

---

*Washburn was, until 1982, a member of the Federal Communications Commission, after a career as deputy director of the United States Information Agency, U.S. ambassador to the Intelsat Conference, and consultant to the Office of Telecommunications Policy.

was to agree on a symbol, around which they could build a full-scale campaign. They wanted one that could achieve instant recognition and evoke an enthusiastic patriotic response. One image kept coming back into their minds: a bell, not unlike the Liberty Bell in Independence Hall—they quickly came to calling it the "Freedom Bell." They toyed with the idea for a few minutes, compared it with other suggestions they had considered, and finally decided that the "Freedom Bell" would surely be the symbol.

From that point on, ideas came in rapid-fire sequence. They had stumbled onto something exciting and were confident that no restraints would be imposed upon them by the Free Europe committee. The sky was the limit, so their planning was uninhibited. They decided that the Freedom Bell should essentially be a replica of the Liberty Bell in Independence Hall in Philadelphia. They would go to England to try to get the same foundry in England that had cast the original Liberty Bell to cast the new Freedom Bell. Once it had been cast and transported to the United States, they would travel it across the country to stimulate public rallies where thousands would sign "Freedom Scrolls" and pledge "Truth Dollars." Finally they would send it to Berlin where it could ring out the sounds of freedom in the middle of that city divided between freedom and repression. Eventually they were describing their effort as a "Crusade." The whole venture became a "Crusade for Freedom." Details still had to be worked out, but Washburn and Crabtree were ready to go back to talk to the committee.

Committee members responded with enthusiasm and expressed eagerness to get on with the program. They also suggested that a logical man to lead the Crusade would be one of their members, the hero of the Berlin blockade, the man who by mounting a gigantic airlift had challenged the Soviet Union's efforts to drive the Western allies out of the divided city. Clay was himself a symbol of freedom, a fervent believer in carrying the message of freedom beyond the Iron Curtain.

Poole and the Free Europe Committee encouraged Washburn and Crabtree to go immediately to Asheville where the general was living to persuade him to take a recess from his writing efforts and head the crusade. The challenge was irresistible. Clay eagerly accepted the invitation, but on *his* terms. He insisted that the Crusade for Freedom and Free Europe needed a broad base of support from the American people and from leadership in every state and every important city of the country. He reaffirmed his support for RFE: "We need another voice—a voice less tempered perhaps by the very dignity of government [than the Voice of America], a tough slugging voice, if you please."[1]

The first elements had fallen into place, but there was much to do and very little time. The Crusade needed a staff. A designer had to be employed for the bell. A trip to England was required to determine whether the original foundry that cast the Liberty Bell was still in existence and, if so, whether it would accept the assignment. Plans for the Freedom Train had to be drawn, local committees organized so that the train would obtain maximum exposure in each community where it stopped, and key personnel selected to endorse the venture and participate actively in stimulating public response. Finally, it was not too early to start planning for installing the Freedom Bell in Berlin and staging a massive Freedom Rally in that city.

The first disappointment came in England. The foundry that had cast the Liberty Bell had long since disappeared. Within only a few miles, however, of the site of the old bell maker was another with a worldwide reputation. Among its accomplishments, Gilett and Johnston, Ltd.—which had been in business for 107 years as one of the world's great bell foundries[2]—had cast the largest bell ever, a massive instrument weighing 18¼ tons and with a carillon of 72 bells, installed in the Riverside Church in New York. A contract with Gilett and Johnston was approved at the May 18 Free Europe board meeting.

Walter Dorwin Teague, a widely known New York industrial designer was selected to design the bell. His first sketch showed a laurel of peace encircling the top of the bell and an inscription taken from Abraham Lincoln, "That this world under God shall have a new birth of freedom," encircling the bottom. Above the base and encircling the main body of the bell, Teague designed a frieze of five figures in relief, representing the five major races of the world. They stood "with arms outstretched passing from hand to hand the torch of freedom until one day it shall light the whole world."[3] Teague's sketch was quickly accepted and by the end of July 1950, just three weeks after the first RFE broadcast to Czechoslovakia from Lampertheim, the bell was cast. There were some anxious moments as molten metal was poured into the molds that had been created in advance. Too much heat or too little might have caused the bell to crack or distorted the shape. An error in mixing the proper formula of copper and tin could have affected the tone. The U.S. ambassador to Great Britain, Lewis Douglas, and the workmen at the foundry waited for four hours while the molten metal streamed into the mold. It took another ten days before the metal was sufficiently cooled to remove it from its shell. This was the crucial moment, when it might crack or chip. But it turned out to be what the workmen described as a "lucky bell."[4] On August 26 it was pronounced completed by the foundry executives. On August 27 it was on its way from Croyden to the docks. And on September 6, immediately after its arrival in the United States, it was ready for its American tour.

New York was its first stop. On September 8 it was the honored guest in a tickertape parade up Broadway. A massive rally on the City Hall steps greeted its arrival in the nation's largest city. It was then loaded aboard a trailer for stops in Pittsburgh, Cleveland, Detroit, Chicago, and Kansas City. In Kansas City the bell was placed aboard a flatcar for the Freedom Train tour that would take it to Denver, Salt Lake City, San Francisco, Los Angeles, Phoenix, El Paso, Houston, New Orleans, Birmingham, Atlanta, Charlotte, and Richmond. Then came Washington, Baltimore, Wilmington, and Philadelphia. Finally, on October 8 it was back in New York where there was a rally before shipment across the Atlantic and on to Berlin. The dedication of the bell in Berlin on October 24 was the culmination of a frantic but enormously successful effort.

Some 400,000 Germans gathered in the Schoenenberger Platz in West Berlin outside the Berlin Rathaus, in whose tower the bell would be installed. At least 25 percent of the 400,000 in the Platz had crossed the line from East Berlin to participate in the ceremony. When the square had been packed, thousands began to fill the six main thoroughfares leading into the square. At 11 o'clock the bell rang out for the first time in its new, permanent location. The East Berlin leadership, which had been condemning the whole venture vociferously for weeks, organized a noisy demonstration in the Communist-controlled eastern part of the city only a couple of miles away from the Rathaus in an effort to disrupt the ceremony, but their efforts had no impact. The ceremony went on, featuring an impassioned speech by Clay followed by an eloquent message from West Berlin's mayor, Ernst Reuter.

On the bell's trip across the United States, people who had come to see it and attend rallies in its honor had been asked to sign Freedom Scrolls. One of the features at the ceremony was the delivery of these Freedom Scrolls to the Rathaus tower. Some 100,000 signatures were in the package delivered to the Tower.

With the completion of the Berlin ceremony, the Crusade was moving ahead under full steam. As Clay had insisted, organizations were set up in every region, every state, and in every major city in the United States. Full-time field offices were established in 16 cities. The headquarters staff was kept at a relatively low level, but hundreds of Americans volunteered their services. They worked as organizers, fund raisers, and public relations assistants. In some cases they were compensated by being taken on trips to Berlin, Munich, and some of the transmitter bases; in other cases there was no compensation of any kind.

Shortly before the Berlin ceremony, on September 28, the board had decided to make the Crusade a separate corporation. By February 28 articles of incorporation had been filed and a board of directors elected. On the board were Poole, Altschul, C. D. Jackson, and Washburn. Later Clay was added to the board and elected chairman. Washburn was elected executive vice chairman. In that role he became the Crusade's chief executive officer.

American media were consistently generous to the Crusade from the very outset. The Advertising Council, an organization of American advertisers, advertising agencies, and media began to support the Crusade as early as 1950. Many Americans long after the campaigns ended still had recollections of a filmed announcement showing an East European boy behind a barbed-wire fence listening to Radio Free Europe. Advertising Council officials estimate that the dollar value of the advertising and public service announcements contributed during the most concentrated periods of the campaign totaled between $9 and $17 million. And some of the television public service announcements produced as late as the early 1970s were still being seen on some stations as late as 1977. The only cost to the Crusade was the out-of-pocket expenses involved in the production of the print advertising and television and radio spot commercials by the participating advertising agencies.

The Crusade became involved in another activity that served two important purposes: to deliver information to Eastern Europe and to further publicize its own organizational and fund-raising activities. The publications division of Free Europe was printing thousands of pamphlets and leaflets written by its exile staff, but there was no practical system available for transporting them to the East European readers for whom they were intended. The SPG, at that time part of the CIA (later absorbed by the OPC with Wisner's appointment as director), had begun in early 1948 to stockpile balloons capable of carrying loads of printed materials over the Iron Curtain and releasing them. In an effort to get their leaflets and pamphlets to the readers for whom they were intended, the Free Europe committee decided, probably with some prompting from the "friends in the South," to use the balloon delivery process. The decision was made while the Crusade was gearing up for its intensive national campaign. It was only logical to involve the Crusade because of the dramatic publicity value inherent in transporting hundreds of thousands of publications to Poland, Czechoslovakia, and Hungary by this novel and precedent-shattering method.

Washburn was able to bring additional expertise to the venture. General Mills, the company he had just left, was deeply involved in manufacturing polyethylene products, which constituted a key ingredient in large balloons. He also knew of a manufacturer in his home state of Minnesota who made balloons of a smaller size. The potential public relations value of the enterprise convinced the Free Europe board that the Crusade should become the project manager and beneficiary of the widespread public reaction even though the publications division created the material.

Two types of balloon were used in the venture. Large polyethylene versions rose to altitudes of 30,000 to 40,000 feet carrying heavy loads of leaflets. At a predetermined altitude, the balloons exploded, dropping their leaflets over a wide area. The smaller units, made of plastic, were designed to spring leaks at lower altitudes and drift to earth with their payloads. The first launching was scheduled for an August night in 1951 from an open field near Regensburg in West Germany. The columnist Drew Pearson was there, Harold Stassen, C. D. Jackson, a number of representatives from both Free Europe and the Crusade offices, and a crew from RFE in Munich.

As Washburn describes it, on launching, the balloons ascended majestically into the night sky and drifted slowly toward the Czech border. That was to be the signal to set off a celebration. But before the celebration began the observers saw the same balloons drifting in their same measured progress directly back toward the takeoff point. Before dismay replaced the euphoria that had followed the launchings, however, the balloons, now directly overhead, rose higher in the sky and once more reversed direction, this time moving without deviation to the Czech border and beyond. The kegs of Bavarian beer that had been carefully brought from Munich for the occasion tasted particularly good.

During the years from 1951 to 1956, some 300 million leaflets of various sorts drifted into the villages and cities beyond the Iron Curtain and fell into the eager hands of East European residents—some 400 tons of reading matter. Balloons were discovered as far away from West Germany as Turkey.[5] At least one was caught in an air current that carried it to Scotland, prompting an irate Scottish farmer to write angry letters to British newspapers condemning the operation.

The Soviets and their East European allies organized a chorus of violent condemnation of the venture. Protests were registered through international organizations and directly with the U.S. government. During his presidency, Dwight D. Eisenhower replied to one protest by denying any responsibility for the balloon flights. He described the Crusade as an organization of American citizens, not of the government.

The balloon flights came to an abrupt end in 1956. Opposition from the East, which had been building to a crescendo, suddenly found evidence that could be used for even more violent protest. A Czech airliner went down in a vicinity where balloons were in flight. It was easy for Eastern propagandists to blame the crash and its loss of life on illegal interference in the airspace of a neighboring country. Since RFE by this time had built its broadcast facilities to a high level of efficiency, it was delivering information to the East more effectively than the balloons could, so the balloon operation was discontinued.

The balloons had served a useful purpose. They had been a stop-gap delivery system while RFE built its transmitter and antenna facilities. They had furnished another focus for Crusade activities and had been a colorful vehicle for continuing the public relations activities of the Crusade.

The Crusade continued to function, part of the time on its own, part within the American Heritage Foundation, until 1965, when it turned over its organizational structure and its assets to its successor, the Radio Free Europe Fund. The Crusade had done its job. It had focused massive attention on the activities of the Free Europe Committee. It had made RFE a byword across the United States. It had been highly successful in creating the illusion that the activities of the Free Europe committee were in fact supported by funds donated by public-spirited citizens. It had built the illusion so strongly that it was impossible for East European and Soviet propagandists successfully to identify the Free Europe Committee with the government of the United States. And it had furnished ready ammunition for supporters of RFE who, when questioned to their embarrassment about the source of funds, were able to respond, with some element of truth, that Free Europe was an organization supported by the people—although many knew better.

We now know that some open general governmental funding was available for the Crusade effort. A General Accounting Office (GAO) report, delivered to the Congress of the United States in 1971, shows that the U.S. government contributed a little more than $2.3 million to the Radio Free Europe Fund in the fiscal years 1951 and 1952 and another $800,000 in 1953.

Once the Crusade was under way, "Truth Dollars" started arriving in considerable volume. In fiscal 1951 contributions totaled more than $1.3 million (expenses were in excess of $900,000.)[6]

The Crusade costs for an 11-month period from April 1, 1951, through February 29, 1952, amounted to almost $2 million, but contributions barely exceeded $1.75 million—a loss for the period of a quarter million dollars. Over a 15-year period, from 1951 through 1976, receipts totaled about $50 million and campaign costs about $20 million, for a net of approximately $30 million, only a tiny fraction of the total sum required to operate Free Europe. Washburn points out candidly that fund raising was only one of three goals. The first was to acquaint citizens of the United States with efforts to preach the virtues of freedom to peoples behind the Iron Curtain. The second was to obtain some limited funding to help support the effort. A third was to provide cover so it would appear the funding was derived from the general public and not from any governmental source, particularly not from the CIA. The last objective seems in retrospect the most important one.

NOTES

1. Free Europe Committee, *The Story of the World Freedom Bell* (New York: The Committee, 1950), p. 18.

2. *Ibid.*, p. 20.

3. *Ibid.*, pp. 14, 15.

4. *Ibid.*, p. 20.

5. Allan Michie, *Voices Through the Iron Curtain* (New York: Dodd, Mead, 1963), p. 163.

6. A detailed description of the effort may be found in pp. 121–69, internal memorandum presented to "Radio Free Europe Fund Board," included in Agenda Book for April 1977 Board Meeting, Archives of Hoover Institution.

7
The Stalin Era
Is Coming to a Close

R ADIO LIBERATION WAS SPAWNED in the same international political climate that gave birth to the Free Europe Committee: the Communist takeover of Czechoslovakia, the threat of a Communist victory in the 1948 Italian elections, the Berlin blockade, and the urgent necessity to do something about the hordes of hungry and restless exiles from the Soviet Union living off a limited U.S. largesse in the U.S. occupation zone in Germany. The stimulation for the creation of both came from the highest levels of the U.S. government: the Department of State, the Department of Defense and the NSC operating through the OPC under the firm direction of Frank Wisner. But there the similarity ends.

In the formative stages, Wisner himself was the point of contact between the OPC and the group forming the Committee for a Free Europe. One of his aides, Franklin A. Lindsay,* performed the role for a similar group that was forming to work with exiles from the Soviet Union. Lindsay made the original contacts, identified the first persons to be invited to be directors, arranged for invitations to be extended, selected the first general counsel, and commissioned the drafting of the first articles of incorporation of the American Committee for Freedom for the Peoples of the USSR, Inc. In the case of Free Europe, Allen Dulles, Wisner's wartime boss and a key figure in writing the pattern for the nation's intelligence machinery, was instrumental in bringing together the New York establishment figures, mostly lawyers and former OSS

---

*Lindsay is the recently retired chairman of the board and chief executive officer of the ITEK Corporation. During and immediately after the war he was an OSS officer in southeastern Europe, Wisner's wartime turf.

personnel, who constituted Free Europe's first board. Lindsay, clearly responding to government policy, recruited an entirely different type of cast, including Russian-speaking journalists who had been stationed in Moscow, publishers, and leading educators as the nucleus of the Amcomlib board.

Dulles's law firm, Sullivan and Cromwell, drafted the articles of incorporation and bylaws for Free Europe; a New York lawyer friend of Lindsay, John F. B. Mitchell, Jr., an associate in the less prestigious firm of Hawkins, Delafield and Longfellow, drew up the papers for Amcomlib. DeWitt Poole, possessing both State Department and OSS credentials, took the lead in recruiting a board of directors for Free Europe; Lindsay went outside the intelligence and diplomatic community to select a vice president of Time, Inc., Allen Grover, to aid in setting up organizational meetings for Amcomlib as it soon became known. (Grover, an assistant to editor-in-chief Henry R. Luce, was generally regarded as chief of staff to Luce, but he lacked the public standing and experience at high levels of government reflected in the Free Europe leadership.)

The stark contrasts between the two organizations, both products of the same government intelligence agency and assigned almost identical functions, resulted from several obscure differences in the émigrés and their potential audiences as perceived by the OPC leadership. The Soviet Union offered a far more complex set of problems, both in the composition of its exiles and the diversity of its land areas, than the countries of Eastern Europe. It was farther removed physically from the United States and from Germany. There were few cultural similarities or affinities with the West. Language was a major problem. Few of the exiles knew English or any West European language. Maintaining cover was regarded as an important element. Assigning Amcomlib the same high visibility group that directed Free Europe could at best raise eyebrows and at worst give away the whole game. It was decided to operate the venture on a low key, in contrast with Free Europe's razzle dazzle.

There was another, more subtle factor. It was believed in Washington that a unified council of exiles would evoke more sympathy among Soviet citizens and create more consternation among the Kremlin leaderhip than could an American-led body. It was also assumed that broadcasts, which would inevitably constitute the most effective form of reaching Soviet citizens, would carry more credibility and exert more influence if they were clearly identified as the output of Soviet exiles. Less visible American direction was an important ingredient in building the illusion.

The solution was to look to less publicized Americans who were Soviet experts to lead the new organization. They understood the internal divisions. They had observed the Kremlin in action and they sincerely disliked the Soviet system and its leadership. Since returning they had written extensively about their detestation of the Soviet government. It was entirely reasonable

that they would enthusiastically enlist in a new, ostensibly privately supported organization to aid exiles in opposing the regime in Moscow. The very
existence of a unified assembly of exiles, passionately opposed to the Kremlin
leadership and working together to topple it, was calculated to shake the
Kremlin to its foundations—or so it was hoped.

The first tentative efforts to organize an American committee to deal with
émigrés from the Soviet Union began almost simultaneously with the first
moves toward creating the Committee for a Free Europe. In contrast with the
relative ease of setting Free Europe in motion, however, a very considerable
amount of preparatory work was necessary before efforts to unify the Soviet
emigration could have hoped to succeed. More than a year before Amcomlib
was chartered, and several months after Free Europe had been organized,
the Institute for the Study of the USSR was established in Munich under OPC
guidance and with OPC support; its purpose was to use the Soviet émigrés as
sources of basic research on the Soviet Union. The institute was to be the
intellectual arm of the effort.

There actually were two American teams of researchers at work in
Munich during 1950 and early 1951. The so-called Harvard group was the first
on the scene. It was supported by the Rockefeller Foundation and the U.S. Air
Force Historical Project. The purpose of the institute was to interview exiles
in an effort to develop a view of the Soviet Union from the exiles themselves.
It was planned to analyze the responses and prepare scholarly publications
and pieces for the popular press.* When it came on the scene, it rented a
small, comfortable suite of rooms equipped with a typewriter, a mimeograph
machine, and an interview room. Institute personnel made it a comfortable
place for exiles to come to and in so doing established a central physical location around which Amcomlib could later be formed.

During the summer of 1950, Lindsay began assembling a board of directors for a committee still to be formed. He requested John Mitchell to start
drawing up the necessary documents that would be required for incorporation.

The first informal meeting of the group selected to serve as directors took
place on January 12, 1951, in New York. Grover took the chair. In attendance
were Eugene Lyons and William H. Chamberlin, both of whom had been correspondents in the Soviet Union; William Y. Elliott of the Harvard University
faculty; and William L. White, publisher of the Emporia, Kansas, *Gazette* and
son of the famous William Allen White. Grover asked for support for the project and made a number of announcements. A representative of the committee, which did not yet formally exist, he reported to his colleagues had been

---

*After the founding of Amcomlib and the establishing of headquarters in Munich,
the Institute became a semiautonomous adjunct of the American Committee for Liberation.

employed the previous fall and sent to Germany as the committee's European representative. Money had been cabled twice to the representative, Spencer Williams, to help him meet expenses and "to enable him to render small support to émigré activities." There was no explanation regarding the source of the funds or how they could be transmitted by a nonexistent organization. Grover also reported with what would later prove to be more than slight exaggeration that "movement for unification among certain émigré groups had attained considerable impetus," and that "groundwork [has been] started by émigrés for a new unification which should lead to the broadest possible representation."

In an effort to stave off questions that might arise later about sources of funding, the potential directors were told that there would be no public solicitation of funds, "most of which will come from personal friends of committee members, most of whom have already expressed an interest in the work of the committee." These "friends of committee members" were known to Free Europe directors as "our friends in the South"; Grover referred to them as "the Confederates." It was also announced that there was to be no publicity attaching to the work of the committee. Any mention in the media would be directed to "the activities of the Russian emigration abroad."

The first meeting of the Amcomlib incorporators took place one week later, on January 19. There were five present: Grover, Lyons, Chamberlin, Elliott, and White. On February 8 Lyons was elected president, Chamberlin and Elliott vice presidents, Grover secretary, and White treasurer. As expected, Mitchell became general counsel. Isaac Don Levine, another old Russian hand, was elected to the board and sent overseas as European director. It would become his responsibility to cajole, wheedle, and strong-arm the quarreling factions in the emigration to work together. Not much, it was thought then, could be done before a unified coordinating council could be hammered together so that it could take the final responsibility for broadcasts, publications, and other such activities as the committee might decide to undertake. Despite its desire to avoid publicity, the committee felt it necessary to make some report to the media. Broadcasting was not specifically mentioned as one of the purposes as outlined in its first press release. The first objective was to "aid the worldwide Russian and nationalistic emigration in its effort to sustain the spirit of liberty among the peoples of the USSR." The second was "to preserve and sustain the historic cultures of Russians and the nationalities." The third was "to aid the emigration in seeking to extend understanding of the West within the USSR." This third objective could be accomplished best, of course, through radio.

The mechanism for accomplishing these purposes was to be a Center for Unified Action. The center would establish a program "to communicate" with the peoples of the Soviet Union. One method of communicating would involve radio broadcasts of "both news and analysis." But it was clearly understood that such broadcasts would be a function of the exiles and not of Amcomlib.

With all the legal details out of the way and an official announcement released to the media, the committee was in business. Now with OPC and CIA assistance* it had to make good on its promises. The greatest share of the responsibility rested on Levine's shoulders. His was a mission complicated beyond all expectation. The first intention was to form a Council for the Liberation of the Peoples of Russia, but the exercise proved futile. At times it seemed that an uneasy unity might prevail, but then hopes collapsed swiftly. The morass was too tricky and too deep. There were too many long-standing animosities among the émigrés, too many false hopes of nationalism and revenge, too wide a gap in the age levels, in their experiences, and in the length of time they had been out of the Soviet Union. There were too many purely selfish objectives, a bewildering array of splinter groups and splinters off splinter groups.

It looked, in mid-August of 1951, as if an agreement arrived at in Stuttgart to form a Council for the Liberation of the Peoples of Russia might constitute the elusive unified body. Five disparate Russian groups, the extreme right-wing National Labor Alliance (NTS), the left-wing Unification League of Struggle for Peoples' Freedom, Kerensky's Novodniki, the Vlasovites, and the Malgounov group, agreed to a shaky alliance. The picture looked even more favorable when six non-Russian organizations, including Georgians, Azerbaijanis, North Caucasians, Belorussians, Armenians, and Turkistani joined in with the Russians. The announcement of the enlarged council was made on November 7, 1951, the anniversary of the 1917 Revolution. But the signatories failed to submerge their rivalries. Unrest simmered just beneath the surface.

Levine shuttled about in Germany and on to Paris and London and back to Germany, trying to apply enough glue to make his fragile fabric stick together. He was sufficiently successful, even in view of the continuing tensions, that Amcomlib was able to announce in early summer of 1952 the formation at Starnberg of a radio council to function as an arm of the council for the anti-Bolshevik struggle. There had already been signs of stress in the council, however. The NTS had withdrawn prior to the announcement. Peter Khruzhin (still a member of the RL staff as this is written, at that time a member of the council representing the Vlasovites) points out that the NTS would

---

*As of early October 1950, the new CIA director, "Beetle" Smith had brought the OPC administratively under CIA control. In early January 1951 Allen Dulles accepted appointment as the executive in charge of both the OPC and the Office of Special Operations. Nominally, then, OPC was a division of the CIA. In actuality Wisner was able to operate with some independence for several months while the new organization chart was being implemented. Dulles, however, from this point on became the central figure in supporting both committees.

have settled for nothing less than a monopoly of political powers. Its objective was to avoid cooperating with any other political organization. It wanted nothing to do at that stage with a democratically directed organization. The NTS defection still left ten groups in the fold, however, including four Russian and six non-Russian nationality units. This body was in the judgment of Amcomlib sufficiently comprehensive to proceed with the establishment of a radio station, even though the prognosis for a successful broadcast operation was something less than wholly favorable. Khruzhin, Russian himself and not entirely free of charges of prejudice at the time, pointed out that many of the nationalities' representatives were so anti-Russian they did not even want to sit down with the Russians at a conference table. And it is notable that the largest of the non-Russian states in population, the Ukraine, was nowhere represented at any of these negotiations. The Ukrainian emigration was composed of elements so antagonistic to each other that they could not agree on a delegation to represent them.

By August 1952 the ten organizations cooperating in the coordinating center had dropped off to nine. The Ukrainians were still outside, still difficult and obstinate. Ten months later, in June 1953, the nine split into two hostile camps, one Russian, the other non-Russian. At that point Amcomlib, frustrated in its efforts to turn over the responsibility to the coordinating center and the émigrés, announced that the Committee had no alternative but to recognize that "there is no immediate prospect for the formation of a united front of the emigration. . . . It is regrettable that the political forces of the emigration have not had the foresight and statesmanship to lay aside their internal differences and unite in presenting a common front to the Kremlin."

The committee continued to hold out an olive branch, however, pointing out that it still desired the participation of qualified forces of the emigration in the broadcasting activity. It made a number of compromises in an effort to placate the adamant exile groups. For example, since the name, "American Committee for Freedom for the Peoples of the USSR," was an irritant to some influential leaders among the Russian exiles (they insisted that the use of the designation "USSR" connoted recognition of the Soviet Union), the designation was changed by board action in May 1951 to the American Committee for the Liberation of the Peoples of Russia, Inc. But there was little hope. Four years, including the two years before the incorporation of Amcomlib and the two years afterward, had been spent in persuading the emigrant groups to work together, all to no avail.

Lyons remained as president for one year. In February 1952 he was replaced by Admiral Alan G. Kirk, who had served as U.S. ambassador in Moscow. Mitchell had resigned in the fall of 1951 when he accepted assignment as assistant general counsel on the CIA staff in Washington. It was felt by "the Confederates" that agency backing would be unduly exposed if he remained in the position, so he was replaced by another New York attorney, Henry Root Stern.

The CIA reorganization of 1950 and early 1951 under "Beetle" Smith tightened control over the OPC. Dulles, as Wisner's immediate superior, now had final responsibility for both Free Europe and Amcomlib. Separate oversight was maintained, however, below the Dulles and Wisner levels. As the CIA expanded its range of operations, an international operations division under the direction of Thomas Braden kept watch on Free Europe.* Amcomlib remained a ward of the Soviet bloc division, where Henry Varnum Poor was the point of contact with the committee's board.

Cord Meyer, who later became the responsible CIA officer watching after both organizations, believes that Dulles and Wisner had important reasons for what appears an awkward separation of two organizations with similar goals. Some are obvious: the constituencies were clearly dissimilar and required different treatment; cover was less likely to be broken if they were kept compartmentalized. Meyer, though, sees another motive. He believes that both Dulles and Wisner had learned much from the Free Europe experience. One thing they were apprehensive about was the strength and independence of Free Europe's board of directors. The "old boy" atmosphere created by the common experiences of many of the board leadership as former OSS officers, current members of the Council on Foreign Relations, the Century Association, and the closely knit fraternity of New York lawyers gave them a level of prestige that was desirable to Dulles and his aides from one point of view but troublesome in regard to the exercising of tight control. There was actually, Meyer says, some ambivalence within the CIA about Free Europe. It was regarded in some circles as relatively uncontrollable. Among its leaders were too many prestigious influentials who had been in and out of government and knew how to circumvent government orders. The CIA leaders felt they had to step gingerly in creating a new organization in the image of RFE. Dulles had seen enough of the Free Europe Committee and its high-powered leadership to recognize that a different type of relationship with Amcomlib would make life easier.

The excruciatingly slow progress toward unification forced the committee in early 1952 to reconsider its goals and objectives and its plans for achieving them. Could it afford to wait indefinitely for the exile groups to purge their differences, at least to the extent that they could work together in some loose organization? Should it proceed to create its own organization to publish and broadcast in the event that the coordinating center was never formed? If

---

*Braden recently told the writer, "I had nothing to do with RL. I never knew anything about RL and Durkee [Braden's assistant] didn't know anything about it either. I knew it existed, but I had nothing to do with it."

there was still hope for unification, could the board continue to delay leasing real estate, requisitioning broadcast equipment, and employing support staff against the day when unification could be achieved?

It was evident that Amcomlib could not continue to function simply as a small committee in New York with a few field agents struggling with what might turn out to be an insoluble problem in Europe. It was time to start building for the future, with or without a unified council of the emigration, if the committee hoped to accomplish any of its objectives.

As early as May 1951, only four months after the incorporation of Amcomlib, the committee had decided to bite the bullet and proceed with the hope that the unruly units of the emigration would eventually fall into place. It had announced that, come what may, it would "undertake broadcasts in Russian and other languages of the USSR at the earliest practical moment." It still, however, had not been prepared to furnish more than the shell of an organization: the building and physical facilities necessary to carry out the mandate. A press release in that same month had announced:

> The American committee does not plan to undertake any major activities directly on its own. . . . [It] will remain a relatively small and cohesive organization and it proposes to keep itself in the background leaving the foreground to the centralized Russian organizations through which it will channel such material and friendly guidance as it can muster.

On July 24 it had announced the appointment of Forrest McCluney as its director of broadcasting. McCluney had already negotiated for property for RFE, approved building plans, supervised construction, and employed technical and administrative staff. It was now his assignment to perform similar services for RL. McCluney was to spend approximately a year in the New York office, engaged largely in planning for the inauguration of broadcasts; then he was off to Munich in early summer of 1952 to oversee plans for building studios and recruiting a support staff that would make it possible to develop a broadcast schedule.

Writers, editors, and producers had been recruited in New York to start producing experimental programs that would later be converted to on-the-air material. Boris Shub, a Russian-speaking American was enticed away from RIAS in Berlin, where he had been programming director, to hammer a program staff into shape. From a barren loft in New York City's diamond district, Shub and his rag-tag crew started to wrestle with program production.

Most of the U.S. activity in Munich had been devoted to patching up quarrels among the exiles and pleading with them to get together, but some preliminary moves had been made toward building a shell of an American supervisory program staff. Manning Williams had been transferred from the

Frankfurt area, where he had been editing an American-supported newspaper, to take over the program directorship. Francis F. Ronalds, Jr., a Russian-speaking member of the staff of the foreign affairs section of *Time*, joined him. Williams hired the first Russian to be employed by RL in Munich, a former Soviet artillery captain, Boris Orshansky, who had defected to West Berlin shortly after the war. Orshansky became "talent assistant."

The stepped-up activity was evident to the émigré groups. Peter Khruzhin, who was active in the Vlasovite organization, and later joined the RL staff, says that a large group of people came from the United States in 1952 to set up the station. He reports that there were program specialists under Williams's supervision, an administrative group, and a personnel group. There was apparently no resentment at the American invasion. The emigration, Khruzhin says, "very much wanted the station, but had wanted it formed along democratic lines." Democratic lines could lead to chaos, of course.

In June a press release from committee headquarters in New York announced that McCluney had arrived in Munich "to supervise construction and prepare for the opening of radio station Radio Liberation." The extent of the preparatory efforts is reflected in a report that had been made to the annual meeting of the members of the American corporation on April 23, 1952. As of that date the total personnel complement stationed in New York had increased from 19 to 46, and in Munich from 4 to 274. In all, in April 1952, Amcomlib had a payroll of 320, contrasted with 23 the year earlier.

If the plans for the creation of a unified coordinating center had come to fruition, recruitment of all program production personnel would have been the center's responsibility. Without the center, the burden fell on the American staff. Some of the exiles joining the staff, including Orshansky, were not affiliated with the contentious factions, but many were, and that left American management with the problem of maintaining some sense of harmony if any results were to be achieved.

There still was no positive process toward unification by the time the first two 10-kilowatt transmitters were installed and ready for testing at Lampertheim in January 1953,* so the committee decided to go ahead with its inaugural broadcast. By this time Admiral Kirk had resigned the presidency to be succeeded by another admiral with experience in the Soviet Union, Leslie C. Stevens. The Kirk administration, no matter how much it had been frustrated by the endless feuding of the exile factions, had succeeded in laying the foundation for what could be a functioning broadcasting arm. By August 1952, when Kirk resigned, the basic decision had been made to go forward with or without the coordinating center. A rather fragile council of exiles was

---

*RL had purchased the RFE base from RFE, which in turn moved to nearby Biblis.

feeling its way, even though continuing tension inhibited decisive support for the broadcasting programs.

March 1, 1953, was designated as the date to transmit the first program in Russian. The program fare was to constitute a mix of news and commentary, most of it prepared in New York under Shub's direction.* Munich, however, was prepared to participate. The committee had hired an old Moscow hand, Edmund Stevens, to organize a news department and prepare it for the opening air date. Stevens had been a correspondent in Moscow for the *Christian Science Monitor* and spoke fluent Russian, enabling him to communicate with his Russian staff. Facilities were limited. United Press and Deutsche Presse Agentur press services were available; the RFE news service could be picked up by a taxi ride across the city. A monitoring service, moreover, had been created to overhear and record Soviet radio. News personnel, however, were in short supply. Journalists working for Tass, the Soviet news agency, and for newspapers of the Soviet Union, were employees of the state. Few of them were likely to defect, so Stevens had to train nonjournalists to perform journalistic tasks.

The first broadcast on March 1 was uneventful. It did not represent a brilliant use of broadcast facilities, but that was probably unimportant. Ten kilowatts of power with only a temporary antenna was hardly enough to shake the foundations of the Kremlin.

Only four days later, RL by blind luck was face to face with one of the greatest news stories of the postwar era: the death of Josef Stalin. Even with its limited resources, it passed the test. A combination of wire service reports, RFE's news service, and texts of Soviet broadcasts overheard by RL's own monitors backed up by Shub's background material from New York enabled it to provide a running story and stay ahead of Moscow radio and Tass. It suffered, however, in competition with other Western shortwave radio broadcasts to the Soviet Union. It simply could not compete in getting on the air as quickly. There was no effective communication link between the limited quarters occupied by RL's news offices in Munich where the news department was housed and the 10-kilowatt transmitter at Lampertheim more than 200 miles away. Copy was prepared in Munich, recordings were made on tape, and the tape was dispatched to Lampertheim by motorcycle courier (a trip which took a minimum of five or six hours to complete). RL personnel were not too much concerned by the time lag, however, since Soviet media were

---

*Shub's small New York production unit was shipping scripts by air mail to Munich for transshipment to Lampertheim. These tapes were edited into the program output for the half-hour inaugural.

notoriously slow in covering major events. Proving that they could furnish running coverage of a major story provided a growing sense of professionalism. And that in itself was a significant accomplishment.*

Three months later, RL was able to test its muscle against another dramatic event: the East Berlin riots of June 17. A news crew went to Berlin for on-the-spot coverage and sent back material that Amcomlib's president Stevens described as "reaching a level of real brilliance."

Some of the news items, however, got a bit contentious, perhaps a little more so than policy guidelines would have encouraged. One broadcast, addressed to the Soviet troops in the streets of Berlin, pleaded:

> Soldiers and officers of the Soviet Army, the German workers struggle against Kremlin oppression is unfolding before your eyes. . . . [On] order to fire on the demonstrators remember they are not enemies of our country but are defenders of freedom. They seek liberation from the same yoke which oppresses our fathers, mothers, brothers and sisters. . . . The workers of East Berlin are fighting for the cause of all mankind and for the delivery of the whole world, including our motherland, from communism. Help them!

During these first few months on the air, RL was broadcasting as the "voice of the emigration," in anticipation of the ultimate solution of the coordinating council's problem. The committee had taken action earlier in the year to stifle some of the carping criticism. It had voted to change the name of the corporation from the American Committee for the Liberation of Russia to the American Committee for Liberation from Bolshevism, in order to make it easier for the Ukrainians, who had been standing on the sidelines and had no intention of participating, to enter the center along with the almost equally adamant Belorussians. The change, however, backfired: it just incensed the Russians.†

---

*If one of Shub's more daring suggestions had been followed, coverage might have been vastly more dramatic. He proposed some days before RL went on the air that the Russian service feature on each of its broadcasts a metronome. The metronome would tick on and an ominous voice would intone "the Stalin era is coming to a close." There would then be more ticking by the metronome and the voice would repeat "the Stalin era is coming to a close." Unfortunately, Shub's idea was never given a chance. Someone on the staff pointed out that Stalin might live on for years—perhaps even outlive the metronome. The idea was abandoned because no one expected the dictator's death so close to opening air date.

†The committee seems to have been unaware that "Bolshevism" had been Hitler's favorite term of disparagement of the Soviet Union. RFE later issued a directive to its news staffs banning the use of the term for this reason.

Stevens had been intrigued for some time by the prospect of going to India, studying Hindu, and writing a book on India as he had done earlier on Russia. He could not leave Amcomlib, however, until his successor was chosen. At a meeting at Dartmouth College in Hanover, New Hampshire, in the fall of 1953, he ran into an old acquaintance, Howland Sargeant, who had until recently been assistant secretary of state for information. In that office Sargeant had been responsible for managing the cultural and international communications functions of the department, including the VOA. Sargeant had left State when his units had been absorbed into the new U.S. Information Agency in midsummer of 1953. He was mildly interested in the prospect, but only on his terms. Serious negotiations between Sargeant and Stevens began shortly afterwards. In consideration of the prospect, Sargeant talked at length with Dulles, Wisner, Braden (who by then had the prime responsibility for watching over Free Europe and Amcomlib), and Meyer, his assistant.* Sargeant told the CIA executives bluntly what his terms were. "I am not a coordinator of exiles," he told them. "If you are genuinely interested in creating an instrument of communications of a type different from an official radio, I would be willing to take a look at it and see what I can do. On the other hand, if it be an organization for the care and feeding of exiles, there are more competent people than me to do the job."

By this time the CIA executives were frustrated enough over the discord among the exile groups to agree with his analysis. They were particularly disturbed by the split in June 1953 that had forced the committee to recognize that there was no immediate hope for the formation of a united front. They agreed, however, that the future of Amcomlib was to be in radio communications. Before he would accept the assignment, Sargeant insisted that the radio operations be given top priority, and that he be given assurances he would not find himself bogged down in endless negotiations with irreconcilable exile groups. He did offer, however, to keep in touch with the exiles and their leaderships and expressed the hope that he could find in the exile group personnel who would contribute substantially to the editorial side of broadcasting to

---

*Amcomlib had originally been the responsibility of Henry Varnum Poor. Poor served the CIA's Soviet Bloc (SB) division and in that position assumed direct responsibility for overseeing Amcomlib, as Braden, the director of the International Organizations Division, did for Free Europe. When Poor resigned to practice law in New York and incidentally accepted an assignment as legal counsel to Amcomlib, direction of the organization was transferred to the International Organizations' unit.

Braden had joined the agency in 1951 after serving as the chief executive of the American Committee for a United Europe. When the International Organizations Division was formed, he brought in his old assistant at the American Committee, William P. Durkee, as his deputy to oversee Free Europe. When Durkee left two years later, Meyer filled his post, later becoming director when Braden resigned. Meyer then acquired the responsibility, following Poor's departure, for both Free Europe and Amcomlib.

Russia and the nationalities in the Soviet Union. There was a final essential demand: "No order is to be given to any employee of the radio unless that order is given through and in the name of the President of the Committee or that it is withheld until it bears his countersignature." He was determined that if he took the job he was going to run the organization himself and that he was not going to be second-guessed, undercut, or masterminded by CIA executives or field agents. On his terms he was offered and took the job, reporting to the president's office in late September 1954.

In retrospect, Sargeant feels he didn't inherit much. "Nobody," he says "took the Radio seriously." It was grinding away with its two little 10-kilowatt transmitters at a time when 50- and 100-kilowatt units were commonplace, and 250-kilowatts not unknown. (And this was well after Peter Mero had warned Free Europe that the spectrum was getting crowded.) The antennas at the Lampertheim base were still temporary and produced a comparatively low gain, although that could be rectified with greater power and taller, higher-gain curtain units. Program departments had been established but, as Sargeant puts it, "In 1954 they didn't correspond to any program department with which I had been familiar."

The Shub group in New York was competent enough, but it was far removed from Munich. And Munich had very little contact with the group. Furthermore, the programmers were shipping their tapes, as Sargeant puts it, "by slow boat." The needs were considerable in both personnel and equipment. The first step at acquiring some additional professionalism in Munich was the hiring of Richard Bertrandias as program director. Bertrandias had had some commercial radio experience and had been the director of the Far East Broadcasting Company, a U.S. government operation with intelligence ties similar to RFE and RL. Its signals were aimed at Japan and China. Bertrandias thus had had experience in a related operation. Shortly later, Barry Mahool went to Munich as assistant to Bertrandias. Mahool had been one of the program executives at RFE during its early formative stage and after that had functioned as a communications advisor to the government of Egypt. He added additional depth to the program department that was further supplemented by the employment of some of Bertrandias' aides from Far East Broadcasting.

The next step was to induce an innovative army colonel with extensive experience in electronic communications to join RL as head of the technical operations department. Colonel Steven Y. McGiffert had worked with Sargeant at the VOA and with Bertrandias at Far East Broadcasting. He knew shortwave, its problems and its strengths. He had designed facilities and had drawn up specifications for acquiring equipment. Further, he had a wide range of acquaintances involved in radio programming as well as in facilities and transmission. McGiffert's arrival was particularly timely because Sargeant regarded building up his technical operations capability as his first and highest priority. There was no point pouring resources into programming if the signal was to rise a few feet from the earth at the Lampertheim base and fall back again unheard. McGiffert was assigned to work with representatives of A. D. Ring in identifying the optimum site for a major shortwave broadcasting base and to design the facilities to be established there.

The emigration, whether unified or shattered, would have to remain the main source of program personnel. An American staff would lack not only the precise language capability, but, more important, an intimate knowledge of the target audience, its interests, culture, informational background, and the vocabulary it used. How to use the émigrés without turning over total control to them was RL's main headache—how to develop enthusiastic cooperation without abdicating leadership or responsibility. Sargeant took the position with the émigrés: "We want you here. We want you to work with us in a joint cause. But we don't want your internal quarrels invading our premises. When you come to work here, check your six-shooters at the door."

He took even a tougher position with the NTS. He declared that no NTS member who supported the NTS constitution could work at RL or for Amcomlib. The charter of the NTS called for the creation of a Great Russian chauvinism, dominated by Moscow, with minorities regarded only as lower-class citizens. Discipline imposed by NTS leadership was sufficiently firm that transgressions by NTS members were unlikely. "We could not be a Great Russian Radio," Sargeant says. "If we took NTS people who support NTS goals, we could be planting seeds which could defeat our own purpose." Some NTS personnel were later employed in RL positions, but only if they were free of NTS discipline when they worked for the Radio.

Relationships with the CIA, in Sargeant's mind, could also become sticky. He had made it clear at the outset that no one at CIA was to issue orders to his troops. He created mechanisms, however, to keep CIA headquarters informed of day-to-day developments. A "green copy" of all memoranda and correspondence flowing through the president's office was forwarded from Amcomlib to CIA headquarters in Washington. A CIA employee was placed in Sargeant's office as assistant to the president in order to insure that the flow would be unimpeded. In all, the CIA connection was a bundle of contrasts. There was little direct program control over RL but there was constant surveillance of the actions taken by RL management. Budgets were controlled, but generally management was on its own. From an analysis of the method by which RL operated there was little evidence that it was not what it purported to be: an independent organization of U.S. citizens concerned with the problems of exiles from the Soviet Union and broadcasting into the Soviet Union. Dulles and Wisner and their associates apparently had confidence in Sargeant and had no time or desire to enter directly into the radio business, so RL could legitimately operate as an independent radio entity.

As RL completed its first 18 months of broadcasting in September 1954, with Sargeant firmly seated in the president's chair, it was painfully apparent that vastly increased power and the acquisition of additional radio frequencies would be required as soon as possible to put a signal into the Soviet Union that could be easily heard, jamming or no jamming. Transmitters and antennas were desperately needed, and something had to be done quickly if the progress made since 1953 was to yield any positive long-term results. The mechanisms were in place for delivering a program schedule designed to support Amcomlib's goals, but facilities were sorely lacking. Lampertheim did not have the muscle to deliver the message. Some facility with vastly more power would be necessary to reach all the target audiences, along with additional frequencies to permit several signals to be transmitted simultaneously.

8
Franco Pays Off

I T WAS EVIDENT from the outset that Lampertheim was only a stopgap transmitter base for Amcomlib's broadcasts to the Soviet Union. The site was too close to the borders of the Soviet Union for delivery of the signal strength required to reach the main population centers. Since the base was on an east-west axis, moreover, it was not able to take full advantage of twilight immunity* to mitigate the effects of jamming. And finally, there was fear that the Korean War might erupt into full-scale international conflict involving the Soviet Union, thus endangering any facilities in West Germany, which might again become a major battlefield.

The A. D. Ring Company, which had helped select Portugal as the operating base for the Free Europe Committee, had also been requested to prepare propagation studies for Amcomlib. The optimum site, according to Ring, would be about as far northeast from Gloria as Moscow is north and east from Warsaw and Prague. It was clear that either Spain or North Africa would offer the best possible sites. There were several possibilites in Spain: the high plateau around Madrid, the Balearic Islands in the Mediterranean, including some that were virtually uninhabited, and the rugged Costa Brava extending northward from Barcelona to the French border. American consulting engineers had started visiting Spain in search of an operating base for the newly formed Amcomlib as early as 1951.[1] They had been assisted by engineers from the Spanish Directorate General of Radio.

Twilight immunity is a term used by electronic engineers to describe a period in each day when powerful sky-wave jammers lose effectiveness because their jamming signals are diverted from an accurate bounce off the ionosphere by the change from daylight to darkness. The greater the distance from broadcast transmitter to target, the longer immunity lasts. See Chapter 22 for a more detailed discussion of jamming.

The Department of State, however, was apprehensive about Spain. The department had discouraged Gregory Thomas of the Free Europe Committee from going to Spain and was reluctant to permit Amcomlib to go there because it was politically sensitive. Memories of the Spanish Civil War and of Franco's Hitler-tilted neutrality during World War II were too bitter to disappear so soon. And dictatorship in itself was distasteful to many Americans. The engineers, however, were not giving up. In early 1954 an Amcomlib engineer from Munich, Ralph Harmon, visited the Ministry of Information and Tourism in Madrid to confer with engineers there and explain the project to them.

This was the status of the search for a transmitter base for Amcomlib when Howland Sargeant assumed the presidency of the committee in September 1954. The Lampertheim base was operational but with pitifully small power output. The most powerful of the nine transmitters by then in place delivered only 20 kilowatts of signal strength. Combined, the nine totalled a miniscule 86 kilowatts. There were two rhombic antennas that were totally inadequate to deliver the antenna gain required to override jamming or even to project a clear signal well within the USSR. Fortunately for the fledgling base, the worldwide rush to high-powered transmitters and the crowding of the spectrum by national governments was only beginning. However, as Mero had reported to the Free Europe board, the Soviet Union in particular was expanding its shortwave usage rapidly.

It was evident to Sargeant that steps had to be taken soon to acquire the property for a facility comparable to the one that the Free Europe Committee had built at Gloria in Portugal. RL could never transmit more than a feeble and indistinct voice until aggressive action was taken. Engineering data pointed to Spain as the prime choice, and notwithstanding State Department opposition and possible public reaction against dealing with the Franco government, Sargeant was determined to go ahead. With his long State Department experience he understood deparmental thinking well enough to be able to assess the risks involved in taking the chance.

Cord Meyer reveals in his book *Facing Reality* that Dulles agonized for a long time over the expenditures that would be required to build a major new shortwave base, whether in Spain or elsewhere, although he eventually gave in to pressure from Sargeant and his own subordinates. It was clear that RL would amount to only a futile but costly exercise unless it had the power to reach the intended audience.

The Amcomlib president took off in early June 1955, accompanied by Harry Varnum Poor, the corporation's legal counsel, on a mission of undetermined duration. The only deadline they faced was the customary departure of virtually the entire leadership of the Spanish government for the mountains or the seashore for summer vacations. The exodus from Madrid would normally take place in mid-July. This would leave about five weeks from the departure from New York to complete the mission.

Sargeant carried with him a number of bargaining chips he hoped to cash in upon his arrival. In 1951 he had been the chairman of the U.S. delegation to the UNESCO General Conference in Paris. Franco, anxious to win friendship in the West, decided to use an application for membership to UNESCO as an opening gambit. The United States had decided to support the Spanish application, and Sargeant became the instrument through which it would apply its leverage.

A powerful ally soon appeared on the scene. Sargeant struck up a warm friendship with the papal nuncio to France, one Angelo Cardinal Roncalli, whom the world would later come to know as Pope John XXIII. Cardinal Roncalli was an invaluable ally. He had a wide circle of friends among delegates. The two made a powerful and effective team. Spain won its membership on a vote that Sargeant says "wasn't even close," and Sargeant at the same time won Franco's attention. The generalissimo was so pleased that he sent Sargeant a personal message of thanks. The message would be Sargeant's hole card in his negotiations in Madrid.

The mission started as an experience in frustration, if not futility. Government leaders below the generalissimo's level could not see any reason to accommodate a nonofficial visiting American on a mission they did not fully understand. Moreover, Sargeant was pretty much on his own: the State Department's calculated hands-off policy toward both Amcomlib and Free Europe discouraged active embassy participation. The Spanish minister of information and tourism, who would have to make the ultimate decision, was concerned that installing transmitters and antenna towers could be a powerful magnet for Soviet missiles and wanted to have no part of approving so dangerous a base.

Sargeant decided to play his trump card. He called at the generalissimo's office and asked for an appointment to pay a courtesy call, using as a door opener the note he had received almost four years earlier from Franco. Just three weeks after his arrival in Madrid, his request for an interview was granted and a time was arranged. He expected that he would only be permitted to pay his respects, exchange a few pleasantries, and retreat. It was exactly one hour and 20 minutes after he entered Franco's office that he emerged following a cordial discussion in which he had had an opportunity to state his case in detail.

The opportunity to explain his request to Franco, however, was not nearly as important as the secondary impact of the conversation. Cabinet ministers, functionaries in the dictator's office, and a wide variety of government officials frequently measured a visitor's importance and the significance of his project by the length of time he spent with the generalissimo. One hour and 20 minutes in Franco's office was enough to impress even the most unenthusiastic. Doors that had been shut tight suddenly opened. As Sargeant puts it, "The time I spent with Franco elevated my political clout."

The mid-July date for the exodus of government officials was quickly approaching, but with Franco's help Sargeant obtained an "agreement in principle" that if Amcomlib could find a suitable piece of property measuring up to the requirements established by the engineering consultants, then Amcomlib could proceed to negotiate a specific agreement to purchase the property. The agreement was signed with only days to go before the lengthy summer holiday.

The purchase would have to be made in the name of the government of Spain. Spanish law specified that the ownership and operation of shortwave broadcast facilities including ownership of the land were the exclusive right of the government. A decree of the Spanish government and approval by the Cortes, the Spanish parliament, was required before the Ministry of Information and Tourism could enter into a specfic contract. Amcomlib would pay the purchase price for the property and turn the deed over to the ministry. The equipment used on the base would also eventually become the property of the Spanish government. The agreement, although apparently only a first small step, was enough to permit the search for suitable property to go ahead. And implementation of the decree would not only permit the construction of an operating base, but also granted RL the right to use desperately needed broadcasting frequencies that were reserved by the ITU for the government of Spain.

The Ministry of Information assigned Ernesto Marrero, who had worked with both Ralph Harmon and the consulting engineers who had visited Spain in 1951, to aid the Americans in their site search. Marrero had covered much of the terrain himself in search of operating bases for Spanish government broadcast facilities. It was specified by the ministry that once a suitable piece of property was found, one that would satisfy Amcomlib, Marrero would be the one to negotiate the terms and conditions of the purchase with the property owner.

Just five weeks after leaving New York, Sargeant was back in the Amcomlib offices with his "agreement in principle" in hand. But the job had only begun. Still ahead was the search for the site, negotiation for acquisition of the property, obtaining a definitive agreement from the government, including approval by the Cortes, designing transmitter facilities, writing specifications for equipment and accepting bids, completing construction, and obtaining a license to operate.

Sargeant's first step was to assign his old associate from the State Department and VOA days, Colonel Steven McGiffert, whom he had hired as Amcomlib chief engineer, to work with Marrero on the quest for a suitable site.

As a result of his previous experience, McGiffert was acquainted with the Ring Company studies and with the efforts dating back to 1951 to find suitable sites in Spain. It was his job now to work with Marrero to comb through the favored areas in Spain to uncover specific plots of land likely to meet the requirements.

The Costa Brava was the first choice. It was not heavily populated. Although it had not yet been discovered as a prime vacation spot, it was close to the metropolitan center of Barcelona. A trunk rail line that ran from Barcelona to the French border just a few miles inland would facilitate the shipment of heavy equipment that could either be manufactured in Barcelona or shipped in through the Barcelona port. But most important from the engineering point of view, a spot at or near the beach could furnish an unobstructed path for a signal to take off in the direction of the USSR. A low angle of fire with no hills to surmount would be ideal. Reflecting the signal off the water would enhance its strength. It was also hoped that property could be located in an area remote enough so that work would not be impeded by throngs of curious onlookers.

Theirs was a tedious, time-consuming job. There were inadequate roads or no roads at all in many of the beach areas of the Costa Brava. McGiffert and his associates walked through woods and fields and used small boats along the shore. As Sargeant puts it, they "crawled" through much of northeastern Spain. At least ten sites were discovered, each of which would have been satisfactory, but the best by far was a beautiful piece of flat beach near the little village of Palafrugell in the province of Gerona. It was on a wide, half-moon-shaped bay, with a heavily wooded gentle ridge behind it. There was no road leading to the beach and virtually no habitation around it. Best of all, the beach lay at right angles to a direct path toward Moscow, Kiev, and Leningrad, ideal for a low-trajectory signal that would receive an added boost from reflection off the Mediterranean.

The property owner had no great enthusiasm for selling but saw no long-range possibilities for the development of the property. There were no roads, no electric power immediately available, and little tourist interest. An agreement to sell was signed on July 15, 1957, a few days more than two years after Sargeant had received an "agreement in principle" to negotiate for the property. By early fall of 1957, Amcomlib had the property it wanted.

It took another two years before the base began to operate. First it was necessary to build a road into the Playa de Pals. Antenna towers were ordered from steel mills in Barcelona so as to make maximum use of Spanish industry. The first 100-kilowatt transmitter was ordered from the German company Telefunken, which had a unit ready for immediate delivery. Rhombic antennas, much less complicated to install than curtain antennas, which required tall towers, were decided on for the first stage. Electric power was a major problem; but the Spanish power monopoly, sensing a great marketing opportunity, agreed to bring transmission lines in from the nearest substation at Palafrugell, only approximately 8 kilometers away. One concession was made by Amcomlib: by the time power-company personnel began to string the lines, tourism promoters had begun construction of a golf course almost surrounding the Amcomlib property on the inland side. Amcomlib, at the request of the power company, agreed to let the golf club take power from the Amcomlib line and reimburse the station for the amount used.

The danger that curious onlookers might suffer serious injury from contact with power lines was avoided when Marrero went to government officials and received permission to close off the beach fronting on the transmitter site. The Spanish navy assigned patrols to prevent small boats from approaching closer than 200 meters from the shoreline.* Spanish personnel were recruited from the Spanish high school of technology,† from Radio Espana and from the Spanish Ministry of Information and Tourism for the highly specialized engineering jobs involved in installing transmitters, switching fields, communications links, and power lines. Life was not easy for the engineers recruited. The closest towns of any size were nearly an hour away and roads were inferior. Some of those original employees who came to the Playa de Pals in 1959, however, including Chief Engineer Rafael Morena, the manager of the technical support department, Andres Llorento, and Fernando Friol, manager of administrative services, are still on the staff as this is written.

Once installation of the first transmitter and antenna field was completed the government of Spain granted Amcomlib a license to broadcast from the new base. The price was $10, payable annually.‡ Broadcasting began on March 23, 1959, almost four years after Sargeant had arrived in Madrid to open negotiations. The 100-kilowatt output of power was nearly equal to the entire power output then available at Lampertheim. Furthermore, the site

---

*A commission later visited the site and decided that the public had a right to use the beach, thus putting an end to the prohibition. The entire beach remained open until 1981 when RL erected a steel fence at the edge of the antenna emplacements, thus discouraging passersby from risking their lives in the midst of the power lines, but at the same time enabling them to use the beach at will.

†In European terms a "high school for technology," is a graduate school for science, technology, and engineering, comparable to MIT or Caltech in the United States.

‡The lease for the property, however, was billed at an annual rate of $270,000.

was so conducive to shortwave transmission that Amcomlib could finally feel confident that it was putting an acceptable signal into the Soviet Union and at least temporarily had an edge on Soviet jammers.

The intention from the beginning was to make Pals the source of sufficient shortwave electronic energy to force the Soviets to pay attention. Plans went forward to introduce the most powerful shortwave transmitter ever in regular usage: a unit boasting a power output of 250 kilowatts. To amplify the signal for the 250-kilowatt transmitters and direct them toward targets in the USSR, Amcomlib built the most impressive antenna field yet known: a gigantic curtain array hung from steel towers more than 550 feet high. Orders were placed with Continental Electronics in Dallas for four of the monster transmitters. The first was in operation 18 months after the Pals base opened; the second, three weeks later. Two more began operating by April 1961. The fifth, which, when in place, gave Pals more than 1.3 million watts of power, was added in 1964.

McGiffert's dream, though, was to deliver power in excess of anything achieved. He visualized tying together the four 250-kilowatt transmitters into one enormous megawatt giant. By July 2, 1967, engineers at Pals had built a "combiner" that enabled them to tie two 250-kilowatt transmitters together to deliver a massive 500-kilowatt output. A second "combiner" joined the two others into a single 500-kilowatt output. A year later, engineers had completed a third "combiner" that enabled the two 500s to merge into one of a million watts. This was the most powerful shortwave signal ever transmitted in the burgeoning contest among the nations to tell their stories across international borders. Test reports came in from the Soviet Union reporting that the signal boomed in, overpowering jamming. But it proved to be an extravagant use of power. It concentrated too much effort on one frequency. Amcomlib officials came to the conclusion that their objectives would be better served, except in cases of extreme urgency, by broadcasting over as many frequencies as they could with the available equipment rather than by concentrating all of their power into one frequency. With 15 languages of the USSR to cover, they needed as many transmitters as could be made available and as many frequencies as those transmitters could carry. They also concluded that broadcasting a single program on a number of frequencies could cause more trouble for the jammers than devoting all of their resources to one overwhelming thrust of power. This would force the Soviet jamming command to scatter its facilities across the spectrum, thus tying up both personnel and jamming facilities.

Relationships with the government of Spain, which could have been sticky, turned out to be remarkably smooth, primarily because of the deep interest in the project demonstrated by the two executives of the Ministry of

Information and Tourism who were assigned under terms of the license* to manage the project, Manuel Garofa-Duran and Marrero. Garofa-Duran was designated by the Spanish government to be director of the station, and Marrero, chief engineer of technical services. If they had taken their assignments literally they could have forced U.S. management out or into subordinate positions.

Amcomlib officials were confident, however, that Garofa-Duran and Marrero would consider their responsibilities limited to cooperating with Americans assigned to the base. There was a constant fear among Amcomlib personnel, however, that Garofa-Duran and Marrero might be replaced by more ambitious Spanish officals, in which case there might have been some serious arguments concerning rights, prerogatives, and management.

A more sensitive issue related to the content of RL's broadcasts. Government authorities in Madrid were nervous about possible inaccuracies in broadcasts carrying news of Spain and concerned that there was not enough favorable Spanish coverage. As a result of their concerns RL management agreed to send a correspondent to Madrid who would cover Spanish events on the scene and report directly to the RL news department in Munich.

It was anticipated from the beginning that security would be a problem. There was concern that even though the Playa de Pals was an isolated area with little public access, curiosity seekers would eventually discover the futuristic forest of antenna towers and high-voltage electrical cables. Shortly after the road into the Pals base had been completed and construction started, their worries were justified. The Costa Brava achieved new status as an "insider's" area for vacationers and vacation homes. The completion of the 18-hole golf course in the pine woods surrounding the base started a land rush to the Playa de Pals area. Construction of high-rise condominiums started to advance along the coast, encroaching on the Amcomlib area. More and more vacationers from Barcelona and from France and Germany began to use the beaches on either side of the Playa de Pals base and eventually began to walk up and down the beach itself. When the government decided it could no longer prohibit use of the beach, traffic increased. A chain-link fence surrounded the property on the land side. Personnel from the Spanish civil guard manned the gate. Dogs were eventually brought in to patrol the fenced area

---

*The agreement had been negotiated and signed before May 23, 1959, when the station first went on the air, but signatories had failed to date it. George Dennis, the Amcomlib representative in Madrid starting in 1960, and government officials noted the oversight in early 1961 and mutually agreed that the most logical date for the 12-year term to start would be the date of the first transmission. RL was thus cleared to broadcast from Pals without further negotiations until March 23, 1971, 12 years after the first broadcast from the base. A five-year extension was signed on that date. Since March 22, 1976, RL has operated without a lease, but it has continued to pay the $270,000 annual rental fee.

along with guards,* but the beach side was open. In view of the doubtful legality of the order prohibiting traffic on the beach, the government felt it necessary to rescind its prohibition.

With approach by either sea or land wide open, executives at the base were concerned not so much about sabotage as about persons getting too close to the high-voltage power lines crossing the antenna fields. Any potential marauder could have walked the beach, turned into the antenna field, and committed an act of sabotage, but no such event ever took place. The only problem the base encountered took the form of a number of mysterious power outages. Power lines were being stripped of their insulation, causing them to short-circuit. It was a vexing problem until it was discovered that rabbits were fond of eating the insulating material. A less appetizing insulation material ended this form of sabotage.

The lease for the property, first signed in 1959, was renewed in 1971. Government officials, except for Marrero, seemed too busy to pay much attention to Pals. RL's broadcasts continued unimpeded.

As for Generalissimo Franco, once the purchase agreement was signed and the license to broadcast issued, there was no further contact or even any positive recognition that Amcomlib or the Playa de Pals base existed. All contact with the Americans was left to Spanish officials at the ministerial level or below. The only cabinet member to show any genuine interest was Manuel Fraga Iribarne, for a long time minister of Information and Tourism. Fraga was not only interested but also remained a good friend of Amcomlib as long as he was in government.

It was evident that as long as Franco remained in power, RL's position was secure. What would happen when he was no longer in command remained a question—one that has still not been answered as this is written.

NOTE

1. Unpublished manuscript described as "A Briefing Report" prepared on January 31, 1966, by George Dennis, personal representative of Amcomlib's president Howland Sargeant, in Madrid. Since Amcomlib was not chartered until February 1951, it is clear that some agency of government, was anticipating the need for a Spanish transmitter base. Archives of the Hoover Institution.

---

*Antonio Reigosa, the station manager starting in 1978, who had been at Pals from the beginning, points out that the first nonhuman employee was placed on staff in 1976, a German Shepherd given the name "Rinty" for the movie dog Rin Tin Tin.

9
Years of Transition

T HE YEARS FROM 1953 to 1956 were a time of transition for both Radios. RFE had almost a three-year head start on RL, but it was still learning. RL could profit from RFE experience in some areas, including staff organization and news coverage, but it was still unable to move ahead aggressively because of the bitter wrangling among the exile groups on whom it thought it was going to depend for its program service.

Both Radios still held essentially to a hardline approach toward Communist governments, but RFE had started to modify its stance after the first year of "confusing the enemy and embarrassing its leadership." Amcomlib's official name, the American Committee for Liberation from Bolshevism, sounded more belligerent than the product that RL was delivering as the station went on the air, although on occasion it was caught a little short on restraint.

There were a number of changes in the political and international scenes in 1953 that bore a heavy impact on both organizations. Eisenhower was elected president of the United States, replacing Truman; John Foster Dulles became secretary of state, and his brother Allen, the director of central intelligence. The Korean War began to wind down after the first few months of the year. McCarthyism and the repressing of any person charged with having Communist connections began to run out of steam; by the conclusion of the Army–McCarthy hearings in the spring of 1954, McCarthyism had pretty well run its course. There had been no significant Communist victories since the Czechoslovak takeover in 1948. Finally, the conclusion of the Berlin blockade and the winding down of the Korean War had relieved some of the explosive pressure of the late 1940s and early 1950s.

John Foster Dulles took office at the Department of State on the slogan, "Roll back the aggressors," but no aggressive actions were undertaken by U.S. forces to indicate that it pointed to a policy direction. CIA associates of

Allen Dulles suggest that he was restrained in what he ordered at the CIA in order to avoid taking positions that would embarrass his brother.

RFE had actually begun to tone down its harsh rhetoric within its first year on the air. Its policy guidances began to veer from "tearing down the aggressors" to keeping the public in Eastern Europe informed. It was a slow and gradual process, but by early 1953 the trend had clearly set in.

The first evidences of a more restrained attitude had appeared in 1952. Optimism for a roll-back had begun to fade and a different approach seemed necessary. The long-time director of RFE's Polish service, Jan Nowak, says that by 1952 he no longer had any hope of any kind of internal change in Poland: "We were by then resisting any kind of pressure for self-liberation. We thought that a roll-back might only have been achieved right after the war in Iran in 1946 by using American arms superiority to tell the Soviet Union to 'go back or else.' " This profound change in expectations led to an equally profound change in tactics: "We had learned that hard-hitting language is a bad technique, but what was really a mistake was that there was pressure to present us as voices of an internal, nonexisting opposition." In 1952 Nowak thought that RFE could at best merely "slow down the Sovietization."

Cord Meyer maintains that the movement toward a lower-key objective approach that avoided the excesses of the earlier days had started well before his first assignment with the Radios in 1954: "By that time it was agreed that credibility was foremost." He does not think that the shrill and strident approach lasted beyond the first year or so of RFE operations.

He is supported in that view by a member of the Congressional Research Service of the Library of Congress, James Robert Price, who studied RFE in 1971 at the request of Senator J. W. Fulbright, chairman of the Senate Foreign Relations Committee. Price wrote, "As early as 1952 there was evidence that Radio Free Europe policy makers had become wary of the 'liberation' approach. . . ."[1]

The two major events occurring in Europe in 1953 that had furnished RL with so much excitement for its inaugural months of broadcasting, the death of Stalin and the East Berlin riots, had an impact far more significant than listener entertainment. They probably had a more profound effect on attitudes in the countries into which RFE and RL beamed their signals than anything that had been happening in Washington.

The death of Stalin illustrates the point. While Stalin was alive, both Radios had a fixed target. Attacks on the target were certain to gain sympathy among the millions who had lived under Stalinism. With the dictator gone, there was uncertainty. Some of the pressure of being bottled up in the tightly capped dictatorship was released. There was no immediate modification of the absolutes of the Stalin regime, but the public began to ask questions. There was growing evidence that the peoples of both Eastern Europe and the Soviet Union began to experience a new—perhaps slight—sensation of freedom. All of this called for a new approach, a new type of appeal: more rational, more factual, and less pejorative.

The East Berlin riots demonstrated, for the first time, a new skepticism even in the states held captive under the strict controls of Stalinism. Among those in the RFE target areas who listened with fascination to accounts of the uprising against Soviet power, there must have been some who wondered when a similar rebellion could be attempted in their areas.

The failure of the Berlin riots also had a solid impact within the RFE and RL organizations. Price believes that the failure of the Berlin uprising contributed in great measure to the shifted attitude of the exiles making up the bulk of the program staffs of the two Radios, from optimism that they would some day be able to return to a restored democracy toward serious questioning as to whether such a return would ever be possible: "The abortive uprising in East Berlin . . . suggested the futility of any expectation of Western military support of anti-Communist uprisings in the Soviet bloc. This led to RFE's own adaptation of its role as an exponent of 'liberation' to be replaced by 'liberalization.' "[2]

RL was a little slower than RFE to react. It still had not fully settled the question of the unification of the exile groups, and it had barely begun its broadcasting schedule. It still had not built program staffs to the level where there could be much internal disputation, nor had it yet shaken down its management policy guidance procedures, but it, too, in a slower and more cumbersome way was moving away from expectation of a quick liberation to support for a program calculated to liberalize the Soviet Union, even though it still retained the word "liberation" in its title.

There was another event that occurred in 1953 that did not, at the time, receive nearly as much publicity as the death of Stalin or the Berlin riots but contributed enormously to an increase in RFE's listenership and to the instability of the Communist regimes in Eastern Europe. RL also capitalized, but to a lesser extent, on the story. A brilliant coup by the CIA in 1953, even though it was not a major international news event at the time, may have contributed almost as much as the end of the Stalin regime to stimulating questions among East Europeans concerning the stability of their governments.

In December 1953 a colonel in the Polish secret police, Josef Swiatlo, defected to the West at CIA headquarters in Berlin. The CIA kept him in confinement for months while they queried him in detail concerning his experiences in the secret police apparatus. After exhaustive debriefings, Swiatlo was turned over in mid-1954 to the editors of the Polish Broadcasting Department of RFE. Cord Meyer reports, "He turned out to be a gold mine of detailed and accurate information on the corruption and personal scandals that flourished among the leadership of the Polish Communist Party."[3]

Free Europe's Polish service recorded more than 100 tapes of interviews with Swiatlo and broadcast them back into Poland. They were able to report in Swiatlo's own voice the scandals, gossip, and juicy tales of intrigue in Poland's Communist circles and it was all from the best source of all, a man who had been there. In addition, thousands of leaflets were placed aboard balloons and allowed to drift across the Polish border and rain down on Polish cities.

The results were a dramatic demonstration of the power that RFE's broadcasts had built up during the short time that had passed since the summer of 1950 when the first feeble sounds had been projected eastward by the 7½-kilowatt transmitter Barbara. Following the broadcasts, the chief of the Polish secret police resigned, and three of his subordinates were fired. The structure of the secret police was totally reorganized and its powers sharply restricted. RFE executives who had grumbled at the meager fare doled out to them as news in 1950 were exultant at finally receiving a treasure trove of useful information. The broadcasts were to have a profound effect on future events by undermining the confidence of the Polish people in their leadership and exposing the callous disregard for normal standards of human conduct displayed by the luxury-loving leaders.

While the Swiatlo story was largely one for RFE's Polish service, the RFE news wire carried the running account to the other RFE language desks and to RL for use in news items. Read by a newscaster, the colonel's story did not have the impact it gained when told in his own voice, but it was a powerful factor in stimulating questions about Communist leadership.

By the time the Swiatlo tapes were released for broadcast, RL had made substantial progress toward meeting its goals of delivering a complete broadcasting service to the Soviet Union. By mid-March 1954, RL was broadcasting 67 hours weekly in 11 languages from the four 10-kilowatt transmitters it had installed at Lampertheim. More transmitters were on order.

The committee had discontinued all financial support for political groups and their publications and had disengaged from the political elements of the emigration. It had changed the station identification to delete all references to the coordinating center as the sponsor. It substituted the promotional tag-line, "Listen to the voice of your compatriots beyond the border." This reduction in reliance on the emigration as the sole or principal program resource enabled RL to exert more energy in establishing its own resources.

The declining importance of the exiles though did not make imposition of RL's policy controls any easier. RFE had a comparatively easy time ensuring compliance with the less strident approach it had decreed. Policy-guidance personnel, who either knew the language or had interpreters assigned to them, worked directly with each of the language services and were generally able to control the tone of the broadcast. RFE's original campaign to "confuse and destabilize" was to have been carried out through news broadcasts, but in the middle 1950s there was a trend away from looking for embarrassing tidbits of gossip toward using the information resources to deliver something more comparable to hard news.

If RL personnel had wished to carry on the same type of destabilization that RFE had orginally attempted, they would have been even less able than RFE to obtain the embarrassing items of information to "confound and confuse" the leadership of the enemy. They were restrained not so much by caution or professional standards as by the difficulty of gathering information of a scandalous or embarrassing nature. RFE enventually succeeded in obtaining damaging gossip by establishing its information centers. But a similar plan was not likely to provide much pay dirt for RL. The Soviet Union was one tier of countries removed from Western Europe. The East European countries served as a buffer, making it more difficult to maintain lines of communication. Information sources were more tightly controlled. Travel was more tightly restricted. Sailors and businessmen were held on a tight leash. Emigration was likewise restricted, and defections were more dangerous. RL personnel were thus required, frequently against their intentions, to carry on with a more rational approach based on research and analysis rather than scandal mongering. Since their sources of news were largely limited to Western news services who prided themselves on objective reporting (supplemented by RFE's news service, which also tended toward the objective), there was little raw material for the pejorative approach.

Non-news programs were a different matter. They had to be rigidly controlled by management, and this was not easy. RL did not have a sufficient number of Americans who were fluent in Russian or any of the other languages of the Soviet Union in which broadcasts were being directed to maintain adequate control, no matter how hard they tried. The difficulty in imposing policy was exacerbated by the chauvinistic emotionalism of the disparate groups—other than the Russians—among the exiles. The Russians were difficult enough and have continued to be so, but the nationality services added another dimension to the difficulty of control. These émigrés were intensely loyal to their ethnic origins but were frustrated by the iron grip of the Kremlin over what they regarded as their homelands. Frequently, in fact, these homelands had no geographical boundaries; they were simply areas in which the preponderance of population was of their own ethnic origin or spoke the same language. They understood that their hopes of creating a homeland could be realized only in the event of a cataclysmic event in Moscow. Their objective, thus, was not restoring democracy in the Georgian, Tatar-Bashkir, Kazakh, or Turkmen Republics, but rather the total dismemberment of the Soviet state, the obliteration of the government in the Kremlin.

Perhaps fortunately, there were few accomplished broadcasters in those exile groups from which RL drew its language personnel or its signal would have been more pejorative, more prone to encouraging violence than was RFE at its most strident. There was, also perhaps fortunately, a shortage of editorial raw material that could have been converted into combustible material. As a result, the programs on the air tended to be at least marginally milder than those on RFE at that organization's earliest stage.

Notwithstanding the difficulties encountered in harnessing the more recalcitrant among the exile programmers, Amcomlib management moved toward a more liberal policy. By September 5, 1956, it changed its corporate name from the American Committee for Liberation from Bolshevism to simply the American Committee for Liberation. The committee members explained that the new title was "less cumbersome, more understandable by more people." It also softened the impact of the word liberation by blurring the target.

While the committee was moving toward a less combative approach, however, RFE was moving swiftly toward the greatest test of its policy. The events occurring in Europe since the death of Stalin had created an attitude of unrest in Eastern Europe. People began to question their Communist leaderships. They thought they could begin to see evidence that the forces that controlled them were relaxing a bit. The day seemed closer when they could break the bonds. Early in 1956 it was possible to see some evidence that Communist leaderships were on shaky grounds.

NOTES

1. John Robert Price, "Radio Free Europe: A Survey and Analysis." (Washington, D.C.: Congressional Research Service, Library of Congress, February 29, 1972), p. 22.

2. Ibid, p. 23.

3. Cord Meyer, *Facing Reality* (New York: Harper & Row, 1981), p. 120.

10
An Excess of Exuberance

RADIO FREE EUROPE'S crucial test came in the summer and fall of 1956. In early summer its policy advisor in Munich, William Griffith, had warned Cord Meyer at the CIA that forces were bubbling up in Eastern Europe that would inevitably lead to an eruption. Meyer called Griffith's warning to the attention of his boss, Allen Dulles, and Dulles checked it out with his policy and analysis personnel and with their counterparts at the Department of State. All were inclined to feel that serious events were in the making, but they felt that it would be premature for RFE to take any vigorous action. It would be more in order to let events unfold as they would.

The forces that Griffith and his staff had been observing had been building for more than three years, since the death of Stalin on March 5, 1953. The removal from the scene of the Soviet dictator left a vacuum in both the Soviet Union and Eastern Europe, and the contest among his former lieutenants to succeed him compounded the problem. The turbulence that followed left an unsettling effect that was felt not only in the Soviet Union but in the East European satellites as well. The contest for the leadership, involving Lavrenti Beria, Georgi Malenkov, Vyacheslav Molotov, and eventually Nikita Khrushchev and Nikolai Bulganin, removed the main prop from the stability that had kept Eastern Europe under tight rein. The first explosive reaction came in East Berlin on June 17, 1953. The riot in the streets demonstrated that dissident feelings had not been totally eliminated.

Two years later the Soviet Union and its satellites were shaken by a speech made by Khrushchev before the Twentieth Congress of the Communist party, in which he laid bare Stalin's unscrupulous and cruel deeds and crimes against the state. The speech might have passed by entirely unnoticed had the CIA not succeeded in obtaining a copy and smuggling it out of the country and back to the United States. Among the agencies later obtaining copies were RFE and RL. RFE promptly went about the process of broadcasting it into all of its target countries in Eastern Europe. It was beamed in excerpts and highlights as well as analyses and commentaries, and the broadcasts were frequent enough for most listeners to have become familiar with the contents of the speech. The shockwaves can only be guessed. The bonds that held Eastern Europe under tight control were plainly loosened a bit; the leadership of the Soviet Union was proved a little less than omnipotent; the icy cruelty and swift retribution that characterized the Stalin regime gave way to the more moderate style of his successors. They appeared a little less confident, less decisive than Stalin had been—and perhaps a little less cruel.

The Swiatlo case is also assumed to have had a profound destabilizing effect behind the Iron Curtain, particularly in Poland. The RFE broadcasts in the summer of 1954 furnished East European listeners the first tangible evidence of the venality of their leaders. After Swiatlo's confessions, it was easier to believe in the fallibility of cabinet ministers, prime ministers, military commanders, and lesser government authorities. It was a bitter blow to governments that depended on absolute allegiance from their subjects and whose decisions were not to be questioned. The quelling of the rebellion in East Berlin had demonstrated that the Soviet Union could still move quickly and brutally, but as events unfolded in late 1953 and on into 1954 and 1955, the Kremlin seemed a little less sure of itself. There seemed slightly more room for liberalization, if not for freedom. Hungary had seemed on its way to a more liberal regime with its "new course" in late 1953 when Imre Nagy replaced Matyas Rakosi. Rakosi had been a hardline Stalinist; Nagy was hardly a Western democrat, but he was somewhat more inclined toward relaxing the iron grip a bit.

During this period RFE was watching events with utter fascination. It had been functioning long enough to have developed its own information sources, supplementing the news and analysis obtained through wire services and newspapers. It kept a close watch on developments through information centers in 18 European cities, from Stockholm to Vienna and Rome, with at least one experienced journalist assigned to each city, bolstering the efforts of the exile staff. Its news department in Munich processed news from all its sources. Its monitoring service was able to eavesdrop on all the East European wire services and the Soviet Union's Tass, in addition to recording the broadcasts of some 40 or 50 East European and Soviet radio stations, both metropolitan and regional. Its archives department subscribed to all the more prominent daily newspapers and trade journals published in the target areas. By analyzing all available data from these varied sources it was able to obtain a fairly good notion of what the East European and Soviet regimes were thinking.

The program department in Munich felt that its experienced American broadcasters had made spectacular progress in training performers, developing formats, creating schedules, and converting print-oriented journalists and academicians to writing for radio. Content was the function of the policy advisor's department. William Griffith was nominally only policy advisor to the RFE European director, Richard Condon, but Condon, who was an engineer, was more interested in administrative and engineering problems and realized his lack of background in policy and research matters and, consequently, was quite content to give Griffith his head. And Griffith was not shy. As one of his aides, Paul Henze, pointed out, "Bill abhors a vacuum."

Griffith, by force of his personality, became the director of research, analysis, and evaluation in addition to policy. Presumably he was a notch lower in the echelons of authority within the Free Europe Committee than the policy director in New York, but in point of fact his staff paid little attention to the daily guidances they received from Reuben Nathan, who had the title of policy director. They worked within the broader parameters of the less frequent policy papers written by Lewis Gallantiere, whose function was to produce general recommendations without prescribing specific approaches to daily events. Nathan had come to RFE from psychological warfare and Griffith and his group saw too much of the psychological warrior's approach in his telexes to be willing to adapt them directly to their broadcasts to Eastern Europe.

The Griffith staff had been carefully created from acquaintances Griffith had made during his career in the army, where he had been a military interrogator, and at Harvard while he was working on his doctorate degree after the war. Paul Henze, whom he had known both in the army and at Harvard, became his deputy; Ralph Walter, a classmate of Henze's at St. Olaf College in Northfield, Minnesota, joined the staff in 1953. Two other acquaintances, William Rademaekers and Ernie Schneider, had been language specialists in the army.

The mood among the exiles in Munich as Free Europe entered its sixth year was still one of optimism that the Communist regimes would eventually fall and the East European staff members would be able to go home to resume their former lives. But in 1956 RFE received the ultimate jolt, the event that demonstrated very clearly that it was in business for a long term—a very long term. The jolt, which had been forecast by Griffith, came in late June in the form of riots in Poland.[1]

Poznan, in southwestern Poland, was the scene of the first of the momentous events that kept tensions high in Eastern Europe throughout the summer and fall of 1956. Workers in the ZISPO locomotive-building plant in Poznan had been dissatisfied for approximately three years. Their workloads had steadily increased, along with the cost of living, but their wages had remained on a plateau. On June 27, while a foreign delegation was visiting Poznan, the workers were informed that their work "norms" were to be increased, with no increase in salary. This was more than they were willing to take. Fires of resentment had been smoldering for weeks; the announcement of increased workloads fanned them into flames.

The next morning the workers started a march of protest toward the city center, gathering supporters by the hundreds as they proceeded. As they marched they sang the national anthem and a church hymn. At the town hall they paused for more speech making and hymn singing; then they broke in and hoisted the national flag over the building. Next they went to the radio station, where jamming units were blocking incoming Western signals. The equipment was ripped out of the building and thrown to the street, destroyed. The march resumed and went on toward the headquarters of the secret police. There, trouble erupted. A shot was fired from inside the building, striking a young boy among the marchers. A Polish flag was dipped in the boy's blood and held high by the mob. More shots from the building struck men in the first ranks in the crowd. Soldiers in the Polish army were unwilling to use weapons to stop the unruly mob as it shouted for bread and freedom. Finally, a detachment of the internal security corps moved in with tanks. Antiaircraft guns with their barrels leveled were pointed down the streets and jet planes flew overhead. The overwhelming show of force, supported by arrest of scores of marchers and their leaders, restored order, but the summer in Poland was an uneasy one—a tense period that would persist until late October.

The trials of those arrested took place in late September. The sentences were surprisingly light, considering that the defendants and their supporters had bitterly condemned and demonstrated against Polish communism.

Pressure began to grow for the reinstatement to power of one of the early Communist leaders of postwar Poland, Wladyslav Gomulka. He had been held in confinement since he had been deposed in 1949. Now, after seven years of confinement, he was in a position to strike a hard bargain. He would come back to the Central Committee of the Communist party if a number of high-ranking Communists were dismissed. Pressure had built up to a level at which Gomulka's demands had to be seriously considered. On October 9 Gomulka's main target, Deputy Prime Minister Hilary Minc, resigned. On October 15 Gomulka attended a meeting of the Politburo. On October 19 he and two of his supporters were elected to the Central Committee. At the same meeting the Politburo was dissolved, thus removing from office Poland's defense minister, Marshal Rokossovsky. Rokossovsky was actually a Pole, but he had been a field marshal in the Soviet armies during the war and was installed in the position of defense minister by the Soviet leadership.

Following the October 19 meeting, events happened with dazzling speed. It was announced that Khrushchev, Molotov, and Anastas Mikoyan had landed at the Warsaw airport and were on their way to the city center. Gomulka, Edward Ochab, the party's first secretary, and other high-ranking Poles were conferring about the confused situation when they were told about the arrival of the Kremlin leaders. They left the meeting and went to Warsaw's Belvedere Palace to meet their visitors. A noisy, blustery session followed. Khrushchev was both demanding and threatening and loudly declared that if Rokossovsky and the other ranking party members who had been dismissed from the Politburo were not restored instantly, the alternative would be war. Armed forces, Khrushchev said, were at that moment on their way to Warsaw. The result of holding out any further would be disastrous for the Warsaw leadership and the Polish dissidents.

In the face of this intemperate blast, Gomulka and Ochab held firm; they refused to knuckle under. Tensions continued to run high; war was a distinct possibility. Then the Soviets suprisingly backed down, whereupon Gomulka took over as first secretary of a liberalized Polish Communist party. A major threat to peace within the Eastern bloc had been averted, and for the first time the leadership of the Soviet Communist party had been forced to yield to determined opposition from a satellite nation.

RFE's Polish Service, led by the dynamic and sure-handed Munich desk chief, Jan Nowak, had from the very beginning played a cautious but confident hand in the Poznan events. Nowak's staff told the story in full detail but carefully avoided emotionalism or exaggeration. They counselled against hasty or dangerous action that could damage the cause but encouraged keeping the spirit of freedom alive. The most eloquent tribute to the skill demonstrated by the Polish desk is the fact that during the period of highest tension the Polish jammers went off the air, allowing the signals to come in unimpeded. Weeks later a Gomulka supporter admitted to an RFE reporter in Stockholm that had RFE not told the people to be calm, "we could not have coped with the situation."[2]

Only two days after the crisis in Warsaw, while Poland was beginning to cool down, Hungary suddenly burst into disarray. In a sense it was Poznan repeated, this time in Budapest. In contrast to the situation in Poznan, order could not be restored. A march in the streets in Budapest turned into nationwide revolution that was ultimately stopped only by the use of massive Soviet force.

Trouble had been brewing since 1953. Stalin's death and Malenkov's eventual succession to power had serious repercussions in Hungary. Rakosi, who had been both premier and first secretary of the Hungarian Communist party, gave up the premiership to Nagy in 1953 partly as a result of a nudge from Malenkov in the Kremlin.[3] Nagy tried to implement a somewhat liberalized program under the umbrella description "the new course." But before he could implement the new program, Malenkov was deposed by the Khrushchev coup in Moscow. Rakosi, who had retained the post of party general secretary, put his puppet, Andras Hegedus, in the premier's office, replacing Nagy. All the pre-1953 repressive programs were reinstated.

Later in the same year, Khrushchev made his speech to the Twentieth Congress of the Communist party. Broadcasts of the speech deeply compromised Rakosi, who was a dedicated Stalinist and, in fact, Stalin's creation. Moreover, it demolished the philosophical underpinnings of the Communist faith and left Hungarian party supporters without any basic principles to which they could cling. With the seeds thus planted, unrest grew rapidly. The intellectuals' demand for more freedom grew, as did pressure to oust Rakosi. Mikoyan was sent by the Kremlin to help restore order. He and the Rakosi supporters made an irretrievable error, however: they replaced Rakosi as demanded, but the replacement was an ineffectual Rakosi supporter, Erno Geroe, who was almost as unpopular as Rakosi himself, without any of the magnetism or dynamism. By this time the stage was set.

On October 23 the whole system collapsed. On the night of October 22 grumbling citizens had been meeting all over Budapest. One such meeting, largely of students and intellectuals, resulted in the writing of 16 demands calling for the full reinstatement of Nagy and a number of sweeping reforms. An attempt was made to get Radio Budapest to read the list of demands, but officials at the station rejected it. Students fanned out all over Budapest. Copies of the 16-point program were duplicated in volume and posted all over the city. Budapest had become such a bubbling cauldron by this time that the student activity was all that was needed to stimulate a spontaneous outpouring of citizens. Marchers came from all sections of the city, shouting slogans, singing songs, and converging on the city center. When they reached the statue of Stalin, they tore it down and broke it up in the streets.

Business in Budapest was at an absolute standstill. The stampeding throngs were totally out of control. At one point secret police fired on the crowd and killed a number of people, but the thousands of demonstrators raged on. Soviet tanks promptly came into Hungary and by October 25 the country was involved in what amounted to nationwide revolution. Hungarian troops, in many cases, went over to the revolutionaries; if they did not join the revolutionaries in person, they turned over their arms to them.

There was no central leadership for the revolution and virtually no communication among the pockets of resistance scattered about the country. Regional radio stations were seized by revolutionaries, but most of their signals were too weak to be heard outside their immediate service areas. They were, however, monitored by RFE in Munich and their messages were broadcast back into Hungary. RFE consequently became a critically important communications channel for the revolutionaries.

By November 4 it seemed that the revolutionaries had won. Nagy proclaimed a ceasefire and Soviet tanks began to withdraw. Nagy and Janos Kadar, who was in the Nagy government, together had asked the UN Security

Council for protection, but the Security Council adjourned for the weekend without taking any action.

At this critical period, when it seemed as if Nagy and his supporters might have the situation under control, Kadar and three members of the Nagy government switched abruptly to the Soviet side, formed a new rump government and requested help from the Soviet army to defeat what they described as reactionary forces in Hungary. The Soviets had withdrawn from Budapest, but they had not left Hungary. They simply reorganized outside the city. Some Central Soviet Asian troops had been brought in to replace the Russians who had presumably become too sympathetic to the Hungarians during their tour of occupation duty in that country. Then the Soviets returned in irresistible force.

Radio Budapest was quickly taken off the air and the "freedom stations," so called because they had become the major communications medium for the freedom fighters, went silent one by one as Soviet troops moved in to kill or capture their operators. That was the end of organized resistance; by November 11, it was pretty well all over. (However, nearly 200,000 refugees were still near the Austrian border, and within the next month most had crossed to find freedom in the West.)

RFE's Hungarian service found itself in a position comparable to that that the Polish desk had been faced with just days earlier, but the problems for the Hungarians were much more complicated. Except for the demonstration in Poznan and its bloody aftermath, the Polish issues were fought out largely in government offices. The confrontation between the Polish and Soviet delegations at the Belvedere Palace might have led to bloodshed if Khrushchev and the Soviet delegation had not backed down, but the reticence of the Soviet leadership to force war permitted an exit, though not a wholly graceful one. The Hungarian Revolution, on the other hand, was spontaneous and nationwide. Government leadership was shaky and indecisive. People led by intellectuals and students took the power into their own hands, and emotionalism ran at a fever pitch.

From RFE's point of view Hungary was far more dangerous than Poland because the Hungarian service did not operate under the same sternly disciplined approach that had characterized the Polish service under Nowak's direction. Its staff members permitted themselves to get caught up more tightly in the web of almost hysterical passion that pervaded Hungary. The communications channels on which the service had to rely were chaotic. Most of the press agencies and newspaper personnel covering the revolution were in Budapest and could only report what they saw and heard there—only a fraction of the whole story. The climax of the Polish crisis had occurred in Warsaw where reporters were headquartered and had access to transmission facilities, but the ten days of rebellion in Hungary spread all over the country and, although it might have been possible for RFE reporters to observe some of the turbulence for themselves, they were prevented from crossing the border by policy provisions that restrained them from travel in the countries that were targets of their broadcasts.

RFE had access to one source that was almost exclusive to it: the freedom radio stations in the outlying areas of Hungary. The RFE monitoring service quickly shifted its receiving antennas to lock onto the freedom stations. The broadcasters in these stations were almost all totally dedicated freedom fighters who were emotionally involved in what to them was the prevailing cause. They were not trained observers and reporters and were unable to supply the dispassionate type of reporting that RFE so badly needed at this point. How much attention to pay to the freedom radio stations was a knotty policy problem. Could RFE afford to appear to take sides by giving the freedom radios full opportunity to state their cases and make their demands, or would such a position only lead to disaster by encouraging more Hungarian citizens to risk their lives in what could be a futile cause?

The CIA and the Department of State monitored the fluid situation almost on an hour-by-hour basis. Policy guidances moved from Washington to New York and from New York across the Atlantic. Griffith and his staff were on duty 24 hours a day. Possibilities for gross errors either by excessive zeal or negligence were a constant source of concern. But generally, even allowing for the muddled and chaotic events and the inadequate sources for sound and realistic reporting, RFE coverage at least as reflected in scripts was sufficiently even-handed to remain with only a few exceptions within policy guidelines.

Criticisms of the coverage, however, soon came pouring in. Immediately after the winding down of the Hungarian Revolution, RFE came under violent attack from both sides of the Iron Curtain. Part of the attack was carefully orchestrated by the Soviet Union, part by the Kadar government in Hungary, part by the West German press, and part by frustrated Western liberals who looked for a scapegoat when Nagy was forced to succumb to the power of the Soviet tanks.

The Soviet Union began the assault. The charge was that RFE had set up the headquarters for the revolt and given instructions and orders to the revolutionaries. The theme was played out in the Soviet Union and in the United Nations where Anatoly Kuznetsov, the Soviet ambassador to the UN, aggressively condemned Free Europe. The Soviet attack was picked up by some West German newspapers and likewise by some individual American newspapermen.

Analyses of RFE's conduct were instituted by the West German government, a special committee of the Council of Europe, and internally by RFE itself, stimulated in part by questions asked by the CIA concerning the RFE performance. Generally, the analyses resulted in a more or less clear bill of health for the Hungarian Broadcast Service. The West German chancellor,

Konrad Adenauer, announced on January 25, 1957, that RFE had not incited revolution with promises of Western aid. The special committee of the Council of Europe assigned to investigate the broadcasts reported, too, that the charges were baseless.

RFE's own internal analyses, however, did not clear the Hungarian desk and its executives quite so glibly. The critical question remained: did or did not the Hungarian desk promise that Western aid was forthcoming or already on the way? Examination of the scripts broadcast reveals that no promise was ever made quite that bluntly, but there were some broadcasts that might have encouraged an excited freedom fighter to infer such a promise. There is a wide gap, of course, between implications that aid is forthcoming and an actual promise that it is on the way.

The Hungarian desk was clearly vulnerable on one count, however. In a program called the "World Press Review," an excerpt from the *Observer* of London could easily have been interpreted by emotionally aroused freedom fighters as suggesting the possibility that Western aid would soon be on the scene. And it provided grounds, even if somewhat shaky ones, for the critics. The quotation was from the Sunday, November 4, *Observer*, and it was broadcast on that same day. The text of the RFE press review story read as follows:

This morning the British *Observer* published a report from its Washington correspondent. The situation report was written before the Soviet attack early this morning. In spite of this the *Observer* correspondent writes that the Russians have probably decided to beat down the Hungarian Revolution with arms. The article goes on, "If the Soviet troops really attack Hungary, if our expectations should hold true, then the pressure upon the government of the United States to send military help to the freedom fighters will become irresistible." This is what the *Observer* writes in today's number. The paper observes that the American Congress cannot vote for war as long as the Presidential elections have not been held [elections were scheduled for Tuesday, November 6]. The article then continues: "If the Hungarians can continue to fight until Wednesday [the day after the elections] we shall be closer to a world war than at any time since 1938."

Nowhere did the press review item specifically say that help would come, was on its way, or was even a distinct possibility. But there was a mighty strong hint in the line "pressure upon the government of the United States to send military help to the freedom fighters will become irresistible." It was a quote from the *Observer*, but quotation marks cannot be seen on radio. The item apparently did not have much effect on the Hungarians. RFE research shows that a vast majority of refugees who had been freedom fighters were not influenced by this article or by any other broadcast. But the story had two disturbing results: in the first place , it furnished ammunition for critics, and second, it delivered direct and incontrovertible evidence that RFE writers were skirting dangerously close to making an outright statement that aid would be coming and that war was imminent. The interpolations created the impression that the RFE Hungarian Service broadcaster who read the piece was in complete agreement with the *Observer* and was simply using lines from the *Observer* item to support his own point of view.

The evidence is clear that the Hungarian Service did not apply the same skillful, thoughtful talents to their broadcasts that the Polish Service did to theirs. Cord Meyer writes, "There was a more exuberant and optimistic attitude than the circumstances warranted." He continues:

> I am satisfied that Radio Free Europe did not plan, direct or attempt to provoke the Hungarian Revolution. The spontaneous combustion of a popular revolution does not fit easily into the conspiratorial theory of history, but in this case it is the best explanation of what occurred.[4]

RFE's own internal analysis, stimulated largely by the request of the federal government of Germany for information for its own investigation, indicated that of some 308 separate items studied, 16 were careless enough in construction to be considered suspect even though not outright violations of policy. Another four, including the *Observer* item, were judged guilty, at least inferentially, of giving military advice to Hungarian freedom fighters. Of these, the *Observer* item was judged as the most flagrant violation.[5]

Griffith ascribes the failure of the Hungarian desk to measure up to the standards of its Polish counterpart to two causes: first, the quality of personnel generally did not meet the same high standards, and second, the chief of the Hungarian desk, Andor Gellert, became ill in the early stages of the rebellion and the desk was leaderless during his absence. Griffith's aide in charge of policy for the Hungarian Service, William Rademaekers, worked night and day but was simply unable to read every item before it was put on the air or to subdue the emotional exuberance of the staff members. The four items in question thus slipped by without any prebroadcast clearance.

Questions have been raised about another RFE broadcast during this period. At one point during the most hazardous moments of the crisis, RFE staffers summarized the demands being made by the freedom fighters. These demands among others insisted that all Soviet troops be withdrawn from Hungarian soil, that the secret police be totally dissolved, and that Hungary be withdrawn from the Warsaw Pact. RFE executives had considered the wisdom of broadcasting this list and had in turn requested guidance from the CIA and the Department of State. Permission had been granted on the basis that the broadcast was in total conformity with U.S. government policy. This action, approved by the highest levels of the U.S. government, may have had a sharper impact than any of the more publicized items.

There were other contributing factors to the perception that RFE had, as it was charged in the Soviet media, "fomented, organized, and directed the revolution." U.S. foreign policy as the revolution broke out still called for rolling back the aggressors and lifting the Iron Curtain. Vestiges of the cold war environment still prevailing in Washington continued to be an emotional motivation for members of the exile staffs. Exile staff members still were optimistic that they could return to ther homelands in due course and they had been encouraged by attitudes expressed by high U.S. government officials. The very names assumed by the RFE broadcast services were also indicative of the abiding hope that freedom would come soon: the Polish Service, for example, used as its identification "The Voice of Free Poland"; the Hungarian Service was "The Voice of Free Hungary"; and the Czech Service, "The Voice of Free Czechoslovakia." Not only did this nomenclature affect the employees of the various services, but it certainly must have had some effect on the listeners in the target areas as well.

Unfortunately also for RFE, the combination of frustration and chaos created by the Polish and Hungarian upheavals and the almost simultaneous British, French, and Israeli attack on the Suez area created an embittered environment that was ideal for nurturing violent criticism, mistrust, and suspicion. The attacks from the Soviet Union and its allies encouraged suspicion and mistrust. The consistent antipathy of U.S. citizens to any activity to which the word *propaganda* could be applied created a fertile climate in which to nourish seeds of complaint.

In the spring of 1957 the controversy had pretty well run its course, but the suspicions of RFE that had been aroused by the events could not so easily be put to rest. The perception of RFE as a "cold warrior" and propagandist troublemaker persisted for years. (As this is written it still surfaces from time to time.) The series of events in the summer and autumn of 1956, however, led to profound changes in the organization, its objectives, and its management. Perhaps even more important, there was a drastic shift in the attitudes of its employees. Hungary and Poland were, in the full sense of the word, a watershed in RFE's affairs.

Griffith in retrospect sees the optimism of the exiles on the RFE staff evaporating almost like boiling water in an open pan. They no longer hoped for a quick end to the Communist governments of the East European countries. They had a full realization that life in Germany, and broadcasting for RFE, was not ephemeral: it was to extend into the foreseeable future.

RFE's structure and policies, too, began to change. (This was not an isolated phenomenon: the cold warrior theme that had permeated the U.S. government was now being replaced by a trend toward more cautious accommodations with Eastern Europe and the Soviet Union.) RFE's drive to liberate Eastern Europe was being replaced by a philosophical attitude that called for "liberalization" of the policies of Eastern Europe, rather than for "liberation."

Changes in management also followed in the wake of the traumatic period. And tensions between New York and Munich rose to new levels of intensity. W. J. Convery Egan, the RFE director in New York, terminated Condon and Noel Bernard, the director of the Romanian service. Eric Hazelhoff, a swashbuckling, flamboyant ex-fighter pilot in the Dutch air force, most recently at NBC in New York, was sent to Munich as European director, replacing Condon. The terminations did nothing to improve the mood of Griffith and his staff. They had respected Condon as an excellent engineer and good manager. They did not have similar respect for Hazelhoff and they were totally dissatisfied with Egan's management of the radio organization in New York.

Within less than three years Griffith's entire policy staff was gone: Henze to Washington in intelligence activities, Rademaekers to *Time* magazine, Walter back to Free Europe in New York, and Griffith himself to the political science department of the Massachusetts Institute of Technology. The climate became sufficiently unsatisfactory that remaining in Munich was unattractive. Annoyances of having to work with senior management 4000 miles away could have been brushed aside in the enthusiasm of the pre-1956 summer and fall, but, magnified in the aftermath of the revolts in Poland and Hungary, they grated on the policy staff. The happy enthusiasms of the earlier period were turning into drudgery. Policy direction continued to be important but never again would the strength of personality of Griffith and his associates dominate the organization as they did during the period prior to the outbreaks in Hungary and Poland.

RFE would have to adapt to a changed world. In order to continue to influence events in Eastern Europe it would have to examine both its policies and its operating methods. Hungary and Poland brought to the surface weaknesses that would have to be dealt with. Internal methods of policy enforcement would have to be examined; a more professional news-gathering and -processing staff was essential; more emphasis would have to be placed on deep and analytical research in order to furnish broadcast services with the background required to understand and comment on developments in the target areas. Moreover, something would have to be done about the conflicting roles of New York and Munich. The organization could not afford to operate with a head in New York, a body in Munich, and inadequate communications between them. Clear lines of authority were required, along with precise assignments of responsibility. Planning thereafter would have to be for the long term, since the quick collapse of the Communist regimes in Eastern Europe was seen as an outmoded dream.

NOTES

1. See Allan A. Michie, *Voices Through the Iron Curtain* (New York: Dodd, Mead, 1963), for a detailed account of the events in Poland in the summer and fall of 1956 and RFE's coverage of them. Michie had been deputy European director of RFE during the period of the Polish crisis and the Hungarian crisis that followed.

2. *Ibid.*, p. 191.

3. See *Ibid.*, pp. 193–269. Another account of the Hungarian Revolution and RFE's part in covering it can be found in Robert T. Holt, *Radio Free Europe* (Minneapolis: University of Minnesota Press, 1958), pp. 185–199.

4. Cord Meyer, *Facing Reality* (New York: Harper & Row, 1980), p. 127.

5. Michie, *Voices Through the Iron Curtain*, pp. 257–258.

11

The Implacable Struggle

T HE EVENTS IN HUNGARY in 1956 had profound, almost crippling, effects on RFE, radically transforming the station's view of its own role. All of RFE was stung by questions concerning its behavior under fire, questions that seemed to imply that the Radio had been responsible for needless bloodshed. RFE's coverage had been aggressive and forthright, to say the least.

By comparison, RL had seemed uncertain in its accounts of the fighting, indecisive, even vacillating. One critic, Vladimir Petrov, writing approximately 18 months after the freedom fighters had been subdued, commented that "RL didn't know what to say. Actually some foolish things were said." Petrov cited a broadcast that implored Soviet soldiers not to shoot the Hungarians because they too were building socialism. He blamed the weakness in part on RL guidelines that consisted of "don'ts," thus reducing writers and editors to producing nothing but platitudes. "RL," he concluded, "suffers from a distinct lack of character. This was evident during the Hungarian crisis when word went out from management, 'Don't do anything outside the news.' "[1]

RL's staff, however, had indeed made a game effort to cover the events with limited resources. During the height of the fighting they had reoriented their antennas to direct broadcasts to the Soviet troops fighting in Hungary.[2] What they had to say was hardly a cold, detached, and objective view of events. "Comrades, soldiers, officers," one broadcast pleaded, "why are many of our* soldiers helping the insurgents? It is clear why; out of a feeling of solidarity with the workers, students and peasants . . . the ultimate victory of the Hungarian workers and peasants is assured."

Reasons for RL's apparent uncertainty and confusion are not hard to find.

---

*It was still RL policy at this time to use the first person plural to identify the émigré broadcaster with members of the audience in the Soviet Union.

Its management had to struggle against overwhelming odds to keep its unruly and quarrelsome factions in check. Most of the Americans in the program department had been hired on the basis of their familiarity with the Russian language, but checking every script before air time was virtually impossible. In addition, unlike RFE, which had created a highly competent policy control unit under Griffith's aggressive direction, RL was still in the building stage; it did not have nearly so efficient a mechanism in place, nor a sufficient number of competent Americans to ensure compliance with policy. There were no Americans on the staff who were competent in some of the languages used in the nationality services; they were able to spot-check the Russian from which the Caucasian, Turkik, and other minority language translations were made, but they had no means of controlling the output after it left the Russian desk.

The nationality services posed another set of perplexing problems to executives trying to enforce policy. Unlike the Russians, who could debate endlessly whether communism ought to be replaced by a monarchy, a social democracy, a tightly controlled corporate state as envisioned by NTS, or a different brand of socialism, any one of which could conceivably be achieved by overthrowing the regime in the Kremlin, the disparate non-Russian groups were convinced that something far bloodier and on a far broader scale would be required before they could satisfy their national aspirations.* This more belligerent attitude made the problem of applying policy controls vastly more complex.

The Amcomlib management had been moving gradually toward a less strident policy virtually from the time it had abandoned hope for the assumption of broadcast function by the coordinating center of the emigration. Its more objective outlook was signaled when it changed its corporate title from the American Committee for Liberation from Bolshevism to the American Committee for Liberation, Inc. The change was hardly a confession that its original course had been misguided, but it did remove some of the onus of excessive rhetoric. The word *liberation* was still prominently displayed, however, and there was no hard evidence that the more hot-headed émigré employees were sympathetic to the evolving policy—if indeed, it was evolving. RL still identified itself on the air with the Russian word *osvovozhdenye*, which could be translated freely as "liberation by force from abroad."†

---

*Responsibility for the control of the nationality services was left to the Russian desk. Not only was this an awkward procedure, but it left policy enforcement in the hands of members of the émigré community who might or might not be trustworthy. As it turned out, no flagrant policy violations occurred, but there was always the fear of a slip, a spark that could ignite an explosion.

†It was not until May 1959 that a change was made in the on-the-air identification of the RL stations. After that date they were referred to as *stantsiya svoboda*, ("freedom stations").

If RL was never as strident as RFE had been in its earliest days, it was not because the leaders of the Soviet emigration preferred a less bombastic approach. Left to their own devices, there is no telling how boisterous their on-the-air output might have been. Amcomlib's own description of its basic objectives did little to suggest the imposition of restraints. As it went on the air on March 1, 1953, it proclaimed publicly that its aim was to carry on "an implacable struggle" toward the "complete destruction of the Communist dictatorship." (It was not until June 1956 that the phrase "complete destruction" was deleted from the policy manuals, and even then "implacable struggle" remained.) However, there was no cheering section at the Amcomlib board headquarters back in New York egging on the broadcasters as there had been on the Free Europe board during the first few months of RFE broadcasts. And the near hysteria of the late 1940s and early 1950s in the United States was giving way to a more relaxed outlook. The CIA had fully absorbed the flamboyant OPC within its directorate of plans, and Allen Dulles had succeeded in institutionalizing the whole intelligence apparatus. All of this was reflected in management's attitude toward RL's mission.

The elements were present at RL for a hair-raising approach to broadcasting: if each of the squabbling factions had been turned loose to use air time as it saw fit, Amcomlib would have had chaos on its hands. The inability of the emigration to agree on common goals, however, was an effective restraint on the creation of an organization wholly out of control. The quarreling among the factions slowed down the complex organizing process and complicated program production efforts, and the shortage of experienced personnel prevented a brisk start comparable to RFE's first few boisterous months. Valiant efforts by the few Americans charged with getting the station underway were hardly enough to carry the organization. Finding a language fully understood by both program personnel and administrators remained a perplexing problem and restricted intraorganizational communication. And long delays in building up transmitter strength kept RL's voice weak through most of its first decade.

The complexities, while they could have cleared the way for administrative chaos, actually had the opposite effect—they served to make widespread disregard for policy more difficult. Replenishing the employment rolls with new personnel was also a problem. Emigration after the postwar burst was virtually nonexistent, and defections were more dangerous. There was only a trickle of recent émigrés who could update news personnel on current conditions. The Institute for the Study of the USSR, the Amcomlib companion organization in Munich, was a valuable source of program material because it regularly interviewed Soviet exiles, but the supply was limited. Once the immediate postwar defectors had been interviewed by institute interviewers there were too few migrants to maintain a steady flow. RL programmers were required—often contrary to their emotional desires—to adopt a more rational approach to news gathering, based on research and analysis rather than on scandal mongering.

Amcomlib started with another crippling handicap. In addition to their journalistic and broadcasting inexperience, many of the exiles had no acquaintance with English or even with German. United Press International news reports consequently could be processed only by American or British personnel, and DPA, the German agency, only by the handful of Soviet exiles who knew a little German or by the few Americans or British who had had some German-language training.

Few of the exiles were acquainted with Western journalistic standards—or for that matter had any sympathy with journalism as an objective, fact-reporting function. The leaders of the exile groups in many cases were political dissidents, propagandists rather than journalists.* (Most of those who had any journalistic experience had been absorbed into the NTS, whose members, except in special circumstances, were barred from the RL payroll by order of President Sargeant.)

American executives found it almost impossible to create an efficient, hard-hitting news machine. The émigrés' responses to events were normally sluggish, except in the case of a catastrophic event such as the death of Stalin. (Long-time employee Robert Tuck compared the operation of the news department to "a bowl of jelly.") During the 1950s and early 1960s there were only two freshly prepared news broadcasts during every 24-hour period, each repeated 11 times. Besides news broadcasts there were programs involving culture, literature, science, history, and information from the West that were calculated to be of interest to Soviet citizens, but it was news that enabled the broadcaster to react to significant events (or shape them), and news was the commodity that consistently drew the largest audiences and the most attention.

RL suffered in comparison with RFE not only because it lacked the resources and enthusiastic personnel to cover and process events in the Soviet Union, but because of the lack of drama in its news; rebellion and revolution were almost an impossibility in the rigidly controlled Soviet society. RFE on the one hand dealt with explosive situations. There was constantly a chance that the discontented populations that were restrained by force—and were culturally more attuned to the West than to the East—might attempt to throw off their yokes, as happened in Hungary and Poland in 1956 and would happen again in Czechoslovakia in 1968. This added suspense to RFE news; it led to peaks of intensity and surges of drama. In contrast, the most dramatic story to come out of the Soviet Union during the whole lifetime of RL was the death

---

*Most Soviet journalists simply did not emigrate. They were, for the most part, either party members or so directly involved in government as to be part of the party propaganda apparatus and unlikely to defect.

of Stalin and the contest for succession. Events in the Soviet Union involved not bloodshed in the streets but the interplay of personalities, policy shifts and political change—important, significant, but hardly as effective as bloody revolution in commanding public attention. RL looked a little blander, a little more even tempered than RFE—a little less flamboyant.

The events RL covered in the years after its organization were not unimportant or wholly without intense interest. The CIA gave both RL and RFE access to the full text of Chairman Khrushchev's speech to the Twentieth Congress of the Communist party only about four months after it had been delivered. It was RL's biggest news break after the death of Stalin, and gave the station a chance to test its growing strength both in personnel and facilities.

In 1959 the major event was Khrushchev's trip to the United States. One would assume that the émigré staff members would have greeted news of the impending journey as another opportunity to test their strength and to build audience in the target areas; enthusiasm, however, was subdued. In fact, coverage plans struck a sensitive nerve in the organization. Many members of the exile staff argued passionately that the trip be ignored, that coverage would give the Soviet leader undue publicity and imply the concession of legitimacy to the Soviet regime. Khrushchev's projected meeting with Eisenhower further stimulated their opposition: meeting with the U.S. president, they contended, would give the chairman stature he had previously lacked. In the end the trip was covered, however, and there was one scheduled event that was covered and covered well, despite the angry protests of some of the émigrés: when the Soviet leader spoke to the General Assembly of the United Nations, RL broadcast his speech live to the Soviet Union.*

The next year, when the Soviet leader was back in the United States, the opposition from the émigrés on the Radio staff had softened somewhat, apparently on the basis that any damage that could be done had already been done. Again, RL covered his UN speech and transmitted it live, including the now famous episode in which the chairman emphasized a point by taking off his shoe and banging it on his desk, a sound effect the microphone faithfully recorded.†

---

*Not unexpectedly, Soviet jammers were silent for Khrushchev's speech. They jumped into action immediately thereafter, when the U.S. Secretary of State Christian Herter took the podium to reply. The game was continued when Khrushchev went to Washington to speak to the National Press Club. The chairman's formal remarks, transmitted live, were unmarred by jamming. The lively question-and-answer session that followed was given the full jamming treatment of screeches and howls.

†Soviet radio also covered the chairman's speech but on a delayed basis. The delay gave editors an opportunity to delete the shoe-pounding sequence and change the thrust of the remarks to make it appear that Khrushchev had appeared before the international forum as a dignified proponent of peace.

The Cuban missile crisis in September 1962 gave the U.S.-based staff members another opportunity to flex their muscles on a dramatic event. In this case RL management added a new twist to its regular routine. It contracted for two 15-minute periods weekly on the medium-wave commercial station WBT in Charlotte, North Carolina, to broadcast programs aimed at Soviet troops stationed in Cuba. The Charlotte station, operating with the maximum power allowed in the United States and broadcasting on a frequency that blanketed most of the island nation, risked retaliation from Premier Castro, but it permitted the use of its facilities to go on for several months.

Growing tensions between the Soviets and their Chinese allies gave RL another running story that built gradually from the release of the Khrushchev Party Congress speech in June 1956 to a climactic month-long negotiating session in Moscow in mid-summer 1963 that ended in what appeared to be an irreconcilable split. Amcomlib had contracted more than a year earlier with the Broadcasting Corporation of China, the broadcasting arm of the Republic of China on Taiwan, for the use of a high-powered shortwave transmitter to enable RL to reach the maritime provinces of the Soviet Union bordering on the Pacific Ocean and those portions of eastern Siberia extending as far westward as Lake Baikal. Service from the Taiwan transmitter began in 1955. In order to furnish a program service that would not be forced to depend on the slow shipment of tapes from Munich or New York, Amcomlib decided to create a separate program department in Taipei.* The Taiwan site gave the station a close-up listening post in mainland China's backyard. Coverage from Taipei was supplemented by reports from a special correspondent stationed in Hong Kong.

As remarked above, none of these events, although extremely important to RL, incorporated the intrinsic high drama that characterized the Polish and Hungarian rebellions. They placed a burden on the staff but did not tempt unusual emotional outbursts by hot-headed personnel. This may be one important reason why RL gave the impression of being more stolid than its older cousin. Events covered made fewer banner headlines and appealed more to the intellect than to the senses. This lower-key approach, of course, was also in accordance with the U.S. government policy, which had decreed that Amcomlib should stay out of the spotlight of media attention.

The gradually evolving policy calling for restraint and avoidance of provocation to overt action was formally recognized in a revised policy manual issued toward the end of 1958. Revolution was specifically banned as an objective of RL broadcasts. *Evolution* within the Soviet Union was thereafter to be the goal: political change within the USSR was to be encouraged. The new

---

*The Taipei broadcast operations were continued until 1973, when they were suspended after an 18-year run for lack of funds.

guidelines recognized that Soviet society was changing and that RL would have to adjust accordingly to exert influence on its listeners. It recognized that the Khrushchev regime was more concerned than the previous Stalin regime had been with consumer goods and the needs and comforts of the Soviet peoples. It was the beginning of the era of "peaceful coexistence" and the station had to react to the changed attitudes, even though the Kremlin leadership's definition of the term *coexistence* varied substantially from that in the West. Its ability to reach its target audience depended on its ability to understand changing conditions.

The shift in attitude at RL was hardly abrupt, but in the 1958 policy manual it was formally acknowledged. *New York Times* correspondent David Binder 13 years later, in March 1971, recalled the differences between RFE and RL and described the changes at the latter that had occurred over the years:

> The crushing of the Hungarian uprising in 1956 by Soviet armor led to the crushing of cold war agitation by Radio Free Europe and in less dramatic form at the Munich station aimed at the Soviet Union . . . Radio Liberty. At RFE commentators and policy advisors were dismissed or shifted to innocuous jobs. Radio Liberation . . . gradually toned down its more aggressive commentators.[3]

The key word is *gradually*. The aggressive emotionalism of a large part of the émigré staff, the internal quarrels between bitterly divided factions, and the universal hatred of the government in the Kremlin could not be eliminated by printing a sentence or a paragraph in a policy manual—and enforcement would continue to be a problem. But as at RFE, the heady old days of intensive confrontation were over. The "implacable struggle" would go on, but broadcasts would no longer advocate the total destruction of the Soviet state. "Liberation" was giving way to *liberalization*. In December 1963 the Amcomlib board took one more step in this direction. It voted to change its corporate name once more, this time from the Radio Liberation Committee to the Radio Liberty Committee. The change took effect in January 1964.

NOTES

1. Vladimir Petrov, "Radio Liberation," *Russian Review* 17 (April 1958): 112–130.

2. American Committee for Liberation, untitled publication (May 1957), p. 21. (In Hoover Institution Archives.)

3. David Binder, "Embattled RFE Defends Role," *New York Times*, March 15, 1971.

12
The End of Jiggery-Pokery

W HILE STILL RECOVERING from the trauma of the Hungarian Revolution, RFE suffered another shock, this one internally generated rather than externally imposed. It was a shattering experience. Stern measures restored order but only after several weeks of chaos amounting almost to insurrection. There was for a time a serious question whether the radio station could absorb the blows and keep on operating.

The shock was caused by an upheaval in the Czechoslovak Service. The Poles had had their test in 1956 and survived in excellent health thanks to the mature guidance and steady hand of Jan Nowak and the strength of the Polish Service. The Hungarian Service had faltered under pressure and committed errors that took years to live down. Now it was the turn for the Czechs and Slovaks to be tested.

The crisis began in early autumn 1960, when the highly respected head of the Czechoslovak Service, Julius Firt, asked for retirement. Eric Hazelhoff, RFE's European director, replaced Firt with the associate director of the service, Oswald Kostrba. This seemed on the face of it to be a sensible and reasonable move, but it did not look that way to a large majority of members of the Czechoslovak staff. They saw Kostrba as a martinet. His father had been a military officer, and some of the military bearing and behavior patterns had rubbed off on the son. He gave orders in military fashion and demanded that they be carried out. He expected absolute discipline and refused to permit desk editors to question his judgment. His problems were compounded by a history of what some RFE staff members regarded as lax discipline in the service.

Kostrba made a dangerous mistake in selecting for his assistant a Slovak regarded by fellow editors as unqualified for the job. The decision was bitterly opposed by all except a small minority and it led to tension between the Czechs and the Slovaks, where deep-seated animosities constantly threatened to erupt. Only days had passed after the announcement of the appointment before Kostrba's control of the staff was utterly shattered. He resorted to excessive disciplinary measures, but they only drove staff members deeper into the opposition. Attempting to exert his authority and restore order, Kostrba assigned those he regarded as the principal troublemakers to menial jobs on the remote fringes of editorial programming, including correcting grammar and spelling in broadcast material. This was bitter medicine for proud editors who were ideologically committed to the cause of a free Europe. Protests began within the Czechoslovak service, but as they grew in bitterness and volume they began to affect the whole RFE organization.

The dissidents took to writing memos to Kostrba, making sure that copies went to Hazelhoff. The other desk chiefs, led by Jan Nowak, went to Kostrba to warn him that the angry dispute in the Czechoslovak service was beginning to stimulate repercussions throughout the headquarters building. Kostrba was unimpressed. By early December the impasse reached a stage where action was mandatory. Hazelhoff, in a move to restore order, terminated the 18 editors in the Czechoslovak service whom he regarded as the ringleaders of the rebellion. All but a handful of members loyal to Kostrba and his hand-picked assistant desk chief then walked out, leaving the service in total disarray.

New York headquarters had not been fully informed of the problem. Ferdinand Peroutka, the head of the Czechoslovak service in New York to whom Kostrba nominally reported, had little knowledge of events in Munich and felt that he had to back his desk chief. Thomas H. Brown, the RFE director, also based in New York, was even less well informed. But with the service on the verge of total collapse, vigorous steps had to be taken. RFE's legal counsel, J. R. Greenlea, was dispatched to Munich to investigate. CIA director Allen Dulles and his aide Cord Meyer by now saw the possibility that the whole house of cards in Munich would collapse unless aggressive action was taken to restore order.

In early December, approximately two weeks after Kostrba had fired the 18 editors, Hazelhoff and his two deputies, Charles McNeill and David Penn, abruptly resigned or were terminated. The vice president for administration for the Free Europe Committee in New York, retired Major General C. Rodney Smith, was sent off to Munich to restore order. Firt was persuaded to return for another tour of duty as the desk head and Kostrba was shipped off to Vienna as a correspondent. Samuel Bellus, who had been trying to hold the service together during the crisis, was made associate director. Within 48 hours after Hazelhoff and his aides had cleaned out their offices and left for good, the 18 fired members of the Czechoslovak service were back at their jobs, as were the sympathizers who had refused to work without them.

These steps were only a palliative, however. A drastic overhaul of the whole organization, it became clear, was required.* General Smith was on the scene in Munich patching up the wounds. It was clear to the general that the turbulence in the Czechoslovak service and the helplessness of New York headquarters to maintain firm management control pointed to a serious structural deficiency that would require more than a patch-up. His original assignment was to remain in Munich only until order was restored. When some semblance of harmony had been established, however, he was asked by Allen Dulles to accept the Munich appointment on a permanent basis. He would be director of RFE, not merely European director. All RFE offices and personnel, including New York, would report to him. Channels of command would flow from Munich to New York, not vice versa. With those conditions fully clarified, he accepted. The significance of the change was clear. Munich, from its earliest days as a program production center, had only been an outpost, a subsidiary of New York headquarters. Its new status would relieve it of checking decisions with New York. Changes in the organization came rapidly. Smith moved with the confidence and decisiveness of a senior military officer.

The next two years may have been the most challenging in RFE's development after the experimental and risk-taking days of its very early history. The shape of organization was radically altered, reflecting changed conditions in both the East and the West and modification of Free Europe's earlier objectives. Smith had firm ideas as to what had to be done. New York's influence had to be reduced; the New York office below the level of senior Free

---

*At this point the writer becomes personally involved in the story. In early January 1961 I had a call from Tom Brown asking me to join him for dinner in a Westport, Connecticut, restaurant. Brown asked me whether I would consider moving to Munich as European director of RFE. I was mildly curious but reluctant to make so dramatic a move. Within a few days, Archibald Alexander, the president of Free Europe, Inc., and Brown's superior officer, invited me to lunch. Alexander was persuasive in urging me to accept the offer and also made it considerably more attractive by telling me that Free Europe had decided to transfer RFE headquarters from New York to Munich. The job he was offering, thus, was directorship of RFE, not the European directorship. He didn't tell me what would happen to Brown nor did I think it discreet at this point to ask. I was still reluctant. The next call came from Allen Dulles, asking me to come down to Washington to meet him in his office in the CIA headquarters. I arrived at his office about 6:30 one February evening. Cord Meyer was with him as we sat down to talk about the Munich move. Dulles and Meyer were clearly seriously disturbed by the course of events in Munich. They felt it necessary to take decisive action, and obviously it had to be taken quickly. They were certain that RFE could continue to contribute positively to relationships with Eastern Europe for years to come. They were sure that the new Kennedy administration would continue to support RFE; I wasn't so sure. Happily, history has proved me wrong. However, several days after our meeting I decided—reluctantly—to refuse their offer.

Europe executives would be maintained not as headquarters but as a support component. The show had to be run from Munich. The chiefs of the broadcast services in Munich had to be given both prestige and salaries commensurate with the responsibilities they carried, and they had to have full support from management. Smith felt that they should report directly to the director of RFE and not in a confused circular organization chart in which responsibilities were difficult to fix. It was unclear, prior to 1961, whether they reported to a policy advisor (as they did during Bill Griffith's term of duty), to an American program director assigned to the staff, to the appropriate desk chief in New York, or to the European director who in turn reported to the RFE director in New York. The general quickly moved to change the nomenclature so that Radio Free Poland, say, became the Polish Broadcast Desk, and its head would be the director of the "Polish BD." That director would report directly to the director of RFE, not to a policy adviser or a Polish desk chief in New York. Designations applying to the other services were similarly changed. Salaries of directors of BDs were increased as much as regulations would allow (about $1000 annually), but the increases were repeated in subsequent years.

Not only did this move enhance the prestige of the broadcast desk heads, but it placed more responsibility on them for the conduct of their services. The American program directors to whom the BD heads had nominally reported were eliminated. In the early days program specialists had been useful in training desk personnel in production methods and schedule building, but now the training job was done; they were superfluous. Émigré staff members were fully competent to produce programs with flair and imagination. It was assumed that the more grandiose programs of the earlier period would not be continued, thus reducing the requirement for elaborate show-business experience.

The News and Information Department underwent the greatest transformation. Smith was dissatisfied with the administrative abilities of News Director Russell Hill, but he admired Hill's deputy, Gene Mater,* who had the responsibility for managing the central news room under Hill's direction. He reassigned Hill as a correspondent in Washington and made Mater the overall news chief.

Mater was a purist. He had no tolerance for rumors, half-truths, or unverified information passing as news. If a story could not be fully verified by at least two independent sources, he refused to permit his editor to pass it on. The story either passed the test or it didn't; if it failed the test, it was tossed in the wastebasket. "Puritanical objectivity" is the way some of the old-timers

---

*Now a CBS Broadcast group vice president in New York, Mater had been a military interrogator after the war, as had some of the others on the news desk, but on his return to the United States he gained solid newspaper background on a daily paper in California, followed by a five-year period on the *New York World Telegram*.

described the new emphasis on absolute objectivity and the absence of even a hint of conjecture. People who were on the news staff at the time say that there were some "terrible hassles." His critics argued that his rigid standards were creating a dull, drab, gray news report. The new approach to journalism was a little hard to take in an organization that had put a premium on "information" for years and had established an elaborate mechanism for obtaining that information through interviews with émigrés, travelers, and anyone else who had something to offer. Jan Nowak, while subscribing to the theory of objectivity and to the necessity for building a sense of credibility among his listeners, was particularly disturbed to lose this wellspring of attention-compelling items. He had vivid recollections of the success of the Polish service with the Colonel Swiatlo story and with others that had been gathered through the information centers. But General Smith gave Mater his head. It was, as James Brown who became Radio Free Europe Director in 1979 describes it, "the end of the era of 'jiggery-pokery.' "

Mater made one concession, allowing the continued distribution of background and interpretive information through the Central News Department service—but for background purposes only. He instituted a new color-coding system to distinguish between verified facts and information for background uses. White paper was used for news items that had been checked out to the point where news editors were willing to pass them on for broadcast use. Other material was distributed on buff. Edited news copy from the central newsroom went to the newsrooms of the five broadcast services by teletype transmission. There the language news service editors translated them, adding as much pertinent background information as might give the story more substance and appeal in the target areas, and sent them on to the studio for broadcast. No changes in facts were permitted; that would have circumvented Mater's tight control. However, the order in which items were broadcast could be changed and additional, carefully verified background facts inserted in order to appeal to the specific audiences in the countries in question.

Following the institution of the white/buff system, only the white could be used in building a broadcast. The buff material could be used in interpretive pieces and factual analyses but only as unverified information. James Edwards, who became news director in the middle 1970s after serving in RFE's news service since 1956, regards the instituting of the white/buff color scheme as the most important single step in the professionalizing of RFE's news service.

Other steps were being taken, too. The information centers were gradually being phased out and the resources thus made available concentrated in major news bureaus in such critically important news centers as London, Paris, Bonn, and Rome. No more would RFE have information centers in such unlikely bureau points as Graz, Linz, and Salzburg. At the same time Mater began to hire only experienced news personnel with records compiled on major newspapers or wire services. British Commonwealth personnel— English, Canadian, and Australian—began to fill many of the slots as they opened up; they seemed more flexible than Americans in adapting to the job requirements, including relatively low wage scales. The bureaus, however, were managed by Americans.

There was still a conflict with the policy advisor. Richard Burks, a scholar with a CIA background, had taken over direction of the policy function and had brought Ralph Walter back from New York, where he had been transferred to Free Europe's New York headquarters after the breakup of Griffith's policy team. He came back as Burks' deputy. Both Burks and Walter wanted to be sure they had control of news. Mater, on the other hand, insisted on reporting only to the RFE director with no intermediate level between.

Smith brought the contesting forces together and worked on a compromise in which Mater was given full responsibility for news. If any serious question should arise between News and Policy, the matter could be brought to Smith's attention for adjudication. Mater succeeded in getting the terms of the compromise on paper, serving as a small-scale Magna Carta for the news department. There were only a very few times during Smith's five-year tour of duty in Munich when he was asked to settle disputes between News and Policy.

The compromise established a basis for cooperation between the two departments but did not entirely ease the tensions. Walter complained that Mater and Nathan Kingsley, who succeeded him, had a tendency to feel they should not have to consult with Policy; they ran their own fiefdom. Any residual irritations that continued to exist, however, were kept under control.

The Research Department had been severed from News and Information as early as 1959 in the aftermath of the Hungarian trauma. Previously, it had been designated as Research and Evaluation and had functioned as a unit of News and Information, with the primary purpose of checking out reports developed by the information gatherers in the News and Information bureaus. James Brown, who was hired in 1957 by News Director Talbot Hood to serve on the News and Evaluation staff, was not at all proud of his new job. He had accepted it largely because he found himself jobless in Munich and had neither the reason nor the resources to return to his home in England. "Research was not anything at all," he says. "We were just running errands for editors on the desks. Just get the facts. We weren't supposed to think. A Research Department simply didn't exist. We were occupied with evaluating the information items, a large number of which were trash."

What research there was, according to Brown, was really in the domain of the East European editors. Americans served as copy editors (except for Griffith who occasionally did a research piece on his own). It took at least four years after the end of the Hungarian Revolution to shake the preoccupation with field reports. Brown ascribes this reluctance to change to the backgrounds of many of the Americans in key positions both at Free Europe headquarters and in the RFE organization in psychological warfare, CIA service, and counterintelligence units.

He gives Dick Burks a lion's share of the credit for "putting Research on the right track." It was Burks, backed by Smith, who introduced a scholarly approach and changed the relationship between Research and the broadcast desks to make Research a valuable source of analytical papers of impeccable quality for delivery to the broadcast services, either for direct broadcast or background. He encouraged a dialogue between desk personnel and research experts so that, on the one hand, Research would have the benefit of the expertise in East European affairs that reposed in the East European staffs and, on the other, the editors and writers in turn could benefit from the deep, scholarly, and thorough research efforts of the revitalized Research Department. The two departments were beginning to operate on a partnership basis, and Research was well on the way to becoming a unique strength of RFE.

The professionalization of the News Department and the increasing prestige of Research had a profound impact on the entire program schedule. The preoccupation with relatively minor affairs of significance only in the target countries gave way to greater concern with world affairs that affected them. Serious appraisals of economic and social conditions behind the Iron Curtain began to replace the more personal stories picked up from the information sources. Commentary began to give way to interpretation and analysis.

At the same time, the character of the personnel of the broadcast services was undergoing significant change. In the early 1950s émigrés available for RFE employment were largely from the upper economic and intellectual classes; they had fled communism either during the World War II or as communism moved swiftly to engulf their countries following the war. Starting with the Hungarian Revolution, the pattern of migration shifted. More middle-class and in some cases blue-collar workers joined the exodus from Eastern Europe. The shift broadened the horizons of the services, brought them fresh points of view, and enabled them to broaden the base of their audience targets. It also brought in exiles who had worked in the middle levels of newspapers, magazines, and radio stations, not just in the editor's chairs, thus democratizing the services.

Program schedules, likewise, changed. The early emphasis on elaborate schemes for presenting dramatic and serious music programs gave way to more news, analysis, economic and social background, and imitations of U.S. informational variety shows. Program titles like "Panorama" and "March of Time" began to appear.

The unhappy end to the Hungarian Revolution also led to a pronounced change in the attitude of the exile employees. As their dominant concern with return to the homeland gave way to submission to the fact that life in the West was likely to continue for many years to come, their attention turned to their own working conditions, wages and hours, company-supplied benefits, unionization, and disputes with management. Ideological disputes within the exile groups continued, but employees began to show greater concern with making the best possible living under the most favorable circumstances in the West. Settling labor disputes and negotiating contracts began to consume as much time on the part of management as setting down policy requirements.

The Policy Department never regained the predominant position it had held in the pre-Hungarian period under Griffith and his aggressive team. As Research grew in strength it established an analytical background for policy evaluation, thus eliminating some of the need for constant surveillance. Long-term policy guidances continued to be prepared in cooperation with officials of the Department of State and the CIA, but the daily policy guidances were eliminated.

By late 1961 what James Brown calls the "romantic-heroic period" was finished. Archibald Alexander had left the presidency of the Free Europe Committee to be succeeded by John Richardson, Jr., a New York investment banker with a view of RFE's functions well adapted to the new circumstances. The New York staff was scaled down to function as a support unit, and in adjusting to this new role both Reuben Nathan and Tom Brown left the organization. RFE was in a position of relative tranquility that continued until February 1967, when *Ramparts* magazine revealed to the public the secret that had been so carefully protected since 1949: RFE was financed by the CIA.

13
The Security Blanket Begins to Unravel

F REE EUROPE'S SECURITY BLANKET began to unravel in February 1967. It had held together remarkably well over the years. A widening circle of media personnel, former Free Europe and RL employees, members of Congress, congressional staffs, and a substantial number of citizens had learned in one way or another of the CIA connection. But the media had taken no notice of the stations' illicit parentage, even though it was common knowledge among the ranks of publishers and editors.

The unraveling of the cover began innocently enough. A disgruntled executive of the National Students Association who also happened to be a member of the left-wing Students for a Democratic Society learned that one of the NSA's major sources of support was the CIA. He got in touch with a reporter for *Ramparts* magazine, a counterculture periodical published in San Francisco. The result was a detailed report that appeared in the March 1967 edition of *Ramparts*, explaining the channels used by the CIA in passing money on to dummy foundations that in turn channeled it to legitimate foundations from which it went to the NSA.*

---

*It is curious that *Ramparts* referred to NSA executives who had been told the secret as being "witty." They explained that once an NSA executive rose to a level where there was a "need to know," he was informed during a quiet lunch or office session of the connection. This was the process described as being made "witty." What *Ramparts* never caught on to—nor did many of the newspapers that referred to the *Ramparts* piece, nor even CBS news—was that the word that the CIA used was a much more meaningful one: "witting." RFE and RL personnel, when they reached a level where there was a "need to know" went through the same process of being made "witting."

Neither Free Europe nor Amcomlib were mentioned in *Ramparts*. The sole target was the CIA's relationship with the NSA. But Free Europe quickly got caught in the backwash. *Ramparts* was so proud of its accomplishments in tripping up the CIA in another clandestine adventure that it bought a full-page advertisement in the *New York Times* to gloat over its triumphs, and it submitted advance copies of its investigative report to a number of publications.

On Tuesday, February 14, 1967, the *New York Times* front-paged an item that revealed that an NSA executive admitted that the association had been receiving CIA funds. The item also called attention to the fact that *Ramparts* would carry the full report in its March issue. The barrier against reporting on CIA financing ventures had now been broken and the *Times* reportorial staff was free to pursue the story.

On Wednesday, February 15, the *Times* reported that President Lyndon B. Johnson had instructed the CIA to close out all secret aid to student groups. The president also called for a review of all other CIA-funded anti-Communist programs in private organizations. Then came a sentence that pointed in a carefully indirect way at RFE and RL: "It is believed," *Times* reporter Neil Sheehan wrote, "that the Agency provides clandestine aid to anti-Communist labor unions, publications and radio and television stations." In the same issue the chief Washington correspondent of the *Times*, James Reston, underscored the possible results of the disclosure: "It places in jeopardy CIA programs to aid anti-Communist publications, radio and television stations and labor unions." Reston pointed out that such aid had been known to Presidents Eisenhower, Kennedy, and Johnson and to the members of the Senate committee that oversees the CIA. He also revealed that both Senators J. W. Fulbright of Arkansas and Eugene McCarthy of Minnesota had been informed as to what would be revealed in the *Ramparts* article.

Still there is no clear-cut identification of RFE or RL. That was to come six days later, in a February 21 piece. Even then, RL was overlooked. The *Times* story described the processes used for channeling monies through dummy conduits to legitimate foundations that passed funds on to agencies dependent on the CIA. Five organizations were listed as receiving funds from the Hobby Foundation* of Houston, Texas: the American Friends of the Middle East, the Fund for International Social and Economic Education, the Foreign Policy Association, the Institute of Internal Education (by this was probably meant the Institute for International Education), and Radio Free Europe. RFE was listed as a recipient of $40,000 from the Hobby Foundation in 1964 and $250 in 1965. Finally its name was in print.

---

*The president of the Hobby Foundation was listed as William P. Hobby. His mother, Oveta Culp Hobby, had been a member of President Eisenhower's cabinet as the first secretary for health, education and welfare, appointed in 1953.

RL curiously was still in the clear. No mention was made of its sources of support, and apparently no questions were asked. Its consistently lower profile, its avoidance of massive fund drives like the Crusade for Freedom, and the fact that it had never been caught in a crossfire comparable to the aftermath of the 1956 Hungarian Revolution seemed to protect it for the moment. But only for the moment.

The *Washington Post*'s Sunday edition on February 26 added graphic detail in the lead story of its "Outlook" section. A banner headline read: "O What a Tangled Web the CIA Wove." The deck under it read: "Cost Likely/ To Run High/ Into Millions." A large chart in the shape of a wheel covered most of the center of the page. At the hub was the CIA. Spokes radiated out to little-known foundations to which the CIA channeled funds. They were described by the line, "They got it first." Outside this tier was another tier described as "Secondary Conduits." The next tier, described as "The Final Disbursers," included the letters RFE. RFE was not displayed prominently; it was only one of a number of organizations. But it was there in print, and the funding processes by which it had been kept operating through the years were plain for anyone to see. It was clear that the conduits who "got it first" were five funds: Kentfield, Beacon, Edsel, Price, and Gotham. The Hobby Foundation was the "Secondary Conduit." Again, there is no mention of RL or the Radio Liberty Committee and the chart is inaccurate in suggesting that funding went to RFE. The Free Europe Committee, corporate parent of RFE, was the actual recipient.

The *Ramparts* article was potentially damaging because it brought into the open the CIA's funding of Free Europe and showed the methods for that funding. The *Times* added a national circulation composed of an elite readership. The *Washington Post* made the information available to government personnel at all levels, foreign embassy staffs, and correspondents for all media, both domestic and foreign. It took a documentary broadcast on a television network, however, to bring the story to the masses, and the controversy that followed that broadcast kept the story alive and widened its impact.

Shortly after the *Times* broke the news, CBS News assigned one of its best investigative teams to further research the story and to develop it into a pictorial account for broadcast purposes. Executive producer Les Midgeley, producer Ron Bonn, and correspondent Mike Wallace smelled blood and went in for the kill. Their takeoff point was the NSA story, but after detailing the highlights of NSA's affair with the CIA and interviewing Gloria Steinem about her four years on the agency's payroll, they abruptly switched their attention to RFE. The title of the documentary was indicative of the approach: "In the Pay of the CIA: An American Dilemma." It was broadcast by the full CBS network on March 13, just four weeks after the original *Times* item and two weeks after the *Washington Post* Sunday piece. Wallace as the narrator pulled no punches. He described CIA support of RFE as "the strangest of CIA's penetrations into private groups, a project which in effect used you, the individual American citizen, as cover. . . . If you responded to the many appeals for Radio Free Europe on television, in magazines, or even on buses or subways, then you became a part of a CIA cover." In concluding this section of the program, Wallace reported that the CBS Television network "is now studying its policy on public service announcements for Radio Free Europe. The network has broadcast no such announcements since February 15."*

This almost extraneous note dropped into the broadcast set off a flurry of comment in the nation's press, kept the story alive well beyond the time when it could have been expected to die down, and stirred up a hornet's nest within the CBS corporate structure. Editors read into the CBS decision to consider banning RFE Fund announcements a major shift in policy. The apparently innocent line was sufficiently startling to lead reporters to question Wallace and Midgeley, who reported that they had received the information from Richard S. Salant, president of the CBS News division. Corporate President Frank Stanton, however, quickly denied that CBS had taken action and pointed out that an announcement on behalf of the RFE Fund had been carried by CBS-owned station KMOX-TV, St. Louis, since the February 15 deadline. Stanton was in the uncomfortable position of being both the president and chief policy maker for CBS Incorporated and the chairman of the executive committee of the Radio Free Europe Fund whose announcements were in jeopardy.

The apparent rift between the corporate president and the president of the news division, insignificant as it may have been, was considered fair game by the print media. News stories and editorials appeared in a rash across the country. The net result was not so much that CBS's internal inconsistencies were exposed as that by now CIA's funding of RFE had become a secondary target in a nationwide news story. The CBS documentary had succeeded in injecting into the CIA-RFE connection new drama, urgency, and a patina of mystery; no longer could there be polite acceptance of the connection by only a few knowing individuals. There was now the substance for a nationwide cause célèbre.

Free Europe and the Radio Liberty Committee had been able to keep their secret for a surprisingly long time, nearly two decades, but eventually something had to happen that would blow the shaky cover and expose their clandestine source of funds. A disgruntled member of Congress or an opposition publisher could blow the whistle, or the government, anticipating a possible revelation of the secret, could recommend legislation for a new funding method. By the middle 1960s the number of Americans who knew the secret

---

*February 15 was the date on which *The New York Times* hinted that radio and television might also have received government funding through the CIA.

must have been well into the thousands: former employees, journalists who knew the story but kept their lips and typewriters sealed, government personnel who were privy to the facts, and private citizens who had learned in one way or another. Soviet and East European intelligence agencies were obviously fully knowledgeable; their media kept labeling both the Radios as "agents of the CIA." Americans who knew had kept the secret, although it is difficult to explain their silence. Apparently the funding had been going on for so long that it did not seem much of a news story any more.

An important question of propriety had been raised as a result of the investigations that had begun with *Ramparts'* exposé of the NSA, however, and both Radios found themselves in their first real life-or-death crisis. That is, was there any legal foundation for an agency of the government to draw money from the public treasury and channel it out to institutions, associations, or corporations established independently of the government?

President Johnson, according to Cord Meyer, was deeply concerned. He was nervous about the process and deeply worried concerning its legality. And while he had been aware of the existence of RFE and RL and their largesse from the CIA, he had never been much involved or overly enthusiastic; he had too many other pressing problems. In order to obtain a rational basis for deciding whether all funding had to cease or whether there might be a loophole that would permit continuation of the process he did what presidents frequently do: appoint a committee. The members of the committee were Nicholas Katzenbach, under secretary of state who was to be chairman; John Gardiner, secretary of health, education and welfare; and Richard Helms, director of the CIA. The committee went to work at once. Two weeks later, on March 29, their report was in the president's hands.

The language of the report seemed quite clear: "No federal agency, shall provide covert financial assistance or support, direct or indirect, to any of the nation's educational or voluntary organizations." Then it added what would appear to be the clincher: "No programs currently would justify any exceptions to this rule."[1] The president accepted the committee's recommendation without objection and directed that it be implemented by federal agencies. This seemed to spell the instant demise of both Free Europe and the Radio Liberty Committee. If there were loopholes, they were not apparent. If the order were to be carried out as the committee prescribed, it seemed mandatory for CIA support to cease. RL had no other source of funding, and Free Europe was able to derive only a pittance from its Free Europe Fund, not enough to pay the power bill for its transmitters.

Helms, however, was unwilling to see the CIA's efforts over the years evaporate with a stroke of the pen. Meyer says it was Helms's influence that encouraged the president to avoid applying to Free Europe and the Radio Liberty Committee the order that would have been fatal to both. The Radios also had an influential supporter in the Senate. Major General Smith (who by then had left the RFE directorship) credits Senator James O. Eastland of Mississippi with persuading the president to avoid dropping the guillotine on the two Radios. Whether it was Helms or Eastland or both, the Radios escaped and their checks kept on coming out of the CIA budget. (Meyer adds that it was a very close call; the president was never quite sure whether he was for the Radios or against them.) The basis for the favorable decision was the rather flimsy contention that the Radios "were not private and voluntary organizations but rather government proprietaries established by government initiative and functioning under official policy direction."[2]

It would have been reasonable to expect at this point that the public would take up the cry that the Radios be liquidated. The CBS documentary and the controversy surrounding it almost certainly evoked memories of the Crusade for Freedom drives and its exhortations to send "Truth Dollars" and pennies from school children to keep freedom alive in Eastern Europe. Millions of Americans had taken pride and a sense of satisfaction from contributing their parts in the effort. Now they could be excused if they felt they had been duped. Their dollars and pennies did not mean very much if the CIA out of its vast outlay of secret funds was channelling enough to RFE to enable the station to live at least comfortably, if not lavishly. A sense of having been victimized by the top-secret intelligence agency (of which the general public was naturally somewhat suspicious anyway) would have been an expectable result. RFE executives expected a deluge of criticisms and demands for shutting down the Radios. They were astounded, however, that no such thing occurred. "We had to put out a few small fires," says J. Allen Hovey, RFE's vice president for public affairs, "but the storm quickly blew itself out."

Suspicion of RFE, aroused by the CIA disclosure, had been fed by residual distrust resulting from conduct of the station during the Hungarian episode. The revolution in Hungary had been a traumatic experience for millions of Americans who were emotionally tied to the freedom fighters and frustrated by their own helplessness in coming to their aid. Their frustrations found a resolution in the charges against RFE that followed the suppression of the rebellion, some of them carefully nurtured by Communist propagandists. In the desire to find scapegoats and relieve frustrations it was easy to remember the well-publicized charges that RFE had fanned the flames, cheering on the insurgents and promising aid, and by its excessive exuberance condemned thousands of freedom fighters to their deaths. The 1967 disclosures were of a type to rekindle the lingering uneasiness, to give critics a theatrical new angle for tying Free Europe to the world of the notorious spy agency, the CIA. Eleven years earlier, the revelation might have been passed off with a shrug, but this was a different era, one of rioting on campuses and in the streets, popular protests against the Vietnam war, the distrust of government and disdain for authority, and the abandonment of once-traditional values. The connection of the Hungarian Revolution with the currently detested CIA condemned RFE to a prominent position on hate lists and created an atmosphere of suspicion that prevailed well into the 1970s.*

The climate was ripe for a wave of popular animosity that would wash away both Radios. Surprisingly, however, no such thing happened. After a brief flurry of attention, the story died out. There apparently were too many other, more serious and immediate problems demanding attention. The Vietnam war, draft resistance, protests on the campuses, and demonstrations in the streets aroused deeper passions.

Congress turned out to be surprisingly more docile than might have been expected. President Johnson's shaky decision that government funding could continue went unchallenged. No member of Congress raised the issue publicly for almost four years. The media, too, remained generally supportive. However, a seed-bed of suspicion and hostility had passed through the germination stage, and another round of disclosures would bring out unwanted blooms. There was a solid base for subsequent campaigns to destroy the Radios.

The performance of RFE's Czechoslovak desk in the highly sensitive "Prague Spring" and the subsequent Soviet invasion in August 1968 restored some faith in the organization. The cautious restraint demonstrated in covering a situation that was potentially as explosive as Hungary had been in 1956 won the station new confidence from those who were concerned about its future. Its adroit and sure-handed coverage of the violent riots in Poland in 1970 also reflected the efforts of a mature and responsible communications organization.

The lessons learned in Poland and Hungary twelve years earlier had been put to good use. Reporters, writers, broadcasters, policy personnel and management all snapped to attention, worked long, excruciating hours, and never permitted enthusiasms or passions to distract them from their key goal of delivering an unemotional factual report to Czechoslovak citizens in 1968 and to Poland in 1970.

Meanwhile, the unrest that had gripped the United States in 1967 was intensifying. The assassinations in 1968 of Robert F. Kennedy and Martin Luther King, open confrontation between police and rioters in Chicago during the Democratic convention, and the bitter election campaign between Richard Nixon and Hubert Humphrey commanded the headlines. In this charged atmosphere RFE and RL were able to retreat out of range of the most

---

*As late as March 1982, 15 years after the *New York Times* named the CIA as a source of RFE's funding, the Copley News Service distributed an analytical report on the proposed radio station Radio MARTI, including the following: "The U.S. learned its lesson years ago in 1956 when it was said that the programs of the U.S. funded Radio Free Europe on which Radio MARTI is presumably modeled misled the people of Hungary into thinking that the United States would intervene militarily to help them throw off their Soviet backed Communist regime." Myths apparently die hard.

determined attackers; they seemed impervious for the moment to political sniping in Washington. Then in 1971 the signal to attack was being heard once more. But this time it was not in an obscure counterculture magazine or even *The New York Times*, the *Washington Post* or "CBS Reports" that broke the silence. Opposition came from the floor of the United States Senate. The security blanket was in tatters and the Radios fully exposed to the public. The battle was on for their lives.

NOTES

1. Report (to accompany S. 18) Senate Committee on Foreign Relations, July 30, 1971, p. 10 (included in speech of Senator Case (N.J.) delivered on January 25, 1971).

2. Cord Meyer, *Facing Reality* (New York: Harper & Row, 1980), p. 133.

14

The Patient Looks
Awful, Awful Sick

THE SECOND BLOW that nearly shattered RFE and RL and came within the slimmest of margins of causing them to close up shop did not come totally without warning. An uneasy calm prevailed after the resolution of the first crisis over the disclosure of clandestine funding, but there were warning signs for those experienced observers of the Washington scene who knew enough of the Capitol's political climate to forecast impending storms. The most forbidding omen came when Senator Clifford Case of New Jersey employed John Marks as a member of his staff. Marks was a disgruntled former CIA agent who, according to his critics, was bent on tearing down the agency. He was variously described as a young man with a chip on his shoulder and as an opportunist who intended to build his CIA experience into a successful and prosperous career. Marks was privy to the full RFE/RL story and was aware of the narrow escape the two Radios had when they had slipped out of Katzenbach's noose in 1967. Marks's position on the staff of a prestigious senator caused more than raised eyebrows among the cognoscenti. The growing disillusionment with U.S. foreign policy expressed by Senator Fulbright, who held the critically important post of chairman of the Senate Foreign Relations Committee, was another disturbing sign noted by experts in reading the political barometer.

One careful observer was David M. Abshire, a former member of the staff for the Center for Strategic and International Studies at Georgetown University, who was appointed assistant secretary of state for congressional relations in mid-1970. Shortly after assuming his new position, Abshire began to sniff trouble on the distant horizon. "It was in our binoculars that RFE and RL were soon going to be a problem." He reported one day to his immediate supervisor, Under Secretary of State U. Alexis Johnson, that it might be a wise move to bring the Radios out from under cover before they were flushed out by enemies bent on their destruction. Johnson replied that he was of the opinion that the Katzenbach report made it virtually impossible for a government agency to support the Radios. Raising the issue could well lead to a political dog fight that no one wanted to initiate.

Another government official who foresaw trouble was John Baker, a middle-level Department of State foreign service officer, who returned to the department from Czechoslovakia in late 1970 to take up a post as director of East European affairs under the supervision of the assistant secretary for the European bureau, Martin Hillenbrand. In his new post he bore direct responsibility for furnishing policy guidance to the Radios. As a veteran of service in one of the target countries, he was well acquainted with their output and favorably disposed to their continued operation. Baker was one of those uneasy about Marks's relationship with Senator Case. His service in East Europe had convinced him of the worth of Free Europe in delivering information to the Eastern European countries in a way that no government broadcaster could. He was concerned that no good could come from the strong position that Marks had assumed in the Case office but saw no alternative other than to be ready when the blow landed.

The first specific evidence that their fears were solidly founded appeared in Sunday newspapers on January 24, 1971. A story released by Senator Case's office called attention to a speech the senator would deliver on the floor of the Senate the next day. On January 25 Senator Case rose to the floor of the Senate and delivered a scathing attack on the two Radios, formally revealing their CIA ties for the first time. He charged them with practicing deception both on American taxpayers and on listeners in the target area. Echoing the 1967 CBS documentary, he singled out particularly as victims those hundreds of thousands of Americans who had contributed to the Crusade for Freedom drives during the 1950s: "Several hundreds of millions of dollars in United States government funds had been expended from secret CIA budgets to pay almost totally for the costs of these two radio stations broadcasting to Eastern Europe. . . . [At] no time was Congress asked or permitted to carry out its constitutional role of approving the expenditures." Case called attention to the Katzenbach Committee report of 1967, which included those two damaging clauses, "No federal agency shall provide covert financial assistance or support, direct or indirect, to any of the nation's educational or voluntary organizations," and "no programs currently would justify any exception to this policy."

With that, Case introduced Senate Bill 18, which would amend the United States Information and Education Exchange Act of 1948 to include an appropriation of $30 million for fiscal year 1972 to provide grants to the Radios "for administration by the Secretary of State." The last phrase would effectively eliminate the CIA from the scene and shift responsibility for oversight to the State Department.

It was Case who made the first move, but standing not far in the background was Senator Fulbright. Fulbright had been told formally of the CIA financing four years earlier, at the time of the appointment of the Katzenbach Committee. He had not liked the idea then, and he liked it less now. In subsequent months the senator from Arkansas was vitriolic in his condemnation of the Radios and the CIA. Time and again, he turned to a favorite phrase, calling the Radios "outworn relics of the cold war." He criticized them for deception, for interfering with normal diplomatic processes, and for wasting money on an enterprise of at best dubious worth. He permitted Case to take the lead in introducing legislation that would have to be considered by the Senate Foreign Relations Committee because as chairman of the committee he would have a platform from which to attack.

He had two strong allies on the committee: Senators Stuart Symington of Missouri and Frank Church of Idaho. Church explained to colleagues later that he was particularly upset because before he entered the Senate he had been recruited as a principal in a Crusade for Freedom drive in Idaho without being told about the CIA financing of RFE. The deception rankled and drove him straight into the Fulbright camp. The dissident senators also had a valuable ally in the influential chief of staff of the Foreign Relations Committee, Carl Marcy.

RFE and RL managements had not had much time to contemplate the future. Even though they had escaped the *Ramparts* episode without serious injury, they recognized that they had done so only on a technicality as a result of pressure exerted on the president by Richard Helms of the CIA and Senator James O. Eastland of Mississippi. Senior staff members at both Radios were concerned that the uneasy truce could not last, but they were fully occupied with day-to-day activities and helpless to do anything, so the best they could do was wait. As Howland Sargeant put it, "We were so numb from previous crises that we assumed that we could somehow stumble through another one."

Because they had been forewarned about Case's speech, by the time executives of the Radios and interested senior officers at the State Department, the White House, and the CIA reached their offices on Monday morning, January 25, they moved quickly to set in motion whatever machinery they could to take steps to save the stations. At the CIA, Cord Meyer was assigned primary responsibility for preparing a case for preserving the Radios. His instructions were to cooperate with whatever group the Department of State would put together to support the Radios' case, but primarily to work with Abshire in creating legislation to keep the Radios alive.* (The CIA saw enormous value in keeping the Radios in full operation but did not necessarily insist that they be under CIA supervision and supported through CIA funding.) State's strategy included drafting a substitute bill for S-18 that would preserve the Radios' independent status. The project had the full support of Secretary William B. Rogers and Under Secretary Johnson.

The State Department was reluctant to accept long-term responsibility for financing and managing the Radios. Senior officers were convinced that a broadcast program that supported long-term U.S. foreign policy objectives would frequently conflict with short-term goals.† There was a vital need for a mechanism that could break censorship barriers and fill the information gaps behind the Iron Curtain. The long-term goal, therefore, would be the relaxing of censorship and the liberalization of Eastern Europe and the Soviet Union. But the Radios would inevitably come into conflict with the Communist leadership, provoking protests and threats. The department felt that its diplomatic missions could be better pursued if it were ostensibly divorced from such provocations. It could tell its ambassadors on the scene to reply to official remonstrances that they had no contact with the Radios and no control over what the Radios would say. The Radios' management could be shown to be in the hands of private corporations in no way connected with the Department of State.

The product of the combined State Department–CIA effort was unveiled on May 24, 1971. A bill to create an American Council on Private International Communications (ACPIC) was introduced in the Senate by the same senator, Clifford Case, who had introduced S-18 in January. Case offered the Department's bill as a substitute for his original one. The new bill called for the creation of an 11-member council to be appointed by the president, "with the advice and consent of the Senate." The council would be chartered in the District of Columbia as a nonprofit corporation and would receive funds appropriated by the Congress in order to carry out international broadcast activities. The council would employ managers to operate the Radios and would function as a board of directors in the employment and direction of management. The pattern proposed was different in only two essential ways from the existing one. First, funding would no longer be covert; it would be out in the

---

*Abshire also received substantial unpublicized support from NSC Director Henry Kissinger and his assistant, Alexander M. Haig. The NSC continued to work behind the scenes during the period of researching and drafting legislation and put the executive department solidly behind the effort.

†This was the same philosophy that had impelled George Kennan 22 years earlier to encourage the establishment of the Committee for a Free Europe as a private American corporation with covert CIA financing.

open, depending on congressional appropriations. Second, there was no specific provision linking the council to a government agency for policy guidance.

Assistant Secretary Martin Hillenbrand, director of the European bureau, was selected to testify on behalf of the council, but the plan was doomed from the start. The committee went through its motions, but defeat was obviously inevitable. The Senate simply was not going to permit open-ended authorization of funds and expenditures by a nongovernmental agency, particularly one with no clearly defined lines of responsibility to government. As Abshire put it: "Congress simply doesn't like to assign responsibility to boards or independent corporations. They become worried about their own oversight responsibilities. They can't see how they can get their hands on the determination of accountability and really knowing who was responsible."

The only alternative for the Radios' backers was to support S-18, which simply amended the Department of State's authorization to appropriate $30 million for one year for the Department "to provide grants, under such terms and conditions as the Secretary deems appropriate, to Radio Free Europe and Radio Liberty." Curiously, there was no provision in this abbreviated legislation for the exercise of governmental oversight of the Radios. It simply appropriated money to the secretary of state, who in turn would make that money available to the Radios. Significantly, there was no provision for funding for more than one year.

There was great urgency about getting some kind of bill passed, since the fiscal year ended on June 30 and it was now late May. The working group, consisting of representatives from the Department of State, the CIA, and the Radios, redoubled its efforts. Baker at State became the focal point. Evidence for use in hearings was developed by senior staff members at the Radios, by Meyer and his deputies in the International Organizations Division of the CIA, and by various concerned units at State. Abshire was given primary responsibility for soliciting support on Capitol Hill for any bill that would meet the approval of the leaderships of the Department of State and the White House. The presidents of the two Radio corporations were to stand by to testify before congressional committees as required.

Marcy's position was critically important since he was able to control the drafting of legislation and the scheduling of hearings and witnesses. The two most articulate supporters of the Radios in the Senate were Charles Percy of Illinois and Hubert Humphrey of Minnesota.

Opposition was concentrated largely in the Senate. In addition to the Fulbright–Case–Symington–Church group, the Senate Majority Leader Mike Mansfield had reservations but tried to play an even-handed game. If the Radios were to go down the drain, Mansfield would see to it that they went down fairly.

There was scattered opposition in the House, but the leadership there was generally supportive. This was particularly true of the House Foreign Affairs Committee, whose chairman, Thomas E. ("Doc") Morgan of Pennsylvania, vice-chairman, Clement Zablocki of Wisconsin, and influential committee member Dante Fascell of Florida, were counted among the loyal supporters. The Senate Committee met on May 24 and did nothing about the Radio problem. It considered both bills in Executive Session again on June 8. Fulbright, apparently still unwilling to vote support, asked at that meeting that no decision be taken until his committee was in receipt of more information regarding the Radios. He proposed asking the General Accounting Office (GAO) and the Congressional Research Service (CRS) of the Library of Congress to prepare thorough research reports, to be used in determining whether "it is in the public interest to support them with tax dollars." This would mean a delay of several months. Abshire describes the request for further information as "a tactical move, the kind of thing Carl Marcy would do," whose intention would be "to go out and get a hard-nosed report, a report that would tear a program apart on a managerial basis, and the program would die."

The end of the fiscal year came and went and still no action had been taken by either Senate or House. A continuing resolution made it possible to continue operation until congressional action could be taken, provided that the process was not too long delayed. The alternative, liquidating both corporations, would involve substantial severance payments and liquidation costs. Both Free Europe and the Radio Liberty Committee had to assign teams of accountants to determine what these costs might be. Nonfinancial personnel had to analyze potential social and political costs.

There were hopes that the Foreign Relations Committee would take action to alleviate the pressure when it met on July 20. Fulbright, however, told the committee that before any long-range bill could be passed, it was essential that the committee members have on hand the GAO and CRS reports. On July 21, the committee met again. It quickly, as expected, rejected S-1936, the bill that would have established a private council to operate the Radios, but it passed S-18, over Fulbright's opposition, authorizing $5 million more than the $30 million originally requested. The committee report, however, was something less than enthusiastic about long-term prospects for the Radios. The comments were brutal:

> The Committee deplores the fact that the financing . . . has been kept secret from the American people and their elected representatives. . . . [it] is regrettable that the executive branch of government under five separate administrations has deceived the taxpayers with respect to the expenditure of these public funds. . . . The connivance of both private and public officials to lead the American public to believe this fantasy is to be regretted. . . .

S-18 is intended to terminate this deception. It is intended to let the people know what they are paying for and how much.

Only nine days later, on July 30, the full Senate passed S-18, but this did not end the suspense: The House still had taken no action. The Radios, in the meantime, had existed for one month on a continuing resolution, on borrowed time.

The House Foreign Affairs Committee waited until September to hold hearings. On September 14 and again on September 21 it considered the ACPIC bill and rejected it. On September 30 it met again and proposed an amendment to S-18, providing for the creation of a study commission that would have until the late fall of 1972 to examine the Radios and make recommendations for their futures. The bill added that the chairman of the commission and public members appointed by the president of the United States would, as an interim step, receive appropriations and supervise grants to the Radios. This was radically different from the Senate bill, which would have turned the appropriation over to the secretary of state. The House passed the amended bill on November 19. More than four and a half months had now passed since the end of the 1971 fiscal year and the Radios were still running on the tenuous security of closed-ended continuing resolutions. Significant differences had yet to be ironed out.

The House and Senate met in conference committee on January 16, 1972, to try to reconcile these differences, but the exercise proved totally futile. The conferees failed to agree on a formula. Now the period of real crisis was quickly approaching. The latest continuing resolution was due to expire on February 22 and there could be no extension. If there were no appropriations by that date, liquidation seemed the only alternative. Sargeant and Durkee had to put their staffs under full draft to get liquidation plans ready for implementation if disaster actually struck. A conference committee representing the two houses met again on January 26 to make another attempt to reach agreement. The *Washington Post* news item reporting on the meeting describes the "icy opposition" to the House version demonstrated by Senator Fulbright. The session broke up without either side budging an inch. An even more serious potential obstacle was noted. An apparently irreconcilable grudge was developing between the two chairmen, Fulbright from the Senate and Morgan from the House, and no plans were announced for resuming the negotiations.

Only five days before the deadline, still with no action being taken to resume efforts to find a basis for compromise, a column by the reporting team of Rowland Evans and Robert Novak in the *Washington Post* irritated the senator from Arkansas even further. Evans and Novak charged that the studies Fulbright had requested from the CRS had in fact been completed and that they had been delivered to the senator's office in early January. No access to the reports, however, Evans and Novak charged, had been permitted to other committee members. They further charged that members of the senator's staff had returned the reports to the writers with the instruction that they be rewritten.

It was not hard to discover the reason for the senator's displeasure, once the reports were finally released. Their content was replete with high praise for the Radios and unreservedly recommended continuation of the service. Fulbright's reaction was not only bitterness toward Novak and Evans but also his most violent attack on the Radios. "Deceptions and falsehoods have been heaped on the American public," he charged on the Senate floor. "RFE and RL were surely a part of a pattern of falsehood and deception; a pattern of fraud and deceit; a pattern of conspiracy to mislead. The radios are an anachronism. . . . [We] ought to realize that they have outlived any usefulness they once may have had." At that point he pronounced what he may have considered the final rites: "Mr. President, I submit these radios should be given an opportunity to take their rightful place in the graveyard of war relics."

In the same tirade the senator introduced an element that had only been alluded to previously but had troubled many members of the Congress: the absence of financial support from allies in Western Europe, who had shared in any benefits derived from the service. "Why are not our NATO allies interested in putting up some of the money to support them? . . . If the need for these radio operations is as clear cut as some administration officials claim, why is there not some recognition on the part of our NATO allies who after all are much closer to the situation than we are?"

The introduction of this theme was almost instantly recognized by the management of the Radios as striking at a vulnerable point in their defenses. Their West European supporters also recognized the difficulty of building defenses against the charge. It was assumed—rightly, as it turned out—that much more would be heard of this complaint. Efforts were quickly undertaken, in anticipation of further development of this line of attack, to build a credible defense.

February 22 came and went with no further action. Fortunately for the Radios, enough money remained in operating accounts to run for a few more weeks. They had to keep going, even on credit, because they had no funds to pay the substantial liquidation costs that would have been mandated. The day after the appropriation officially ran out, the conference committee met again but once more broke up in total disarray. Antagonisms had if anything been aggravated. There was no agreement to meet again—not even any thought given to a subsequent meeting. Senator George Aiken of Vermont remarked, as he left the conference room, "The patient looks awful, awful sick."

Fulbright made it clear again that he would just as soon see the stations die. He urged that a start toward liquidation be undertaken immediately. Representative Peter Frelinghuysen of New Jersey took a different point of view: "I've heard of the arrogance of power. We saw it misused today." The only bright spot on the horizon for the Radios on February 23 was the submission of a resolution signed by 50 senators urging Fulbright to drop his opposition to the measure under consideration. The resolution had been initiated by the bipartisan team of Senators Humphrey and Percy.

Notwithstanding the preponderance of favorable support represented by the 50 signatories, there was genuine doubt about the Radios' future. Unless the representatives of the House and Senate committees could get together to hammer out a compromise that would be acceptable to both sides, the Radios were likely to die. The State Department–CIA–Radios group supporting continuation was fearful that the the impasse between the two Houses would be fatal, even though they were convinced that there was majority support in both Houses if a compromise bill could be brought to a vote.

The only remaining hope seemed to lie in somehow easing the tensions between the two committee chairmen, Morgan and Fulbright. It was Abshire's assignment, to try to resolve the dispute. In order to do so he had to find a means to bring the two chairmen together. The two had been dueling in conference committee and, according to Abshire, had got to the point where Morgan felt he had absorbed all of the insults he was going to take: "Doc got so mad that he told me, as I recall it was about the Thursday before the weekend that the money would run out, that he would simply not meet again." Fulbright's response was not very heartening either. He said that he would offer a bill that would pay up the salaries and severance and "close the thing out." Fulbright, Abshire learned, intended to take off for vacation in the Bahamas and would stay there until the money ran out.

Abshire decided that the best course of action would be for him to go to see the majority leader of the Senate, Mike Mansfield, who, although certainly not to be described as an enthusiastic Radios supporter, was at the same time unwilling to see the collapse of an institution because of a personality conflict. Mansfield suggested that Abshire talk to Carl Marcy. Marcy, according to Abshire, was embarrassed by what was about to happen to the Radios. Abshire was in a position to promise that the Department of State would accept the oversight responsibility, at least for the time being, to keep the Radios from dying. (Morgan, he knew, had previously made Department of State acceptance of this responsibility a precondition to House support.) Marcy was willing to have a try at convincing Fulbright to agree to these terms. The House would have to give on its proposal to establish a commission to study the Radios' future and turn over supervision of the Radios to this commission until a final decision was taken. The Senate would have to agree that State Department oversight be written into the bill and that consideration be given to funding for fiscal year 1972. Abshire called Morgan to tell him he thought a way could be found out of the impasse.

Marcy, in the meantime, went to see Fulbright who was packed up and ready to leave for the holiday. After some conversation, Fulbright finally agreed to go along with the compromise. Morgan likewise agreed. The crisis was as good as over.

The Senate bill was rewritten to give the secretary of state responsibility for maintaining oversight of the Radios for the duration of the period during which funding would be furnished through the department. With both chairmen in accord, the House conferees agreed to support S-18. They requested only one condition, that consideration be given to a separate bill for fiscal year 1973, which would begin on July 1, 1972, now less that four months away. Money was found to keep both Radios operating beyond the February 22 deadline. By March 22, the full House approved the conference report on S-18, which authorized $36 million for fiscal year 1972, with the "clear understanding that further legislation will be considered before the end of this fiscal year." The Senate approved the compromise, and on March 30 the president signed the bill.

The short-term crisis had ended. The long-term shape of the Radios, however, was still to be debated. Methods for assuring sound management, responsible oversight, full accountability, and levels of funding would still be thorny issues, and the question of West European financing would continue to haunt the Radios, but the future no longer seemed in real doubt.

President Nixon took the next step on May 10, when, picking up on a hint from the House version of S-18 as passed the previous autumn, he announced his intention to appoint a study commission to go to work immediately after its selection and to submit recommendations by February 28, 1973. At the same time, the president asked for prompt passage of a bill that would guarantee continued support for the Radios for fiscal year 1973.

15
I Shall Raise
My Voice a Little

PRESIDENT NIXON'S APPROVAL of a one-year funding bill, which he signed on March 30, 1972, gave the Radios a brief respite from the life-or-death crisis that had prevailed since Senator Case's speech a little more than 14 months earlier. It was possible to breathe a little more easily—but only temporarily. Only three months remained of the fiscal year for which the appropriation had just been passed, and no provision had been made for the 1973 fiscal year or for any subsequent years. The legislation signed by the president mandated that immediate consideration be given to writing legislation authorizing an appropriation for fiscal year 1973, but there were no enforcement teeth in the mandate. Congress traditionally has proceeded at its own pace, unhindered by written commitments.

Senator Fulbright, in the meantime, was no more enamored of the Radios than he had been during the battle over the bill the president had just signed. He had been defeated in his campaign to obliterate the "outworn relics of the cold war" when he agreed to the compromise authorization bill for Free Europe and the Radio Liberty Committee funding for fiscal year 1972. He did not make the concession, however, out of sheer good will and appreciation. His animosity had not been softened by the disposition of the 1972 bill. As a matter of fact, in his angry response to the Evans and Novak column of February 17, he had discovered a new issue that might command more support than charges of fraud and deceit: The absence of West European support. His question raised on February 22 as to why our NATO allies were not "putting up some of the money to support them" was a line of attack calculated to elicit a sympathetic response from many colleagues in both Houses. It would permit members concerned about the future of the Radios to shift the blame for inadequate funding to the Europeans. And it would be a popular program with U.S. taxpayers, who were complaining vigorously about mounting national deficits and high taxes.

RL was in a more or less defenseless position, but it was at best a secondary target. Its low-key approach had kept it in the background and only a small number of Americans even recognized its existence. Free Europe, however, was a different matter. Its super-hyped crusade campaigns had catapulted it into public attention. The pugnacious speeches made by its early leaders, boasting of "confounding the enemy," had left an imprint on the public consciousness. Complaints about the behavior of the Hungarian Service in 1956 remained stored in memories.

Free Europe had taken measures shortly after the Hungarian episode to shore up its position in Europe, and these measures served, too, to defuse some of the complaints about the lack of European financial support. As early as 1959, Free Europe executives had instigated the formation of the West European Advisory Committee (WEAC), made up of political and diplomatic leaders from most of the West European countries. WEAC usually met twice a year—at Free Europe's expense—in various European capitals or conference centers. The sessions furnished opportunities for Free Europe directors and executives to discuss mutual problems with influential Europeans, eliciting their support while at the same time sounding out European opinion at both governmental and public levels. The members of WEAC were influential members of their parliaments, leaders in their countries' diplomatic corps, or editors or writers of high standing. Many of them also held high positions in international bodies including the Council of Europe, the North Atlantic Assembly, and the Atlantic Treaty Association. They were well placed to reflect attitudes of European governments and even to influence them.

The breaking of the *Ramparts* story and its aftermath jolted some WEAC members. The participation and funding of the CIA meant nothing to them. They regarded the U.S. public as naive regarding intelligence activities and they considered the CIA a logical source of funding, since it could offer some freedom from government control, which they considered essential to achieving objectives. But they were worried that the episode might cause serious damage to the Radios. Consequently, they watched with fascination and concern as the story unfolded. Fulbright's February 17, 1972, speech served as the spark to stimulate WEAC to action. It was evident to some of the members that European participation and funding would become a critically important issue.

When it became clear that the Senate Foreign Relations Committee would probably hold hearings in late May or early June, Free Europe President Durkee dispatched Vice President J. Allen Hovey, Jr., to Europe to confer with WEAC leaders about specific methods by which they could support the

Free Europe cause. Free Europe's strategic plan included inviting a delegation of the more prominent WEAC members to pay a visit to the United States prior to the Foreign Relations Committee hearings, at which there might be an opportunity to discuss informally their support for Free Europe with influential members of both Senate and House committees.

The delegation was selected with some care so that it could supply the most leverage in supporting the Free Europe cause. Two Germans were available to make the trip: a prominent member of the Christian Democratic Party, Max Schulze-Vorborg, and an equally prominent member of the Social Democratic Party, Kurt Mattick. Since Germany was the host country for so much of the RFE and RL activity, it was considered important that there be representation from both the major German political parties to indicate uniformity of support from that country. The third member of the delegation was a former member of the Danish cabinet and of that country's parliament, Per Federspiel. He had also been active in the North Atlantic Parliament and the Atlantic Treaty Association and in NATO's affairs. The fourth member, the WEAC chairman, also designated as the delegation chairman, was Dirk Stikker, who had served a four-year term as the secretary general of NATO and was a former foreign minister of the Netherlands.

The four, who would ostensibly be in New York for conferences with Free Europe directors and executives, were to go to Washington to meet with the chairmen of the two committees involved in considering the authorization bills for fiscal year 1973 and with a number of key members of those committees. The Free Europe chairman, General Clay, wrote to Fulbright explaining that the foreigners "would appreciate an opportunity to meet with you and other interested members." What was intended obviously was a series of informal meetings with the key members in which opportunities would be afforded to explain the European point of view and to demonstrate support for the Radios. Fulbright, however, looked at the matter a little differently. He responded with an invitation to Stikker to testify in an open hearing, although, as he explained, "normally the committee does not invite foreigners to testify on an impending bill." This was not what either the WEAC delegation or Free Europe had in mind. Testifying openly in formal committee session, Stikker might be subjected to brutal cross-examination by the senator, but once the approach had been made there was no alternative to accepting the invitation.

On June 6 Stikker appeared at Room 4221, New Senate Office Building, for his session with the committee. Fulbright set the tone in his opening remarks: "Very serious consideration must be given to the apparent lack of interest on the part of our European allies to help shoulder the financial burden imposed by these radio operations. . . . [It] is difficult for me and some of the others on this committee to understand why we should continue to go it alone in support of Radio Free Europe and Radio Liberty." The chairman's dyspeptic mood may have been occasioned in part by his frustration over the CRS and GAO reports, which by now had been released publicly. If Abshire was correct in believing that Fulbright's primary objective in requesting the reports was to "get a hard-nosed report . . . that would tear a program apart on a managerial basis," then the cause of his frustration was obvious. The reports, particularly the one from the CRS, were laudatory; GAO had recommended some major adjustments, but nothing in the document could have been interpreted to suggest terminating the services.

Stikker had barely finished his opening statement when the chairman began to question him on the subject of finances. He opened the topic by asking who had financed the trip of the WEAC delegation. Stikker was forced to respond that the expenses were being paid by the Free Europe Committee. The chairman then wanted to know who had financed WEAC activities since the founding of the committee. Again, Stikker was forced to respond that the bills had been paid by Free Europe.

The question of European financing, however, was by no means the only matter that came up. Stikker was badgered about the presence of any CIA members on the RFE staff, how policy controls insuring compliance with U.S. foreign policy objectives were imposed, and how soon would Europeans start contributing toward general operating expenses. The senator was so persistent on the issue of CIA participation that at one time, in the middle of a particularly annoying query, Stikker obviously became angry: "I shall raise my voice a little," he said, "because . . . you make me excited; you make me angry. . . ." Some Free Europe staff members in the audience were fearful that he might suffer a heart attack. State Department personnel were clearly embarrassed by the way the committee handled the former Netherlands foreign minister. John Baker, who was serving as the Department of State's officer assigned to RFE and RL oversight, says "they were pained by the experience."

Throughout the hearings Fulbright did not conceal his distaste for the Radios and their intelligence agency sponsor. He continually put off requests for recognition from Senator Percy, whom he knew to be a strong supporter of the Radios. At one point, after brusquely rejecting Percy's request a number of times, he finally had to yield to the senator from Illinois. Percy asked to insert into the record a summary he had made of the CRS analysis of the Radios, including strongly supportive quotations from the project's director, James Price, who had concluded that the Radios were guided by a policy of liberalization, not liberation, and were not in any way encouraging the overthrow of any government. Fulbright, apparently recognizing that the statement would aid the cause of the Radios, announced that he wanted inserted into the record a biographical sketch of the author of the report. His reason was apparent to committee members and staff: Price had been employed in the past by the CIA. The chairman could not resist the opportunity to get in his dig. The colloquy revealed deep-seated antagonisms toward anything or anybody with a CIA connection.

The amount of useful information elicited by the inquiry was negligible, but one clear conclusion could be drawn: the issue of European participation in the funding effort would not quietly fade into oblivion. Even Percy, who had consistently been a strong Radio supporter, made his plea for Europeans to share the burden.

The issue of financing could no longer affect the outcome of the legislation for fiscal year 1973; even Fulbright conceded that the authorization bill would pass without significant opposition. The committee sent the bill to the floor with only three dissenting votes. The full Senate approved it on June 16 by a vote of 58 to 2. On August 7 the House voted at 375 to 7 in favor of the bill. On August 10 President Nixon announced the names of the members of the commission he had appointed to examine the long-range future of the Radios. The chairman of the commission was to be Milton S. Eisenhower, brother of the former U.S. president and a president emeritus of Johns Hopkins University. Other members of the commission were to be John P. Roche, professor of politics at Brandeis University; Edmund A. Gullion, dean of the Fletcher School of Law and Diplomacy at Tufts University; Edward W. Barrett, former assistant secretary of state for public affairs, dean of the Graduate School of Journalism at Columbia University, and director of the Communications Institute of the Academy for Educational Development in New York; and John A. Gronouski, former postmaster general, former ambassador to Poland, and dean of the Lyndon B. Johnson School of Public Affairs at the University of Texas. The commission was charged to deliver its report by February 28, 1973. The bill appropriating funds to support the previously approved authorizations had cleared both Houses by late October 1972. The issue, thus, was settled for another fiscal year. Not much could be done now toward the reorganization of the Radios or the submission of new legislation until the commission's report was in the president's hands. This was not likely to occur until at least six months had passed.

The hiatus in Washington and New York, however, did not throttle demands for European participation and funding. Free Europe and the WEAC had pledged to launch a campaign, and some WEAC members, including Stikker, had expressed optimism that support could be obtained. The sampling of congressional attitudes demonstrated by the hearing clearly indicated that some affirmative action would be required, no matter what recommendations might later be made by the Eisenhower commission. Fulbright at one time had suggested that he would be willing to support RFE and RL if Europeans contributed 50 percent or more of the total funding required to maintain the operations. This was taken by Free Europe executives and WEAC personnel alike as a ploy to kill both Radios, since funding at that level was as likely as obtaining a grant from the Kremlin.

However, Stikker's commitment to raise funds was firm and unequivocal and even mildly optimistic. In answer to a question from Chairman Fulbright, he had replied, "I am willing to make an effort [to raise funds in Europe], but we cannot start working on this effort unless you have made up your minds . . . definitely there is going to be a continuation. The date that decision is taken, I can assure you that we will start an organization to try to raise money in Europe."*

There was not much doubt that prompt action on the European funding question was required, regardless of action the Congress might take. While Stikker was testifying before the Senate Foreign Relations Committee, the other members of the WEAC delegation had been busy sounding out other congressional leaders, including the chairman of the House International Relations Committee, "Doc" Morgan. The message conveyed to them was essentially the same as the one that Stikker heard in the Fulbright committee. Support for the Radios was strong and funding would be continued, but some European participation in funding of the Radios would be critically important in efforts to obtain long-term financial support from congressional appropriations.

The full membership of WEAC met in September to consider courses of action. They concluded there were four possible sources of financial support: direct contributions by government, subventions from international organizations representing West European countries and the Atlantic Alliance, foundations, and corporate and private donations.

One stumbling block was apparent from the beginning: WEAC was a creation of the Free Europe Committee and had no relations with the Radio Liberty Committee. Many of its members were suspicious of RL and had no enthusiasm for irritating the Soviet Union. European businesses at this time were aggressively trying to exploit Soviet markets. West Germany was engaged in its *Ost Politik* move, and there was hesitation about allowing annoying broadcasts from West German soil to thwart the plan. From a philosophical point of view, there was recognition that East European countries were fair game for broadcasts because they had been forcibly brought into the orbit of the USSR and their governments superimposed on the people, but the government of the USSR, on the other hand, was indigenous, even if not democratically selected. It was considered one thing to upset a government illegally imposed by force in a country that had no choice and quite another to provoke a leadership that ruled, however arrogantly, through its own power and not as the result of pressures exerted from abroad.

---

*Earlier, Stikker had responded to a question from Fulbright as to whether anyone in Europe had made a commitment to support the Radios. Stikker had replied, "I know about several people who are willing to contribute . . . but they have to wait until finally a decision has been taken also by your committee."

Not all members were so strongly against RL, but there was never any great enthusiasm expressed for including it in any money-raising efforts that might be successful.

Per Federspiel was pessimistic about the whole venture. He completely ruled out grants from European governments on the grounds that any government making a contribution would demand a share in policy making, if not in management. Governments in Europe, he pointed out, are subject to no end of audits, committee inquiries, and the like: "You would get endless questions that would jeopardize independence." At a later time, Federspiel reemphasized the point: "For heaven's sake don't get too many elements involved or invariably you will get political interference." His concern was that any substantial funding from Europe would invariably lead to a demand for more political control, "and that I believe would be fatal for the Radios." From the beginning Federspiel had taken the position that obtaining any substantial funds from Europe was a hopeless cause.

An approach was made to the Atlantic Treaty Association, which expressed sympathy and moral support but deemed the idea of general funding totally impractical. The Council of Europe showed a slight spark of interest, but that spark was quickly extinguished. The chairman of its Political Action Committee, Erik Blumenfeld, a member of the German Bundestag, had introduced a recommendation to the council's member governments that they give financial support to the two Radios. The resolution was brought to the floor for a full debate but was amended there to specify that the recommendation should include broadcasting to Spain, Portugal, and Greece. With that, the measure was sent back to the Political Action Committee for further consideration. The question of any broadcasting to those three countries was finessed in the resolution finally brought to the floor, which vaguely suggested that the council "consider ways and means of insuring, either by increased Western European participation in, and responsibility for, the two existing radio stations or by setting up new organizations, that the voice of democratic Europe be heard in other European countries." This was not a very attractive proposition from the Free Europe point of view and surely would not have satisfied congressional critics. Free Europe, however, was spared the necessity of rejecting it. The council voted 33 to 28 to return the resolution to the Political Action Committee for "further study." With that, it quietly disappeared and was never heard from again.

Attempts to interest the North Atlantic Parliament yielded even fewer positive results. Senator John Tunney of California proposed a resolution in the Information and Cultural Affairs Committee calling for NATO governments to give financial support to the two Radios. It was defeated 12 to 4. Blumenfeld, who was also chairman of the Political Committee of the North Atlantic Assembly, introduced the same resolution that had been defeated in the Council of Europe. By a tie vote, members of this committee indicated they did not even want to vote on the resolution, so it was buried deep in the committee's records.

Herman Van Roijen, like Dirk Stikker a former Dutch senior diplomat and a businessman, succeeded Stikker as chairman of WEAC in the autumn of 1972. Shortly after assuming his new position, he informed the Free Europe board that both its fund-raising and advisory functions would be strictly limited to RFE and would exclude any relationship with Radio Liberty Committee. Van Roijen's decision, which was not contested by the committee, effectively removed RL from participation in any European fund-raising efforts.

The new WEAC chairman made a significant move, however, toward establishing a mechanism that would be in a position to accept grants and pass them through to the Free Europe board. He commissioned a prominent Dutch international lawyer, Pieter J. W. DeBrauw, to draw up articles of incorporation for a nonprofit Dutch corporation that could accept tax-free grants. The corporation was given the ostentatious name of The Foundation for the Promotion of the Free Flow of Information. Members of WEAC would also become directors of the foundation. The creation of the foundation, however, turned out to be less than a magic key unlocking the door to European riches.

Governments were not likely to participate, even if they were asked, because they felt that in supporting their own shortwave broadcasting functions, they already assumed as great a burden as their limited resources would allow. Any hopes that international organizations would come to the rescue were dashed by the actions taken by the North Atlantic Parliament, the Council of Europe, and the Atlantic Treaty Association. That left only foundations, corporations, and individuals as potential sources. A contract was signed with a fund-raising firm to survey possibilities of uncovering lucrative sources. The principal finding was that the cost of money raising was so high that the percentage of receipts that went to meeting costs would constitute an unacceptably large share of the total intake; it was hardly worthwhile to proceed along this line. The Free Europe directors had had enough experience with the Crusade for Freedom and its successor, The Free Europe Fund, to understand the wisdom of that conclusion. Nearly 30 percent of all the Crusade's income had gone to administration and miscellaneous costs—and this at a time when the "Red scare" prompted major corporate contributions and the momentum for supporting RFE as a private venture was running at flood tide.

Free Europe's aspirations were also hampered by the fact that there was no tradition in Europe, as there has been in the United States, for either corporate or private giving, and tax structures had not been modified to furnish tax relief for donors. Foundations were few and far between and heavily committed. WEAC members made a half-hearted attempt to survey grant possibilities, but they achieved no tangible results.

Van Roijen may have had an additional motive in mind, however, in creating The Foundation for the Promotion of the Free Flow of Information. His instructions to DeBrauw to draw up the articles of incorporation were given at approximately the same time that the Council of Europe was considering Blumenfeld's proposal that it take a 50-percent ownership position in the Free Europe Committee. De Brauw insists that he was instructed by Van Roijen to write the foundation's articles of incorporation in such a way that the foundation could assume ownership of RFE in the event that congressional backing were denied and if European financial support were obtained. (However, there was never a chance to test the foundation's capability for performing this role.)

There was one other channel through which funds might be obtained: members of Congress and a number of WEAC representatives had wondered out loud whether the output of the research departments of the two Radios might not be distributed at a profit to governments, interested public citizens, and educational institutions. During the June 1972 hearings, Senators Fulbright and Percy had both pointed to the research output as a potentially profitable item if properly distributed. No action was ever taken, however, for two principal reasons. In the first place, creating a marketable product that would have returned enough revenue to make a substantial contribution to operating costs would have demanded substantial expenditure of funds. There was little chance for the success of such a program without employing specialists for packaging, marketing, and distribution of the product in a commercial manner, and the resources for such an effort were never available. Trying to produce an attractive product within the existing personnel structure would have detracted so much from the broadcast output, the principal reason for the Radios' existence, that it was only given perfunctory consideration.

Thus, as 1972 came to a close WEAC and the Foundation for the Promotion of the Free Flow of Information were looking for grants that would never materialize. The State Department was looking forward to the day when responsibility for maintaining the oversight function would be removed. The Eisenhower Commission was busily engaged in preparing recommendations for the Radios' long-range future. The Radios management and employees alike were anxiously awaiting the report that the commission was obligated to deliver by February 28, 1973. There was little doubt that the commission would recommend some form of continuation of the service being performed by the two Radios, but what kind of structure it would recommend was a mystery.

16

Not Inconsistent
with Broad U.S.
Foreign Policy

THERE WAS LITTLE DOUBT after the appropriations bills for fiscal year 1973 had been passed and the Eisenhower Commission members appointed that RFE and RL would continue to function in some form or other. The overwhelming support for the Radios as reflected in House and Senate votes and in White House statements were clear indicators that the threat of extinction had passed. That was hardly enough, however, to ease the pressures and reduce the level of apprehension that gripped staff members, particularly those who were exiles from the target countries. They had been living in an atmosphere of crisis since the *Ramparts* revelations nearly six years earlier. For nearly two years, since the Case speech of January 25, 1971, there was hardly a moment of respite from the fear that the whole Radio structure would be demolished and the exile employees cast out to fend for themselves in a society to which many of them had never become fully acclimated.

Some of the exiles had acquired U.S. citizenship, but many remained stateless. They possessed skills that were finely honed for the tasks they were performing, but there was little call in Germany or the United States for specialists in writing, editing, or producing programs for Czechoslovakia, Poland, Hungary, or the Soviet Union. Only the other Western international broadcasters, including the BBC, the VOA, and Deutsch Welle, would be likely to be able to find immediate use for their talents, and they were well stocked with personnel.

The sense of foreboding was intensified by actions taken by Radio management to keep budgets within reasonable limits in an era of constant inflationary pressures. In the five fiscal years since 1968, 438 employees had been terminated out of a total staff of approximately 2800, nearly 16 percent of the total work force. All indications were that further sharp cuts were inevitable. Wage scales were lagging behind inflation, maintenance was being reduced to a level barely able to keep the organization in operation, and contributions to pension fund insurers were being skipped.

The first union to organize at RFE, the German Union of Employees (DAG), was recognized in 1957 in the wake of the Hungarian crisis. In 1959 the New York local of the American Newspaper Guild (ANG) had established a chapter in Munich and recruited workers from the news and program staffs. A third union, the Bavarian Journalists Association (BJV), came in the early 1960s. The euphoric period of the early and middle 1950s was plainly past history. Pay scales, working conditions, employee benefits, and pension programs had become major issues as living comfortably in a new environment replaced the elusive goal of returning home to a restored democracy. Dollar-paid employees suffered another sharp blow when the U.S. dollar started to plummet against the German Deutsche Mark, reducing the purchasing power of their paychecks.

Both Radios suffered from another phenomenon that inevitably follows staff reduction. The aging staffs, which had been recruited in the early 1950s, were beginning to lose some of the enthusiasm of the earlier period and also losing touch with the rapid changes occurring in their former homelands. The broadcast services during the 1950s had been kept alert, vigorous, and innovative by constantly adding newer, younger, more enthusiastic, more idealistic newcomers with an intimate knowledge of changing social conditions and recent modifications to the written and spoken languages. When terminations became mandatory, managements were forced to apply the "last in–first out" policy, thus losing the new blood that was designed to keep the services at a high level of enthusiasm, relevance, and creativity.

This was the somber climate that prevailed in January 1973 as the Eisenhower Commission pushed ahead to meet its deadline. The squeeze was on again as it had been in the two previous years. Congress had four months from the February 28 delivery of the Eisenhower report until the fiscal year ran out in which to analyze the commission's recommendations and write new legislation, supported by appropriations, for continuing the Radios. Members of the commission went to work almost immediately after its appointment on August 9, 1972.*

---

*Only one of the five commissioners had had direct experience with international political communications: Barrett had been director of overseas operations for the Office of War Information during World War II and had served as assistant secretary of state for public affairs from 1950 to 1952. One of his responsibilities in that post had been the direction of the VOA. In addition, he had been elected a member of the Free Europe Corporation in late 1949. Upon accepting the appointment as assistant secretary of state, he resigned as a member of the corporation in early 1950. The other members were no less impressive, however. Gullion had been a career foreign service

They quickly identified the major issues with which they would have to contend. The first related to détente: did the Radios encourage or deter it? Second, how could a procedure or mechanism be established to ensure that the Radios operated "in a manner not inconsistent with broad United States foreign policy?"* Third, what federal agency should be designated to receive appropriations from the Congress and pass them through to the Radio management? Finally, how much financing could and should be obtained from European sources to supplement appropriations from the Congress?

Except for Senator Fulbright's complaints that the Radios were "a useless deterrent to East/West relations" and that they were "meddling in the internal affairs of other countries," there was relatively little controversy over the first question. The commission concluded that "the broadcasts of Radio Free Europe and Radio Liberty had not deterred but rather contributed to the search for long-term détente."[1]

The commission's reasoning was based on the assumption that "peace is more secure in well informed societies than in those that may be more easily manipulated," and that the Radios "by providing a free flow of information have enabled peoples to whom they broadcast to remain informed and to judge for themselves which policies may contribute to social change and genuine improvement of peaceful relations."[2] East European party leaders, the commission members concluded, had been obliged increasingly in recent years, since the establishment of the two Radios, to take popular pressures into consideration in policy making.

No such clear-cut response was possible to the fourth issue. The commission came down firmly against seeking governmental support from European governments. It foresaw that if such contributions were accepted, the Radios would be faced with accompanying demands for participation in management, thus jeopardizing the professional independence of the stations by making them responsible to a number of governments not necessarily committed to the same principles. They were also fearful that decision making

---

officer before accepting appointment as dean of the Fletcher School at Tufts University. Gronouski had served as ambassador to Poland before moving to the Lyndon B. Johnson School at the University of Texas. Roche had been a special consultant to President Johnson and wrote a widely circulated syndicated newspaper column in addition to serving as a professor of politics at Brandeis University. Eisenhower, because of the prestige he had acquired as a public servant and educator, seemed an ideal choice for the chairmanship.

*Eisenhower is credited with having formulated the statement embracing the double negative. It was so phrased to give the Radios considerable latitude in establishing their policies, not to be constrained by the statement to follow minute changes in U.S. foreign policy, but rather mandated to avoid deviations from "broad" national foreign policy.

under a multinationally supported program would inevitably reflect the lowest common denominator among the participating nations.

During a visit to Munich in November 1972, the commission had met with Van Roijen, chairman of WEAC and the Foundation for the Promotion of the Free Flow of Information. He was not optimistic about the possibility of soliciting substantial contributions from European sources, but he felt that some private contributions and "possibly some public funds" might be available if they were aggressively sought.[3] The commission concluded that WEAC should be encouraged to seek funding actively from private sources, even though it was admittedly less optimistic about realizing any meaningful sums. Marketing the product of the Radios research departments, however, could be a potentially lucrative endeavor, the commission felt. It recommended that the Radios create a Soviet and East European research organization to "receive monies for the purpose."[4]

The commission overlooked, however, the magnitude of the effort required to create and distribute the product in such a way that it would yield a measurable return. No recommendations were made for any appropriations that would be required to establish the recommended profit-oriented research organization. Enthusiasts for marketing research also took a simplistic view of the objectives of the existing research departments. Research seemed to be regarded by commisssion members as a valuable commodity only remotely related to the broadcast effort, rather than as an integral element in keeping staffs informed regarding developments in countries they were forbidden to visit and where sources of news and information were limited at best. No critic apparently realized that diverting manpower from its support function would inevitably weaken the broadcast effort. Only by superimposing a separate unit on the research department, one that would assume the responsibility of converting the research byproduct to a salable commodity, could research become an attractive product in the marketplace. Trying to accomplish this purpose with only the existing personnel would inevitably damage the Radios in the performance of their primary tasks.

The greatest conundrum the commission had to wrestle with involved determining how a procedural mechanism could be devised to operate the Radios "in a manner not inconsistent with broad U.S. foreign policy" and, in so doing, determining what federal agency could be designated or created to accept funds from Congress and pass them on to the Radios. The commission members were aware of the ill-fated proposal of the Department of State in 1971 for the creation of the American Council for Public International Communications that went down to quick defeat, apparently because it proposed making appropriations directly to a council that would function independently of government. They also might very well have been governed by the feeling that Abshire described when he said that "Congress simply doesn't like to assign responsibility to boards or independent corporations. They become worried about their own oversight responsibilities."

The commission's letter of submission to President Nixon stated the problem succinctly: "The critical problem is how can Federal financial support be granted to private corporations in such a way as not to impair their professional independence, credibility, and effectiveness while retaining assurance that the broadcast will not jeopardize the objectives of the United States foreign policy."[5] There were five possible alternatives for establishing a future slot for the Radios by which they could continue to operate with federal financing. They could continue to operate under the general supervision of the secretary of state, merge with the VOA under the United States Information Agency, operate in parallel with the VOA under USIA supervision, become a new federal entity, or, finally, function under a new, independent government agency established to serve as a nexus between the public, the Congress, the Executive Branch, and the stations. The commission opted for the last. A new oversight agency, it felt, could best meet the criteria the commission had laid down. Only this course would preserve professional independence and integrity and permit continued operations free of direct government supervision and control. (The commission considered this freedom an essential element of continued successful operation.)

During its approximately six months of existence, the commission interviewed some 50 experts in formal sessions, talked more informally to scores in one-on-one situations, went to Munich to observe how the Radios worked, and talked to management and programmers, sat in lengthy sessions to share ideas and arrive at a consensus, and framed answers to the questions they had posed to themselves. Since some of the members questioned the strength of the commission's staff, they wrote much of the material for the report themselves and edited their draft efforts as a group.

By mid-January, they were ready to draft the final report. The report went to the White House 23 days ahead of the president's deadline, on February 5. The commission proposed an entirely new structure in government. It borrowed some elements from the State Department's ACPIC plan, preserving the essential independence of the Radios as private American corporations, and recommended leaving their boards of directors intact. To meet congressional demands for assured accountability the plan provided for the creation of a Board for International Broadcasting (BIB) that would serve as a nexus between the government and the private corporations. The board would receive appropriations from Congress, pass them on to Radio managements, and oversee them to the extent that the money was well spent, the broadcast corporations operated efficiently, and the program output was "not inconsistent with broad U.S. foreign policy."

Had the goal been to create an organizational chart that was clear, precise, and easily understandable, the plan would probably receive an "F" from a professor in a graduate school of business. The suggested structure appeared awkward and cumbersome and could give rise to an unending series of quarrels and misunderstandings that could conceivably threaten to tear down the whole edifice. It clearly could not function smoothly unless both the BIB staff and the Radios' managements entered into the relationship with a desire to cooperate and a willingness to yield some prerogatives they might have regarded as their own. There is no precedent for the arrangement in textbooks; it was easy to marshal up convincing arguments that it would not work. But commission members believed that it would preserve the unique character of the Radios and enable them to carry out most efficiently their role as the champions of free information: "We realize that able men of good will can make about any organizational arrangement work; and, conversely, that even the finest organizational arrangements do not guarantee efficient and effective operations."[6]

The report was generally favorably received by the Radios' worried and frustrated employees. The recommended continuation of the service into the indeterminate future allayed their fears of an abrupt termination. Some specific suggestions for structural changes, however, rekindled old fears. For example, borrowing from the GAO report of 1972, the commission urged managements to examine carefully the possibility of consolidation of both headquarters' space and functions in areas where both had personnel and facilities. The commission had considered recommending outright merger of the two corporations but rejected the idea on the basis that savings under merger would be relatively small and damage to morale and operating procedures extensive. The two corporations had grown up independently of each other; what limited contact there was had been established largely in the top echelons, and even at that level it was limited. The mere thought of combining the organizations in one set of physical facilities set off concern for protecting one's own turf. The commission believed, however, that a consolidation must be accepted.

A second recommendation urged the proposed BIB to "work closely with the stations in exploring new possibilities for economy and efficiency." The words "economy and efficiency" sent waves of apprehension coursing through the organization. Rocked by the nearly 16-percent reduction in workforce over the previous four years, employees tended to fear the worst. The prospect for long-term survival was now favorable, but that did not allay fears that a period of turbulence lay ahead and that the Radios that emerged might be almost unrecognizable to the observer who had become accustomed to the old order. A period of painful fat reduction—even some blood-letting—was clearly ahead; obviously, many staff members were going to be badly hurt.

The new BIB could come into being only as the result of congressional action. The time was also getting short for passing legislation required to appropriate monies for fiscal year 1974. A bill to accomplish both purposes was introduced into the Senate by Senators Humphrey and Percy. It authorized the establishment of the board recommended by the Eisenhower Commission and authorized the appropriation of a little more than $50 million for fiscal year 1974, almost a one-third increase over that for the previous fiscal year. Senate hearings were held on June 12 and 23. There never was any real doubt about the committee's final decision, but Senator Fulbright kept up his sharp and frequently acidulous attack. His principal complaint continued to be the lack of financial support from West European nations. His staff, in addition, in probing for vulnerable points in the Radios' defense, had discovered an apparent indiscretion made by a high-ranking RFE employee, and the Senator apparently decided to exploit it to the hilt.

The first person to testify on behalf of the BIB was Deputy Secretary of State Kenneth Rush, appearing before the committee as acting secretary. As Rush was concluding his testimony, he quoted a *Washington Post* editorial strongly supporting the Radios. Fulbright thanked the secretary and complimented him for his thorough and extensive statement. Then he noted that there had been a lot of editorials in support of the Radios. Rush affirmed that this was so, and the senator asked whether the secretary knew "Mr. Jan A. Nowak." When Rush acknowledged that he knew of Nowak by name, Fulbright sprang a well-prepared trap: "Some letters have come to my attention which might bear upon the extensive nature of these editorials, inspired, I think, by Mr. Nowak." He quoted from a number of letters written on RFE's letterhead, datelined Munich, and signed "Jan Nowak." One letter accused Fulbright of having "quieted down briefly after the 1972 hearing only to bring the matter up again and seek revenge on Radio Free Europe for his shameful defeat." In the next paragraph there was a reference to Fulbright's "procommunist sympathies." The letter charged that "he made his first foreign trip after completion of his education to no other place than Moscow."[7] The senator's irritation was plainly stimulated by his assumption that Nowak, an employee of an organization supported entirely by congressionally appropriated funds, was using his position, even the RFE letterhead, to attack a member of the U.S. Senate, an action almost all members of Congress would deplore.

The introduction of this abrasive element apparently had no decisive impact on the ultimately favorable outcome of the hearings, but it caused RFE's executive staff to scurry around for further analysis of the incident, and it left a residue of suspicion concerning Nowak's performance of his job that persisted long after the hearings were completed, the legislation passed, and the BIB created. The incident also gave some members of the committee who were not enthusiastically supportive of the Radios an opportunity to vent some of their misgivings without ultimately affecting the outcome.

President William P. Durkee of Free Europe, Inc., testified that the letter had originally been printed in Poland as part of the campaign to discredit RFE and turn the U.S. electorate against it. Even though the letters were presumably addressed to the editor of a Polish-language publication in the United States, they were never printed in this country. Durkee described one letter as an outright forgery, and evidence was presented to the committee to support this contention.

The case of the purloined letters resulted in a brisk reprimand to Nowak and some shocked responses from committee members, but it proved to be only a momentary diversion in the hearings. Public Law 93-129, the Board for International Broadcasting Act, was enacted into law on October 19, 1973.

It was now up to President Nixon to select the five people, no more than three of them from one political party, who would serve as voting members of the BIB. The chief executive officers of Free Europe and the Radio Liberty Committee, Durkee and Sargeant, would round out the roster of seven as *ex officio*, nonvoting members.

There was no doubt that a major consolidation effort would be required. Expenses, including payroll, facilities, electric power charges, and maintenance would have to be squeezed further. The precise direction the consolidation would take would await the organization of the BIB. Whether "men of good will" could make the awkward relationship work was another problem to be decided by experience.

NOTES

1. Presidential Study Commission on International Broadcasting, *The Right to Know: Report* (Washington, D.C.: Government Printing Office, 1973), p. 27.

2. Ibid., p. 28.

3. Ibid., p. 50.

4. Ibid., p. 51.

5. Ibid., p. iv.

6. Ibid., p. 43.

7. The text of the testimony concerning this incident can be found in U.S. Congress, Senate, Foreign Relations Committee, *Hearings* on S-1914 "to provide for the establishment of the Board for International Broadcasting. . . ," 93rd Cong., First sess., 12 and 23 June 1973, pp. 15, 19. There is further reference to the controversy in *ibid.*, pp. 59, 62.

17

What We Need Most Is a Period of Tranquility

I T TOOK MORE than six months from the enactment of Public Law 93-129 for the creation of the BIB. By the end of April 1974, however, all five voting members had been nominated by President Nixon and approved by the Senate. The chairman was to be David Abshire; he had resigned as assistant secretary of state in 1973 to return to Georgetown University's Center for Strategic and International Studies as executive director, in which post he was eligible for—and enthusiastic about—accepting appointment to the BIB. A second appointee, Foy Kohler, was an expert on Soviet affairs and had served as ambassador in Moscow; he also had been director of the VOA in the early 1950s, and this experience enhanced his expertise in international communications. A third appointee, Abbott Washburn, had been the driving force and innovative genius behind the Crusade for Freedom; he was later deputy director of the United States Information Agency, parent of the VOA, and in 1970–71 had been appointed head of the U.S. delegation to a conference determining the future of the International Telecommunications Satellite Consortium, with the rank of ambassador. Another appointee, John Roche, knew the Radios well since he had been a member of the Eisenhower Commission. Only Thomas Quinn had had no specific contact with the Radios, but he had come to Washington from Rhode Island, where he was a close acquaintance of Senators John Pastore, the chairman of the Senate Appropriations Committee, and Claiborne Pell, an influential Democratic member of the Senate Foreign Relations Committee, who had been involved in the Fulbright hearings beginning in 1971. Presidents Durkee and Sargeant rounded out the roster as *ex officio*, nonvoting members.

There was not much doubt where the new BIB would have to start. The GAO had pointed the way in its May 1972 report to the Senate Foreign Relations Committee. There was little likelihood that members of the committee would soon forget one recommendation that promised to save money: "Since the activities of both Free Europe and the Radio Liberty Committee had diminished to strictly radio broadcasting, it appears the cost of providing an uncensored news service to the peoples of Eastern Europe and the United States of Soviet Russia could be reduced if those organizations were consolidated and some or all of their activities were merged."[1] The GAO report called for consolidation of the Radios' general management, administration, and news services.

The word of the GAO was not law, but it was abundantly clear that the report's recommendations would have a profound impact on Congress, particularly in view of the economies it promised. The report did not go unnoticed in Munich, where many members of both the program and administrative staffs had become voracious readers of any written words from Washington concerning their own futures. An era was finished and what lay ahead did not promise to be nearly as attractive as what had gone before. Consolidation meant commingling two potentially incompatible staffs representing vastly different cultures. The East European exiles who created the program product for RFE had no love for the Soviet Russians who had overrun their homelands, and some of the antagonisms rubbed off on all Russians whatever their sympathies and wherever they might be, in Munich as well as in the USSR. The Russians, who constituted most of the RL program staff, kept pretty much to themselves in Munich; there was very little fraternizing with RFE personnel.

The overwhelming cause for apprehension, though, was economic. Termination slips were being issued in the fall and winter of 1973–74, at a rate that outpaced by a wide margin the staff reductions in 1971 and 1972. In fiscal year 1974, 343 employees lost their jobs, nearly a 15-percent reduction of staff. And the executioner's knife would almost certainly continue to fall as consolidation became reality.

In November 1973 plans were presented by Radio management to the Office of Management and the Budget for a consolidation program in Munich. During that month, the boards of both Free Europe and the Radio Liberty Committee approved plans for a single management for the Radios, common support services and joint operating locations in both New York and Munich. This meant that the Russians from RL would be working under the same management as and in the same headquarters building with the East Europeans from RFE. This was doubly disconcerting because the common language of RL was Russian, while that of RFE was English. Many of the RL staff were monolingual and thus unable to communicate with executives of Free Europe or East Europeans on the Free Europe staff.

Notwithstanding the danger signals, the Free Europe and Radio Liberty Committee boards pushed ahead. In December 1973 they opened negotiations with German authorities for permission to renovate the Free Europe building on the English Garden to accommodate RL as well as RFE. They requested permission to add approximately 2000 square meters to the existing space, at an estimated cost of $945,000. The completion date was expected in October or November 1975, provided plans were drawn and permissions granted within the next few months.

Such was the situation as members of the BIB met for the first time to determine how to proceed. In June 1974 Washburn, Roche, and Quinn made their first exploratory trip to Munich. CIA personnel had always carefully avoided being present on the Radios' premises, to create the impression that the corporations were managerially as well as professionally independent. Department of State personnel assigned to replace the CIA in the policy role during the interim years had also maintained an arm's-length relationship.* Consequently, the delegation of visitors from the oversight board was a new phenomenon. The reception by Munich staff was neither enthusiastic nor antagonistic. There was curiosity regarding the ultimate course of action and suspicion that the new era was going to be cheerless at best and disastrous at worst.

Construction permits had not yet been obtained when Washburn, Roche, and Quinn arrived in Munich, but the direction to be taken was clear. The BIB members talked to management, labor, and workers' councils; inspected transmitters and monitoring sites; examined the headquarters buildings and facilities; and returned to Washington to write their recommendations. Their proposed reorganization plan paralleled the plan presented to the OMB by the Radios' managements in almost every detail. The report was accepted by the full board in November 1974. There was one added stipulation, however (not specifically suggested by the Radios' managements), assuring that the future shape of the Radios would be dramatically different. Both presidents, Durkee and Sargeant, were to resign and a new chief executive to serve both corporations would be recruited to replace them. With that, the die was cast. Consolidation would take place, no matter the misgivings. RL and the Russians would move in with RFE and its East Europeans as soon as building renovations were completed. But now, apprehension and concern for the future affected not only personnel at the working level, but management as well, up to the senior executive echelons.

The pattern that would prevail in the future was now clear. Permissions for building reconstruction in Munich were granted by German authorities in

---

*While the CIA carefully refrained from maintaining any overt presence at either radio headquarters the agency did assign one of its staff members to the U.S. consulate in Munich to maintain liaison with Radio management.

October 1974 and construction started only weeks later. The BIB appointed a committee consisting of Free Europe Board Chairman Jacob A. Beam, RL Chairman John S. Hayes, and Kohler to set up procedures, seek candidates, and make the selection of a new president to serve both corporations. Durkee and Sargeant assumed the unenviable task, as lame ducks, of drawing up reorganization plans that would implement consolidation. In the meantime, terminations continued as part of the plan to reduce the payroll to fewer than 1800 employees, a reduction of 1000 from the base of 2806 in 1968.

Neither Radio was fully pleased with the direction that consolidation was taking. RFE would have preferred to absorb RL with its considerably smaller organization as an operating division. RL, for its part, was fearful that it would lose its identity and become assimilated into the much larger and much more publicized RFE. At any rate, program production functions were to retain their separate identities as would program department managements. It was the support and administrative services that posed problems. The dividing of functions resembled the system by which children choose up sides for a baseball game. FRE selected the director of administration from its personnel roster; RL, the director of fiscal and accounting services; RFE, the director of engineering operations; RL, the budget officer; RFE, the director of personnel; RL, the general services manager. And so it went, through the executive echelons, both in Munich and New York. RFE was granted the better positions to fill because it was the larger organization, although the intention was to balance the key executive positions as evenly as possible.

Jockeying for position was unceasing. Some executives were clearly going to be forced out; others, supplanted by members of the other service, would suffer down-grading. Tempers were kept in check, at least publicly, but egos were badly bruised and jealousies were hard to conceal.

Adding to the climate of resentment and jealousy, there was bickering early-on between senior management and members of the BIB staff. Free Europe and Radio Liberty Committee executives considered the BIB staff members intrusive and abrasive. They were accustomed to the more free-wheeling, relaxed method of imposing controls exercised over the years by the CIA and more recently by the Department of State. They felt that while both CIA and State had confidence in them and so had no need to pry into every miniscule activity, the BIB staff was constantly overstepping the reasonable lines between oversight and management, and they deeply resented it.

It was in this charged atmosphere that both Radios had to make hard decisions for the future, and they needed the help of the BIB. Pensions were a major cause of anxiety. In the period when the tight budgets had kept operations at a bare subsistence level, it had been necessary to forego the regular contributions to pension funds in order to meet payrolls. As budget planning for fiscal year 1975 began, however, it was obvious that the unfunded liabilities would have to be made up or there would be rebellion among staffs, as well as penalties imposed by government. (New pension legislation in the United States was particularly specific on this issue.) Moreover, employee leaders attacked the unfunded pension plans as being inadequate even if fully funded. They pointed to inflationary pressures that had reduced the buying power of those already on pensions to a poverty level.

Economy measures also affected the maintenance of equipment at the Radios. RL's 250-kilowatt transmitters at the Pals base in Spain were still reasonably new, but its Lampertheim equipment was woefully inadequate. It needed more powerful transmitters and at least one new antenna field, if it was to reach its target areas. RFE's Gloria base in Portugal had had no new equipment added since 1964 and was lagging badly in the battle to carve out a position in the shortwave spectrum that would permit it to reach clearly into Eastern Europe. Its Biblis base was as inadequate as RL's base at Lampertheim.

Besides the problem of the decline in the power and efficiency of transmitters and antennas, there was another dangerous prospect: leases for both Spain and Portugal were in jeopardy. The Portugese revolution that overthrew the last remnants of the Salazar government in April 1974 cast a deep shadow over Gloria's future. It was touch and go for almost two years: even if the base was spared a takeover by Communist elements in the country, there was always the possibility the left-wing government might simply refuse to renew the lease that had already run out. However, a Portugese army captain, Tomas Rosa, assigned by the revolutionary government as delegate to RARET, assured Free Europe management that the station could continue to operate indefinitely; apparently the base, which furnished employment, an industrial school, and a hospital with medical service was indispensable to the community, and this protected it from forceful takeover.

The lease at Pals was also approaching renewal date, but Spanish government officials were not disposed even to discuss renewal. The March 1976 deadline for renewal left little time to get negotiations underway or to plan and acquire alternative bases.

RL had a special problem of its own. Soviet migration, following the flood of refugees that washed over Western Europe immediately after the war in the late 1940s, amounted to only a trickle. Soviet policy made it exceedingly difficult to travel abroad and groups outside the Soviet Union were kept under close surveillance to prevent defections. This policy sharply reduced the talent pool from which the station could draw and forced it to rely for replacement and staff augmentation purposes, largely on exiles who had been in the West too long to have intimate knowledge of current conditions in the Soviet Union. There was a desperate need for young migrants, exiles cognizant of current conditions and also possessing the strength and enthusiasm of youth to refresh and renew an aging staff. "What we need most," said Francis Ronalds, RL's executive director, "is a period of tranquility."

The dam that had been holding back Jewish emigration from the Soviet Union broke just as the two Radios were suffering their most traumatic experiences with congressional criticism and budget shortages. RL management reached out to attract as many of the recent Jewish migrants as it could afford under its financially straitened circumstances. But this created a turmoil within its Russian service ranks that was to affect its operations for months to come. Not only were the new Jewish staff members young and energetic, intimately acquainted with current conditions in the Soviet Union, but many were also extraordinarily able. They rose quickly through the ranks of the organization and moved into positions of responsibility, leap-frogging over some of the older, more orthodox Russians. There was a continuing clash between the Jews and the old-line Russians who, as members of the Orthodox church, could not accept Jews as legitimate Russians. The old-line Russians also suspected that the Jewish migrants had been tainted by living under Soviet leadership for so long that they could not be regarded as legitimate anti-Communists.

In the meantime, Durkee and Sargeant and their staffs in New York were struggling with the arduous task of combining two dissimilar organizations, beset moreover, they believed, by an inordinate amount of malicious sniping from the BIB staff. Not only did the two corporations speak different languages, but they had different accounting systems, salary schedules, benefits programs, vacation policies, home-leave regulations, and working conditions. A total adjustment to make them conform was out of the question, but they had to be brought as close to conformity as possible. Bearing the burden of staff reductions was a point of contention between the corporations. Each tried to protect as many of its own employees as possible and slough off layoffs to the other side. RL was particularly sensitive on this point and complained bitterly that it was being discriminated against.

Such were the conditions that prevailed as the BIB's Presidential Search Committee set about to hire a single replacement for both Durkee and Sargeant to be president of both corporations. July 1, 1975, was set as the deadline to have a new president on the job. Scores of names were considered. Biographical data was submitted to the BIB staff in Washington while Durkee and Sargeant labored as fast as they could with their wholly thankless task.

NOTE

1. Report to the Committee on Foreign Relations United States Senate, *U.S. Government Monies Provided to Radio Free Europe and Radio Liberty,* by the Comptroller General of the United States, May 25, 1972, p. 4.

18
88 Million Eastern Europeans Can't Protest but We Can

IT MIGHT HAVE SEEMED to an outside observer that by the winter of 1975 the crisis was over. Senator Fulbright's efforts to eliminate the Radios had been overwhelmingly defeated. A mechanism had been found to maintain the professional integrity of the stations and at the same time keep a tight rein over expenditures. An oversight formula had been devised that would restrict the Radios only to the extent they would not operate in a manner "inconsistent with broad U.S. foreign policy." Presumably, this would have restored peace to the Radios, which had had little respite from crisis since the funding disclosures in 1967, and particularly since Senator Case's speech on January 25, 1971. However, peace was not in sight. A tenuous stand-off seemed to have replaced the hopeless drift, but the Radios could hardly be described as happy ships. If anything, the levels of tension were increasing; the pressure gauge was pushing toward the red line, marking danger.

Three separate developments, all of them directly related to the future of Free Europe and the Radio Liberty Committee, were proceeding on parallel courses. Durkee and Sargeant were pushing to carry out the consolidation program to the point where a pattern would be established before they yielded to the new chief executive. Both felt beleaguered by excessive pressure from the BIB and carried out their unpleasant jobs with deep resentment. Employee unrest was increasing at full throttle; the mood, according to some executives in Munich, was becoming ugly. At the same time the search committee was beginning to screen possible candidates for the presidency. No long-term solutions seemed possible without a permanent new organization under new leadership.

The chaotic conditions stemming from the incomplete process of consolidation were enough to keep both Radios in a state of constant turmoil, but to make matters worse, the leases in both Spain and Portugal, where fully 90 percent of the Radio's transmitter power was concentrated, were in danger of termination. Only the Gloria and Pals sites were far enough removed from their target areas to deliver an optimum shortwave signal; Biblis and Lampertheim were too close and Holzkirchen was effective only because parts of Czechoslovakia and Hungary were within range of its medium-wave transmitter.

The crisis in Portugal deepened as 1975 progressed. In the area from Gloria south to the Algarve revolutionaries were moving on the big estates and expropriating property with no signs of disapproval from the revolutionary government in Lisbon. It was feared that the same might happen at Gloria. RFE's lease on the property formally expired on April 30, but the revolutionary government granted an extension until October; however, it was vague on what might happen after the expiration of the six-month extension. All Free Europe had to rely on was Captain Rosa's assurances that the base was safe.

The impending crises in Portugal and Spain, however, were geographically remote and the eventual outcome beyond the control of the Radios or BIB, so they seemed only a distant cloud on the darkening horizon. There was not much they could do except brace themselves, make plans for carrying on if the storm should strike, and hope it would change its course before severe damage were done.

The labor problem was different: it had already arrived. There were two key issues: staff reductions and pensions. As Evdokim Evdokimov, chairman of the Munich unit of the New York Newspaper Guild, pointed out, the budgetary knife was cutting so deep that the depleted forces remaining were unable to perform their jobs adequately. In addition, it was felt that the existing pension plans, even if they should be funded properly, were inadequate to support retired workers above the poverty line. A strong stand for a revised, more generous pension program became the union rallying point, chiefly because it was a visible cause that could arouse emotional support, and there was a chance of winning.* Union leadership realized that staff reductions would occur whether or not they were protested.

---

*The emotional component of the campaign is difficult to measure, but it is noteworthy that the guild stressed cases of retired workers whose pension incomes were deplorably low. David Taylor, vice chairman of the Munich guild unit, cites other additional evidence of the degree to which the pension plans were a highly charged issue. He points out that when the guild discovered in 1972 that the companies' annual contributions to their fund were being postponed, the discovery was a spark that set off a wave of anger. "That's what got me outraged," he says.

The first salvo was fired on February 28 by the RFE unions, the German Employees' Union (DAG), the Bavarian Journalists Union (BJV) and the American Newspaper Guild. The negotiations between the BIB and the OMB regarding the fiscal 1976 budget were the target. It was assumed that the BIB had acquiesced with an OMB demand that $725,000, designed to provide a "modest improvement" for retired RFE employees already on pension, be deleted from the budget. The BIB was declared the target and the three unions wrote to the director, David Abshire, declaring that the protesting unions would use every channel at their disposal, both in Germany and the United States, to reverse the decision.[1] Abshire dodged the fusillade by rightly pointing out that the process of negotiating internal company disputes was exclusively the right and requirement of the management of the two Radios and that Congress would ultimately decide on the final level of funding. The BIB, however, deeply involved in trying to get a reasonable level of funding for its first year of oversight, had the responsibility for shepherding the bill through the congressional authorization and appropriation process.

Preparing its first budget would have been difficult enough for the BIB staff, but there was an additional twist to the process. In 1975 the government was changing to a new fiscal year that would run from October 1 through September 30. This called for developing a five-quarter budget for fiscal year 1976: the normal four quarters to June 30, and an additional transition quarter to September 30. The additional quarter was included at the same level of expenditure as that for the others, but adding the 25-percent increment produced a figure that seemed inordinately large: $65.7 million. However, the base for the 12-month period was only $52 million (appropriations had amounted to $50 million in the preceding year), and the grand total involved provision for making good on unfunded pension liabilities, increasing salaries, and modernizing the transmitter bases at Biblis and Lampertheim.

Employees in general and the unions in particular spotted what they regarded as two basic weaknesses. First, the amount requested for fiscal 1976 was not sufficient to bring pensions up to a level of minimal acceptability. Second, the four-quarter budget figure the BIB had informally projected for fiscal 1977 was set at only $57 million. This would have marked an increase of almost 10 percent, but the unions thought it was hardly enough to compensate for inflationary pressures, produce some equitable wage policy, and raise pensions to a reasonable level.

It was in this climate of suspicion and antagonism that Durkee and Sargeant went with their senior aides to Washington to determine how they could develop spending patterns that would permit the Radios to live within the $65.7 million spending limit (presumably to be imposed on them by Congress, provided no more cuts were made). They determined the $65.7 million clearly would not permit them to meet their obligations unless an additional $4.1 million could be shaved from projected operating costs. Since more than

80 percent of the costs of operating the two Radios went to wages and sala-ries, the bulk of the $4.1 million would have to come from further reductions in the personnel lists. This meant that at least 100 more employees, probably more, would have to be terminated, voluntarily or involuntarily.

Employees in Munich learned of the impending spate of dismissals and voluntary terminations through notices posted on the bulletin boards in the English Garden headquarters on the morning of May 13. The unions took immediate action. That same day they called a press conference, describing the staff reductions as "irresponsibility" on the part of the BIB and the man-agement in that "neither tried seriously to obtain the requisite financing from the United States Congress." They intended to take their case to the appropri-ate congressional committees. With that announcement, the battle was joined.

On May 20 Harry Fisdell, executive vice president of the Newspaper Guild of New York, testified at his own request before a subcommittee of the House Appropriations Committee that was considering the BIB appropria-tions for the Radios. Fisdell urged congressional support for the $65.7 million budget for fiscal 1976, but he also asked that the schedule of personnel termi-nations be cushioned by making early retirement financially attractive to em-ployees over sixty. He condemned the policy of "nickeling and diming" the employees to death and argued that the loyalty and dedication that em-ployees had demonstrated over the years had been "shamefully exploited," producing a deep sense of demoralization among the staff.

The testimony served as a warning that unless action were taken, the unions would adopt measures that would compel a response. On May 28 Fis-dell wrote to Abshire that the unions had taken the unprecedented step of calling for "industrial action," a term that would mean at worst a strike, at best a protracted demonstration. The union posted a message to all em-ployees on May 30, calling for a vote on industrial action to be scheduled for June 2, 3, and 4. Ralph Walter, the RFE director in Munich, promptly sent the text of the union message to Durkee in New York. Durkee, in turn, relayed it to BIB headquarters in Washington. The message from the unions was hardly conciliatory. It called the economy cuts neither necessary nor responsible and suggested that the BIB's projections for future fiscal year budgeting would "inescapably mean still further staff cuts over the next few years."

The call for industrial action stung Abshire and the BIB staff. Their posi-tion with Congress, they felt, was so precarious that many lukewarm sup-porters who had had misgivings about supporting the Radios in past years might now be tempted to wash their hands of the whole thing. An examina-tion of the text of the hearings over the past three years suggests that few members of either the House or Senate committees fully understood the ob-jectives of the two corporations and what they were doing. It would have been a simple matter to take the position that, if the ingrates at the Radios were not satisfied with the style in which they were going to be supported, Congress should let the effort be dropped. Abshire wrote to Fisdell on June 3, abandoning the position he had expressed two months earlier, that the matter be settled by the Free Europe and the Radio Liberty Committee managements. He explained the budget request in detail, including the fact that some $7.4 million would go into making up unfunded pension liabilities and $150,000 would be dedicated to improving benefit features in the pension programs. He argued that even with the $65.7 million budget, the Radios would still face a deficit of $4.1 million. There was simply no way of extracting that sum of money from operational expenses without staff reductions. He begged for cooperation in working toward a stable budget that Congress would continue to support not only in 1976 but in the years to come.

Abshire's effort proved futile. On schedule, on June 2, 3, and 4 the unions voted. Out of 478 eligible to vote, 403 actually cast their ballots. Only 25 of the 403 voted "no". The remainder, 93 percent of the total, voted for "industrial action." That left only two questions undecided. What form would industrial action take, and when would it be scheduled?

While the unions, management, and the BIB moved inexorably toward a potentially disastrous confrontation, the combined BIB and corporate search committee was preparing to introduce the new president of the corporations. The effort to discover a suitable candidate was begun in January. The three-man committee was ready to make a decision in early April.*

June, following the industrial action vote, appeared to be a quiet month: there were no sharp clashes that commanded attention, no controversy in Congress, no rebellious statements from employees in Munich. But the quiet was deceptive. Senior managements of both companies were pushing forward to pare down the staff to the agreed levels before relinquishing office on June 30. The BIB staff was studying personnel practices and alternative transmitter sites in the event that either Spain or Portugal were lost, and establishing procedures for program oversight.

The unions in Munich had to decide what specific industrial action to take. The 93-percent favorable vote seemed to offer wide latitude, but unknown to the management and the BIB a subsequent development threw the whole procedure into unexpected turmoil. A representative of the DAG headquarters appeared on the scene with disturbing news for the union leadership. He advised that the questions under consideration in the

---

*At this point it is necessary to switch to the first person to continue this account. I accepted appointment as president of both Free Europe and the Radio Liberty Committee in mid-April after preliminary negotiations over terms and conditions of employment, and prepared to take office on July 1. It was agreed that in the interim, I should attend some of the congressional hearings that were scheduled for late April and early May and that I would spend a week in Munich in May trying to absorb as much background as I could before being thrust into the developing combat.

industrial-action vote had been improperly formulated and that a second ballot was required to insure conformity with law.[2] Had this development been known in Washington and New York, it would have been recognized as a major victory, but word of the changed scene never leaked out. The unions, however, faced a critical dilemma: they could either vote again and risk losing face in a second election or avoid the risk and seek an alternative process for making the case without violating the labor law—one that would command attention commensurate with what could be achieved with a strike. A quirk in the law furnished the loophole the unions were seeking: conventional industrial action might be a violation of the law, but a "spontaneous demonstration" by employees would be totally legal because it would not constitute a refusal to work.

The three unions set out to mount a carefully prepared "spontaneous demonstration," the impact of which would be certain to reverberate in Washington. They would have to pick a time and place when the demonstration was certain to attract major media attention, and they would have to make it dramatic enough so that it could not be overlooked. They had no trouble deciding on the time and place; word was passed through the building by management that the new president would make his first official visit to RFE headquarters on July 10.

In his June 3 letter to Fisdell at the American Newspaper Guild, Abshire had promised the unions that as soon as possible after July 1, I would go to Munich to meet with employee representatives and develop proposals for revising the pension plans. The Munich management scheduled a press conference for early afternoon on July 10 in the largest studio in the English Garden building and arranged to have it piped throughout the building and to the RL headquarters building a mile and a half away. Employees of both corporations would hear my opening statement, the questions asked by the media representatives, and my responses to those questions.

As I arrived at the entrance to the building shortly after lunch on July 10, it was immediately clear what course the unions had chosen. Lined up across the front of the building were 100 or more employees carrying banners, placards, and signs of varying sizes, most of them large enough to register clearly on film even when photographers had to work from a distance. The placards and banners were skillfully designed to reflect the protesters' attitudes without it being necessary to back them up with shouted slogans and jeers. In fact, it seemed almost eerily quiet as I walked through the line to take my position in front of some 25 members of the Bavarian and international media.

Since there was no point in failing to recognize the demonstration that had taken place outside, I complimented the protesters on the signs they had prepared and called attention to the visibly rousing welcome. I then read my opening statement and answered questions for nearly an hour. The most difficult question to answer and the one asked in the greatest variety of ways regarded the projected $57 million budget for fiscal 1977. Questioners wanted to know how we could provide improved pension plans, stop personnel erosion, modernize facilities, and stay within what, in view of inflation, seemed to be a wholly inadequate total grant. (The questions apparently reflected the concern expressed by the unions regarding their assumption that the pension plans were totally inadequate; typical of the messages on the placards was one that read: "88 Million People in Eastern Europe Can't Protest, but We Can.") By the time the press conference was finished, at any rate, the signs had all disappeared, the demonstrators were apparently back on the job, and it was possible to sense that a potentially destructive crisis had passed. Meetings the next day with unions and works councils proceeded with neither harsh words nor what management might have considered unreasonable demands.*

By the next day, the peak of tension had been passed. The protests had been made and there had been sufficient media coverage to assure that they would be noted in Washington and New York. It did not mark by any means the end of squabbling between management and employees, but at this writing no strike votes have been taken since June 1975 and no staged protests or demonstrations since July of that year. The easing of the stress in Munich eliminated the threat that Congress might react to a strike by whittling the budget further or even washing its hands of the Radios altogether. The breathing spell from labor disputes permitted concentration on other problems—for example, deciding how to move the headquarters staff from New York to Washington, and how to reconcile the different accounting systems so that a dollar would mean the same thing in the RFE book of accounts as in RL's. The termination process also had to continue.

Always hovering in the background, intruding into every conversation, however, was the possible closing down of the Gloria base in Portugal, either abruptly by force or legally at the expiration of the most recent six-month lease. Pals in Spain was apparently safe until March 23, 1976, but there seemed no disposition on the part of Spanish officials to talk extension. It was clear that a massive effort would have to be undertaken at once to discover back-up base possibilities and plan for their implementation.

---

*There is some indication that the Social Democratic government in Bonn may have had some impact on softening the employee attitudes. One newspaper guild official told me that some guild members felt that the DAG executive from Hamburg who came to Munich during one of the most explosive periods might have had word from Bonn to help keep everything quiet. It is apparent the West German government preferred to avoid a potentially unpleasant confrontation with international implications. Realizing that a work stoppage was out of the question, employees were apparently satisfied to have made their point.

NOTES

1. Letter from the three unions, dated February 28, 1975. A copy is available in the Archives of the Hoover Institution. It was addressed to Abshire and signed by Senator Hans Schaumann for DAG, Dr. Hans Badewitz for BJV, Evdokim Evdokimov for the Munich unit of ANG, and Harry Fisdell for the Newspaper Guild of New York. An appendix describes eight retired RFE employees living on pensions that fail to ensure that they will be able to live "above the minimum existence level."

2. Revealed in June 1982 by David Taylor in conversation with the author. A tape cassette of the conversation is available in the Archives of the Hoover Institution.

19
External Problems Divert Attention

I T WAS IRONIC that the leases for operating bases in Spain and Portugal would expire within only months of each other, just at a time when the consolidation of RFE and RL was nearing completion. The leases in the two Iberian countries had been negotiated independently by separate corporations with different terms and conditions and duration of contract. But now the consolidated Radios were faced with an October 30, 1975, expiration date on Free Europe's base in Portugal and another on March 23 of the next year on RL's base in Spain. The situation was doubly frustrating because there appeared to be little that could be done to stave off disaster. An activist approach might only succeed in antagonizing the governmental authorities in control. That could mean expulsion, in which case orderly liquidation would be jeopardized. Under terms of the original contracts the equipment on both bases belonged, either in whole or in large part, to the host country.

Portugal clearly presented the more pressing problem because of the imminence of the October 30 date, but Captain Rosa, the revolutionary government's delegate to RARET, continued to give assurances that no action would be taken by his government at the conclusion of the six-month extension. A clause in the extension specified that RFE could continue to operate until a new government of Portugal was elected. The clause was a little vague about what constituted the election of a new government and as to when that government might be selected. A specific date for elections had not yet been set as October approached, so there appeared to be nothing to worry about. The country, however, remained frighteningly unstable and it was an open question as to whether a successful coup might be mounted that would bring a new and more radical government into power. To avoid any possibilities of calling undue attention to the existence of the Gloria base the Radios' management decided that the wisest course of action would be no action at all. The lowest possible profile would be maintained: no corporate executives would visit Portugal; American personnel in Lisbon and Gloria would remain as unobtrusive as possible. Nothing would be done to tempt retaliation or even to call attention to the existence of the facility.

While Portugal remained in this state of suspended animation, Spain offered an equally puzzling enigma. The Department of State was preoccupied with renegotiating a lease for the U.S. military bases on Spanish soil and insisted on completing that delicate process before considering RL's problems. The U.S. ambassador, Wells Stabler, preferred that embassy personnel not accompany Radio personnel to visit offices of Spanish authorities, and he was not enthusiastic about Radio personnel doing so either. Embassy officials were to go no further than to help arrange appointments.

Spanish officials were vague in their responses to questions as to when negotiations might start. They were cordial but noncommittal. There were rumors, never fully substantiated, that there were several noteworthy reasons that the lease for Pals would not be renewed.

The first was that the property occupied by RL had become exceedingly valuable. The base was becoming an island in a burgeoning sea of highrises that were encroaching directly on its property lines. Land speculators were said to be casting covetous eyes at this valuable unscarred stretch of smooth beach, a rarity on the rough Costa Brava.

A second rumored motive, with considerable evidence to support it, was that the Soviet government was applying stern pressures to Spain to remove this prickly source of irritation to the USSR in the interests of improved Soviet–Spanish relations. The Soviets were able to offer trade incentives to back up their strong-arm tactics, and they offered to recognize the Spanish Republic.

The third problem was internal. The Spanish government, which was hardly in a secure position, was reluctant to open up a noisy debate on the lease question. Extension could not be granted without a vote in the Cortes, and that, members of the government thought, would surely touch off a boisterous debate that might paralyze the governmental process and even bring down the shaky government. At the very least, the Spanish media would have a field day.

Generalissimo Franco was seriously ill during the autumn of 1975 and unable to exert the authority to support the government in any action it might take. His death on November 20, 1975, did nothing to add to the confidence of government ministers and in fact, if anything, delayed consideration of the matter. In late January 1976 what seemed to be the death warrant for RL arrived in the office of George Dennis, the Radio's personal representative in Madrid. It came in the form of a letter from the Directorate-General of Spanish Radio and Television and informed Dennis the lease would not be renewed. It instructed RL to begin plans for evacuation. Dennis was suspicious that the letter did not represent the considered judgment of the leadership of the government. He thought it might have been posted without adequate checking with the minister of information and tourism and other cabinet ministers. Whether there had been a change of heart after the letter was mailed, or whether Dennis's hunch was right, he was informed unofficially that no definitive decision had been made and that there were no specific plans to make one in the immediate future.

Word of the impending action, however, reached some segments of the Spanish press and through the press, members of the RL staff at Pals. It appeared, from what the employees read, that their jobs were in immediate jeopardy and no specific plans had been made or funds set aside for termination benefits. The responsibility clearly lay, according to the lease agreement, with the Radio. The employees were informed that the Radios were confident that the base would not be closed, but, in the unlikely event that it was closed, the corporation would assume full responsibility for a generous termination compensation program.*

In order to avoid any charge that the Radios' credit was in jeopardy, or that it was defaulting on the agreement management arranged to be certain that the full payment on the lease, due March 23, covering the subsequent six months, would be delivered to the minister of information and tourism at least 24 hours before the deadline. If the check was cashed, management could be sure of another six months without orders to shut down. The money was transferred to a Madrid bank on March 22; the Ministry of Information and Tourism was notified and the money was transferred to the Spanish government's account. It was then possible to breathe a little more easily.

Through the entire period of uncertainty, a search for alternative operating bases went on ceaselessly. Placing transmitters on the U.S. mainland was out of the question. Engineers estimated that no transmitter with less than 2 million watts of power, or eight times the maximum power output of the largest of the transmitters at Pals, would be able to reach the target areas in Eastern Europe, and then only with a serious erosion of signal strength. Time would be required to design and build these superpowerful transmitters, and even then there was no assurance they could successfully be manufactured. And even if they were manufactured, the power for operating a base from the U.S. mainland would require as much electrical energy as a city with at least a 35,000 population. This choice was clearly out of the question.

---

*I made this pledge myself standing on a table in the employee cafeteria at the Pals base at a meeting attended on a national holiday by almost 100 percent of the employees, just a few days before the March 23 deadline.

The BBC was approached and it quickly rejected cooperation. Deutsche Welle likewise would offer no assistance. That left only the VOA as a possiblity for cooperative effort. The Voice was reluctant to permit transmission of an RFE or an RL signal from any of its transmitters for fear that the heavy hand of the jammers would be imposed on VOA programs. At the moment they were free of jamming and wanted to avoid resumption. The alternative would be to acquire leases on property in other countries within target range and build new facilities there. North Africa was a reasonable possibility. The distance from the target areas was within the recommended parameters, but two problems intervened. First, lengthy negotiations would be required with the country selected as the likeliest possibility and there was no assurance that a U.S. proposal would be accepted. Second, building a new base would require a multimillion-dollar infusion of capital and months of research, design, construction, and installation, and it could only be undertaken with congressional approval.

Higher levels of the U.S. government, including the NSC, prodded by the BIB, decided that, as a last resort, the Radios would be offered the use of VOA transmitters in Liberia and at Woofferton in England. At best this would be a makeshift solution. Results would not nearly measure up to those achieved from Pals and Gloria, but it would allow programming to continue without interruption. In the meantime, plans were made to beef up the Holzkirchen base in Germany and to achieve greater flexibility from Biblis and Lampertheim. There was also a low-powered VOA facility in Munich that could be made available, if needed. Implementation of the contingency plan would take time, effort, and money, and the results would plainly be inferior, but there was no alternative except for renewing rights in Spain and Portugal.

In Portugal tensions had relaxed a bit by the first part of January 1976. Gloria was still operating on borrowed time, but it had not lost a second on the air. Rosa assured management personnel that the clause in the extension agreement, permitting continued operations "until elections are held and a new government formed," would prevail. The parliamentary elections were scheduled for mid-April and the presidential election for June.

By late March, however, the Portuguese were ready to start negotiating. It took exactly a year before a new agreement was signed. In March 1977 RARET and the government of Portugal agreed to a new 15-year lease that could not be terminated by either side before 11 years had passed. The new lease included two significant modifications. The first permitted considerable expansion through the introduction of new transmitters onto the base. The second, even more important, permitted Gloria to be used for broadcasting to both Eastern Europe and the Soviet Union. This created a flexibility that would take substantial pressure off operations from Pals.

One obstacle that delayed action for a time was the insistence by the BIB that the lease be negotiated on a "government-to-government" basis and that it be signed by representatives of the two governments, rather than by RARET and personnel representing the Ministry of Information. The Portuguese could not understand why the U.S. government should be involved even if it paid the bills. The Portuguese company of RARET had been created to obtain leases and licenses from the government and to operate the facility, and Portuguese representatives demanded that this arrangement be continued. The BIB finally backed off and was content with a short supplementary statement specifying that both Portugal and the U.S. government approved of the arrangement. Such a short agreement was signed and affixed to the lease.

The Spanish impasse was not so easily settled. Word was transmitted informally from a number of Spanish sources that the best course was to continue the low-profile approach and not to ask for a lease renewal. Government leaders feared that the matter was so volatile that any effort to reach a settlement would inevitably cause violent repercussions in the barely stable Spanish Republic. Radio management made it an inflexible rule that $142,500, half of the annual $285,000 lease payment, would be delivered to the minister of information and tourism on or before March 22 and September 22 in each year as payment for the subsequent six months. This was not a wholly satisfactory arrangement. Modernization projects seemed a poor investment if the maximum expectable lifespan was limited to six months, but, as it turned out, except for the aging of the equipment on the base, Pals has gone on unchanged.*

While the Radios were grappling with problems in Spain and Portugal, the Soviets and their East European allies apparently sensed an opening for launching a new effort to exterminate the irritants or so weaken them that they would cease to be effective. The main target, apparently, was the Radios' planned coverage of the Winter Olympic Games in Innsbruck, Austria, in February 1976, and the Summer Games in Montreal, in July. As a curtain-raiser for their Olympic drama, however, the Communists arranged to stage a brief spectacle in Prague, designed, it appeared, to soften up the opposition. Pavel Minarik, a former employee of the Czechoslovak Service of RFE surfaced in the Czech capital in February and announced that he was an officer in the Czechoslovak secret police who had been assigned to infiltrate RFE. Minarik charged, in a carefully produced interview, that RFE was secretly giving financial support to Alexander Dubcek, who had been deposed as the Czechoslovak prime minister during the Soviet invasion of 1968, along with a number of other Czechoslovak dissidents. He further charged that RFE was continuing to support a number of Czech and Slovak émigré organizations and that representatives of those organizations were on the Free Europe staff.

---

*Contingency plans for Pals and Gloria have since been filed in a little-used file cabinet.

He added the threadbare complaint that RFE was actually an instrument of the CIA.

RFE quickly admitted that Minarik had been a Radio employee since 1968; however, he had resigned after being informed that he was to be terminated at the end of March 1976. Munich management was not totally enthusiastic about Minarik's work and regarded him as being somewhat unstable. It was assumed that he had been frustrated by being unable to find suitable work either in Munich or in New York and had decided voluntarily to return to Prague where he fabricated his spy story. The timing was made to order for Czech authorities, who seized upon the opportunity to flay the enemy in the West. East European and Soviet media elaborated on the theme handed to them by Minarik and orchestrated a symphony of hate against the "CIA spy-nest in Munich."

The Minarik case was beginning to die down when the Soviets struck again, this time with a guaranteed worldwide audience at the Winter Olympic Games at Innsbruck. The Radios had been assigning reporting teams to Olympic events since the mid-1950s. The accelerating interest in athletic events in the Soviet Union and Eastern Europe and the intensive emphasis directed toward victory in international competition by Communist governments made this a particularly attractive target for Radio broadcasts, and the lackadaisical approach of Eastern broadcasters, who were rarely concerned with immediacy or objective coverage, furnished a wide opening the Radios could exploit.

For their part, the upcoming quadrennial games would furnish the Soviet Union and its allies a worldwide forum in which to pull out all the stops in a campaign calculated not only to silence the Radios' coverage, which was obnoxious to them, but also to build a case to drive the Radios out of existence.

The Communist interest in exploiting the Olympic Games to accomplish their primary goal first surfaced in connection with the Mexico City Games in 1968. It was assumed, although there was no specific evidence, that serious delays experienced by Radio personnel in obtaining credentials resulted from some mysterious "political interference." Soviet efforts to throttle the Radios' coverage were gaining momentum by the time of the Munich Games in 1972 and came to a head in Innsbruck and Montreal in 1976. The objective in each of those cases was to bar the Radios from obtaining formal accreditation for reporters and correspondents. Soviet propagandists, however, could hardly have overlooked the opportunity to make their case, too, while media from the whole world were looking on.

The Soviet campaign succeeded in some measure at Innsbruck. Shortly after the games had gotten underway, the Soviets made their first move. The objective was to force RFE and RL personnel to return their credentials. They charged that the applications had not been formally signed by the German National Olympic Committee, although the applications had been approved by the Austrian hosts and badges to permit entry to Olympic venues had been issued formally. Prodded by the Soviet delegate, the International Olympic Committee (IOC) assembly, whose numbers were depleted because many members had left for home, voted by a narrow margin to suspend the credentials. Although this aroused a storm of media protest and in many respects backfired against the Soviets, the decision stood. RFE and RL personnel calmly returned their badges and went back to work covering the games from headquarters they had set up near the Olympic sites. It was not a totally satisfactory arrangement, but they finished the job without missing a beat.

The incident, however, precipitated new tension between the BIB and the Radios. The Radios had not responded as rapidly or as aggressively as BIB thought in order. BIB Chairman Abshire sent a stern cable to the IOC concerning its action and succeeded in inducing Secretary of State Henry Kissinger to follow up with a condemnation of the action. Radio staff were warned by the American Olympic Committee that government intrusion could severely damage the Radios' cause, even though it was common knowledge that the Soviet Union and the East European Olympic committees were in actuality government bodies. The committees representing the non-Communist nations jealously guarded what they regarded as a sacred Olympic principle, that Olympic committees should be totally free of government influence or participation. American Olympic Committee Executive Director F. Don Miller warned RFE and RL personnel that their hopes of obtaining accreditation for the summer Games in Montreal would be in severe jeopardy if it appeared that the U.S. government was taking the lead in promoting their cause. He responded to a letter from Senator Abraham Ribicoff of Connecticut, in which Ribicoff offered to introduce a resolution of support for Radios' cause in the Senate, by warning the senator that "the United States Olympic Committee abhors the entry of blatant politics in any connection with the Olympic Games and we will make a strong effort to resist the incursion of such practices. . . . [Such] a resolution may indicate the involvement of the United States Government, which is tantamount to bringing political pressure to bear on the International Olympic Committee."

Senator Ribicoff introduced his resolution, but Radio personnel played the game cautiously, resisting BIB pressures to become more aggressive and urging BIB to be similarly discreet. They set out as quietly and as guardedly as possible to assure themselves of obtaining credentials for the Montreal Games. It had to be accomplished in a way that could not be challenged. Suspense prevailed almost until the opening ceremony in Montreal. The Soviet Union and its allies at the final pre-Games meeting of the IOC mounted an intensive effort to force the Canadian organizing committee to deny issuance of the badges, which is the final step in the accreditation process.

A protracted debate before the full IOC found the Soviets and their allies attacking furiously in an effort to obtain a majority IOC vote denying the Radios the right to cover the events. It was obvious that the Soviets and their allies had entered the campaign well prepared. In Innsbruck in February and again at Montreal in July the Soviets circulated to Olympic officials and all members of the IOC what they described as a definitive "legal" document, presumably drawn up by one Emil Hoffman, described as a "prominent West German jurist."* "Jurist" Hoffman produced the kind of documentation the Soviets wanted. His brief declared the Radios incompatible with international law: "Any radio station which carries out external broadcasting must belong to the State. Everything else is illegal[;] . . . that applies to Radio Liberty and Radio Free Europe. . . . Since they formally represent neither a nation nor a government, it would appear that for this reason they have no right to exist." Hoffman also argued that the Radios are illegal because "they encroach upon the information policy of the audience countries, although this is irrefutably defined as an internal affair of every state."

The Hoffman document was carefully placed on the seat of each IOC delegate before the debate and vote on the matter of accreditation for the Radios. It was accompanied by a covering note from the USSR Olympic Committee and by letters from Vitaly Smirnov, the Soviet representative on the IOC, and S. Pavlov, president of the USSR National Olympic Committee, making these charges based on the Hoffman brief: RFE was guilty of "interference in the internal affairs of the Soviet state; a violation of the existing international treaties and international law; and in violation of the Convention for Human Rights." The Smirnov and Pavlov letters stressed the presumption that "only national television, radio and newpaper journalists could be accredited. . . . Radio Free Europe journalists could not be accredited as such." National journalists were defined by the Soviets as those "who represent the country in which they are citizens and broadcast or write for the citizens of that country." There were the usual charges in the letters, that Free Europe had distributed false information and malicious slander in order to sow distrust and hostility among countries with different social systems, and that the presence of "Radio Free Europe journalists at the Games would doubtless poison the generally congenial atmosphere at the Games."

The Hoffman document gave the Soviet Union what appeared to be a legal basis for an assault on the Radios' position, but the effort failed. The debate lasted for about three hours. Eight delegates representing the USSR and its allies sounded the Soviet theme. Only two, Douglas Robey of the United States and a Norwegian representative, supported the Radios' posi-

---

*There is some doubt among Western legal circles concerning Hoffman's status as a prominent jurist. An Emil Hoffman residing in West Germany is apparently known in the West as a former Nazi with strong connections with the East. Far from being a lawyer, the Emil Hoffman who is known in West Germany is an international steel salesman.

tions. The full IOC voted 42 to 21 to honor the credentials and issue the badges. The strong affirmative vote ended the debate for the time being.

The attack was renewed, however, almost before the sounds of the closing ceremonies in the stadium in Montreal had faded. This time the Soviets were not trusting to a last-minute vote before the IOC. Their effort was directed at forcing a change in the IOC regulations regarding the issuance of credentials. The new strategy would involve rewriting the IOC accreditation rules. The intention was plainly to bar from obtaining credentials any organization that did not broadcast to its own people in its own country. This would have effectively barred not only the Radios, but the VOA and Deutsche Welle as well. The persistence of the Soviet delegates suggested that in the future applications from the Radios for credentials would be issued, if at all, only after protracted debate with vigorous support from the non-Communist nations.

The depth of the Soviet campaign and the intensity of the effort to deprive two American-owned radio stations an opportunity to cover events with as little ostensible political significance as the quadrennial Olympic Games plainly revealed the near hysteria with which the Western broadcasts were viewed by the Kremlin leadership. The Olympic Games were obviously only a target of opportunity—a big target because they attracted international attention. But the longer-range goal clearly continued to be silencing the transmitters. For that reason, Radio management was forced during the first half of 1976 to devote an inordinate amount of time and energy just to remaining on the air. It was essential to keep the Portuguese and Spanish bases operating and to fight off the challenge at the Olympics, which, if successful, could have formed the basis for a much more broadly based campaign to enforce silence by international political action. It was clear from the Soviet case against accreditation that, were there acceptance by international bodies of the Soviet interpretation of international law, the Radios would be ruled illegal, no better than pirates, and that would surely damage hopes of remaining on German, Portuguese, or Spanish soil and jeopardize support even from the Congress.

Management still had to be concerned first and most intensively, however, with internal problems. Congress was not likely to wait much longer for the completion of consolidation efforts and tight control of the budget. Unified accounting, revised compensation plans and pension programs, reconciliation of divergent work regulations, and union contracts demanded the highest-priorty attention, and unlike the situations in Spain and Portugal and the Olympics, about which relatively little could be done, the internal problems demanded attention leading toward action.

20

Accountability, Nexus, and Fiduciary Responsibility

RELATIONS IN SPAIN and Portugal consumed substantial amounts of management time and energy, as did staving off the Communist attempt to deny the Radios credentials for the Olympic Games, but even though they were life-and-death matters, they were essentially sideshows. In the main tent was the infinitely confusing effort to meld two dissimilar and sometimes antagonistic elements into a smoothly functioning single machine. The two radios had grown up separately, even from their very beginnings in the OPC and the CIA. Their business and management practices, their pay scales and working hours, their benefits programs, and even their organization charts reflected dissimilar backgrounds. Free Europe was an amalgam of loose government controls, a heavy dose of U.S. big business management techniques, adapted to German business and labor laws and East European and German employees. The Radio Liberty Committee originated in a separate compartment of government, developed management practices more oriented to government and applied them in Germany to exiles from the Soviet Union. Limited contact in the upper-management echelons did little to coordinate management techniques and procedures until consolidation began.

Coopers and Lybrand, the accounting firm engaged by the new RFE/RL management to make a thorough analysis of compensation plans, commented at one point early in its study, "You have more pay scales than General Motors"—and that was hardly an exaggeration. There were pay scales for Americans recruited in the United States and sent to Europe, for Germans recruited in Germany to work at home, for East Europeans paid on a dollar scale, and for those paid in Deutsche Marks. There were headquarter scales and executive scales and scales for Portuguese workers at the Gloria base in Portugal. At RL much the same pattern persisted if one substitutes the word *Soviet* for *East European*. Housing was furnished for some employees and not for others, and there was no consistency with regard to education for children, home leave, sick leave, and vacation policies. There was even a problem with 25-year service awards. RL had granted the equivalent of approximately DM 600, or almost $200 in the form of a watch or cash to 25-year employees. In the first year of consolidation, the question arose, whether the awards should also be given to the 25-year personnel at RFE.

The most paralyzing complication, however, arose out of the different accounting systems: cash accounting for Free Europe and accrual accounting for RL. Dollars in the two sets of books had different values, and trying to reconcile the accounts was a nightmare for financial and accounting staff. It made adhering to a unified budget almost an impossibility and reporting to the BIB or to congressional committees almost an exercise in futility. The continuing employee protests about pensions could not be silenced without unified pension plans and hospital and medical benefits, and the systems of benefits were nearly as complicated as pay scales.

There was only one answer that promised a solution that would not be difficult to achieve: merger. It would not make unification and reorganization work instantly, but at least management would then have the tools that would enable it to work through one company rather than two and establish one set of policies rather than two. There would still be bitter clashes ahead with employees and problems with setting up new systems of accounting for the merged company, but at least with one company there was a chance of achieving quicker results.

The Eisenhower Commission had considered merger and had recommended against it. The identities of the two Radios were so precious, the commission had concluded, that they should be protected from the risk of loss in a merged corporation. The GAO had suggested taking a serious look at merging and the BIB encouraged it. Radio management was solidly in favor because almost all members of the executive staff were so frustrated by trying to reconcile the differences that they looked to merger as the only logical possibility to ease the pain. RL personnel had actively fought merger when consolidation was first suggested because they were fearful of being overpowered in the new corporation by the larger, more aggressive Free Europe. Now, however, under consolidated management, they no longer were sufficiently independent to resist.

The decision to merge was made by management in the early spring of 1976. Both Radios' boards of directors agreed that merger was the most logical course of action. Management engaged the Washington law firm of Hogan and Hartson to suggest a plan and draw up the papers. Counsel recommended dissolving the two existing corporations, Free Europe, Inc., and the

Radio Liberty Committee, Inc., and creating a new one that would absorb the assets and liabilities of the old and assume obligations under the existing contracts. There were some 2000 separate licenses and contracts that had to be assigned by the old corporations to the new one. The two Radios were to continue to function as operating divisions of the new corporation with their own program departments and audience and talent research departments, but for all other services they would draw on the resources of the merged corporation.

The decision to merge led inevitably to consideration of a new corporate name. There had been dissatisfaction for years with both the Radio Free Europe and Radio Liberty titles, particularly the former. RL had escaped much of the skepticism about its name when it had changed from Radio Liberation to Radio Liberty more than ten years earlier. The appropriateness of "Radio Free Europe" was questioned, though, in Congress, by the Eisenhower Commission, by the North Atlantic Parliament and by the GAO. The most persuasive suggestion was for attaching the modifier *free* to the word *radio*, rather than to *Europe*, in keeping with Free Europe's abandonment of its earlier hard-line policy.

The Eisenhower Commission, after careful consideration, came down on the side of retaining the traditional names, which had become bywords in Eastern Europe and the USSR after many years of broadcasting. BIB Chairman Abshire at one time considered calling the merged corporation "Radio Human Rights." Others recommended "International Broadcasting Corporation," "International Broadcasting Service," or "Overseas Broadcasting Corporation." A Senate subcommittee urged a change to "East-West Broadcasting Corporation." Some consideration was given to paralleling the name "Corporation for Public Broadcasting," calling the merged Radios the "Corporation for International Broadcasting." Before any action was taken, however, it was noted that the radio corporation would then be referred to as "CIB." This was a little too close for comfort to "CIA." Memories of *Ramparts*, Senator Case, Senator Fulbright, and the stormy period of the early 1970s quickly put an end to further consideration. Title searches were run on "Overseas Broadcasting Corporation," "International Broadcasting Service," and "International Broadcasting Corporation," but in each case there were conflicts that could have caused legal complications. The ultimate decision was to retain the RFE and RL designations for the operating divisions. Too much energy had been expended on building those names. They had acquired too much loyalty in their target areas to abandon them now. The parent corporation was incorporated under the title RFE/RL, Inc. Awkward as it is, and difficult to roll off the tongue, it still describes the corporation, and it offered no problems in obtaining legal clearance.

Merger documents were completed, new articles of incorporation signed and filed, and the 2000 leases and licenses assigned to the new corporation by

September 30, 1976. On the next day Free Europe, Inc. and the Radio Liberty Committee ceased to exist, after 27 and 25 years of life, respectively.

However, while furnishing the tools for a more efficient attack on the horrendous organizational problems facing the new corporation, the merger also stimulated new conflicts with the Congress and the BIB. The words *accountability* and *nexus* suddenly came into popular usage in conversations about RFE/RL, Inc. BIB personnel argued passionately, apparently with considerable congressional support, that the new articles of incorporation did not spell out in sufficient detail the nature of the accountability of the directors and officers of the corporation to the government of the United States from whom it received its operating funds. The question had never been raised in connection with the predecessor corporations, whose articles of incorporation made no mention of the U.S. government and who were, if anything, encouraged to maintain identities clearly separated from government. That theory, however, was now obviously to be consigned to the wastebasket, along with the abandoned corporate charters.

The question of accountability of the new corporation to the U.S. government came to the fore when Abshire wrote to Senator John Sparkman, chairman of the Senate Foreign Relations Committee, on September 24, contending:

> The Board believes that these documents [the articles of incorporation] should spell out the role, duties and obligations (including fiduciary responsibility) of the new corporate directors and should contain an adequate definition of the responsibilities of corporate directors and officers with regard to the use of funds under the Board for International Broadcasting Act.[1]

The chairman of the powerful Senate Foreign Relations Committee took the cue. In replying on September 30, Sparkman furnished the leverage required to project the new corporate charter into status as a major issue of tension in congressional circles. Thus his letter became a powerful club in the hands of BIB directors and staff in their dealings with corporate directors and officers.

Sparkman's letter started mildly. The Senator pointed to the fact that Congress had appropriated more than $717 million over the years, including more than $53 million for the current year. Then he wrote:

> Given this preponderance of Federal funding, it should be clear that the corporation's future activities must be conducted solely within the framework established by the Board for International Broadcasting Act of 1971, as amended, and that the new corporate charter and by-laws should explicitly acknowledge the accountability of corporate officers to the Federal instrumentality created by the Act—namely the BIB.

He concluded, "I would view with grave misgivings a corporate charter which failed clearly to acknowledge the Board's unqualified authority to review and regulate the Radios' management and activities."[2] The word *regulate* added new muscle to the process of oversight and certainly threatened the "professional integrity and credibility of the Radios" that the Eisenhower Commission had so carefully sought to protect. And use of "accountability" furnished a rallying point for a campaign to insist on a clause in the new corporate charter that would spell out the responsibility of corporate officers and directors to the BIB.

A day later Senator Charles Percy, who had been one of the Radios' strongest supporters over the years, wrote a note to Abshire supporting Sparkman's point of view: "I would like to go on record as endorsing completely the sentiments expressed in Senator Sparkman's letter to you."[3]

It was now evident that merger was a mixed blessing from the corporation's point of view in regard to its effort to maintain some degree of management independence and responsibility. The new charter presented an attractive target. The defunct incorporation documents and bylaws of the predecessor corporations had never been challenged. But the simple act of forming a new corporation and registering a new set of documents called attention to the charter and invited attacks because of its high degree of visibility.

Stuart Phillip Ross, the Hogan and Hartson attorney who had served as RFE and RL's legal counsel in establishing the new corporation, was not impressed with the arguments used by Senator Sparkman. He felt that the "merger in no way affects the Board for International Broadcasting's statutory authority over RFE/RL" and argued that "there are now in existence effective fiduciary standards applicable to the corporation's directors and officers." He pointed out that "inherent in the grant process is the ability of the Board to set such terms and conditions as it deemed necessary to ensure that the grants are used for the purposes for which they are made." He described the grant contracts as "binding contractual commitments on the part of grantor and grantee alike."[4] Ross's comments had no impact either on the BIB or on members of the Congress. The voice of a single attorney does not carry much weight when his opinion is in direct conflict with ranking members of the Congress of the United States.

His response, of course, did not answer the "nexus" question, which was high on the list of concerns of the BIB staff. They argued that RFE/RL, Inc., was a self-perpetuating corporation (like a fishing club) that elected its own directors and was responsible only to itself. They contended that the corporation's benefactor, the U.S. government, should have some clearly articulated role in the selection process, not only for directors but for officers as well.

The new corporation, thus, was barely a day old before it was involved in a controversy that threatened to change the fundamental nature of the relationships with government that had prevailed during the lifetime of its predecessors. The Congress and the agency it created were clearly going to use a firmer hand and impose a tougher rein than had the CIA or the Department of State. The question facing the board of the newly constructed corporation, on its first organizational meeting on October 14, 1976, was whether it could resist the pressure or would have to yield by amending its corporate charter and bylaws almost before the ink was dry on the documents creating it.

The requirement that accountability and fiduciary responsibility be in some formal way spelled out in the articles of incorporation of the new RFE/RL had been suggested first at a meeting of the BIB directors in April 1976. BIB staff member Anatole Shub had raised the issue as a question: Since, under the operating trust form of merger that was being considered by the Radio management, the directors of the trust would also be the members. "Would these part-time directors be financially responsible?" he had asked.[5]

Abshire, presiding, had agreed that it was "important to establish fiduciary responsiblity; one could not expect part-time private citizens to assume it." That was all that had been said except for the discussion concerning the advisability of establishing procedures under which BIB members would attend RFE/RL directors' meetings. Attention had been called to the necessity to end the "adversary relationship" between the Radio management and the federal authorities and to the possibility that harmony might be restored in some part if invitations to BIB personnel to attend RFE/RL board meetings were both issued and honored.

The matters of fiduciary responsibility and accountability had come up again at the July 7 and 8 meeting of the board. This time it had been board member Thomas Quinn who had sounded the theme. He had expressed the view that the corporate boards consisted wholly of members appointed by other members. They represented, Quinn had said, only themselves as individuals and there were no real shareholders, so the members were responsible to nobody. Because the U.S. government furnished all the funding required, it was in fact the only shareholder. The corporate boards, therefore, "should be responsible as well as responsive to the BIB." The key word now had become *responsible*. Somewhat petulantly, Quinn had added that the corporate boards seemed to believe they could take positions on issues without recognizing "accountability" to anyone.[6] Quinn's hard-line approach had followed a discussion on employee compensation in Munich that in turn had been triggered by statements made on the floor of the Senate by Majority Leader Mike Mansfield and Appropriations Committee Chairman John Pastore. The two Senators had castigated the Radios for paying Munich employees what they regarded as outrageous salaries.

The provocation for the grim warnings to Radio corporation personnel was a story on RFE and RL compensation practices that had appeared in the *New York Times* a few days earlier. *Times* correspondent David Binder had reported that a middle-level Radio executive in Munich received an annual salary of $67,000 and a secretary more than $36,000.[7] The information on which Binder's story was based had appeared in an unpublished draft of a GAO report on the Radios that was delivered to BIB staff and Radio management several months prior to formal release on June 25 for purposes of eliciting comments and checking facts. The sentence concerning the two presumed salaries had later been deleted on the orders of the controller general because the figures were badly distorted. The totals had included a number of nonsalary items including Social Security payments, pension contributions, hospital and medical benefits, and housing allowances. Published figures concerning government salaries had not included items of this type. Stated as salary, however, the figures had substantially exceeded government norms and had been quickly described by Senators Mansfield and Pastore on the floor of the Senate as "shocking."

The fact that the two senators had called attention to the distorted compensation figures had been seized upon by BIB personnel to make their case that Radio executives were not quick enough to respond to BIB suggestions. The leadership positions of the two senators made their support vital to obtaining further appropriations. Senator Pastore had expressed his outrage when he told the Senate that "the abuses reach the point of becoming almost scandalous"; he had gone so far as to question whether Senator Fulbright might not have been right a number of years previously when he had asked whether RFE had not outlived its usefulness.[8]

The incident had been used by BIB staff as another demonstration that fiduciary responsibility could be achieved only under more active oversight. BIB personnel had adopted the role of the austere parent admonishing the wayward child but willing to forgive, provided it received absolute assurances there would be no more transgressions.

Little more had been heard of the issue until Abshire wrote his September 1976 letter to Senator Sparkman. BIB Executive Director Walter Roberts had requested on a number of occasions that he be kept informed of progress of drafting the new articles of incorporation so that he could be sure they would accord with government legal requirements. He had also delivered a formal request for a copy of the document as soon as it was completed. There had been no further formal demands that either "fiduciary responsibility" or "accountability" be included in the incorporation documents.

Both Abshire and Roberts attended the October 14 meeting of the newly merged RFE/RL board at which the documents were formally approved and a new corporation organized. Abshire spoke at length informally to the directors of the new corporation about the problems that they and the BIB faced jointly. "Fiduciary responsibility" was never mentioned, as such, but Abshire was blunt in calling attention to the fact that Congress was going to be exceedingly tough and demanding about budgets and resolute about insisting on more active oversight, even to clearing line items on the RFE/RL budget.[9] Abshire's message was a clear warning to RFE/RL directors that Radio management would have to yield to tougher and more detailed oversight if appropriations were to continue and if oversight prerogatives were not to be strengthened by legislation rather than by persuasion.

The warning was more explicitly spelled out in the BIB's third annual report to the president and the Congress, which was drafted during the fall of 1976. The report called attention to "inherent or potential ambiguities in the new institutional structure." The "professional independence" that the Eisenhower Commission had so jealously guarded was redefined as "journalistic independence," which the report described as both "unique and precious." The report also specified that "it is the essential responsibility of Radio management . . . to maintain such professional independence and integrity," but it inserted a clause that indicated in no uncertain terms who was in charge. The responsibility of which it wrote was to be maintained "on behalf of the Board."[10]

New oversight responsibilities for the board were spelled out in detail. Quoting Abshire's speech to the RFE/RL board on October 14, the report noted that the BIB chairman had declared the board's ultimate responsibility "in those areas of decision making related to resource allocation and utilization and long-range policy and also key personnel appointments."[11] On the last page of the fourth chapter of the report a sentence was quoted from Abshire's letter to Senator Sparkman, asserting that corporate documents "should spell out the role, duties and obligations (including fiduciary responsibility) of the new corporate directors and officers with regard to the use of funds under the BIB Act."[12]

One RFE/RL director, Douglas Manship, the publisher of the Baton Rouge *State Times and Morning Advocate*, was sufficiently disturbed by the conclusions drawn in Chapter 4 of the report that he wrote to Abshire to express his concern: "Regretfully, I feel it is the purpose of this section of the BIB's third annual report to lay the groundwork and to endorse and recommend the elimination of the RFE/RL Corporate Board under the new combined charter and to receive statutory authority for the BIB Board to manage the Radios on a day by day basis." If such an assumption of power by the BIB were to come about, Manship concluded, "the Radio's integrity will then be no more." The consequence would include providing "Eastern European governments a means of attacking the journalistic integrity of the Radios . . . and enabling them to state that the Radios are only a propaganda arm of the United States Government. . . ."[13]

Manship did not have long to wait for his prediction to come true. Hearings on the BIB fiscal year 1978 budget were called for April 1 by the Senate Foreign Relations Subcommittee under the chairmanship of Senator George McGovern of South Dakota. Since President Jimmy Carter's Democratic administration was in power, replacing President Ford's Republican administration, Abshire had resigned the BIB chairmanship several weeks earlier. At the

McGovern subcommittee hearings, the BIB was represented by Acting Chairman Thomas Quinn, backed up by Executive Director Walter Roberts and other members of the board staff. I was there to represent the Radios. Toward what appeared to be the conclusion of a somewhat perfunctory hearing, Senator Claiborne Pell of Rhode Island asked Roberts, who had played a secondary role in the session to that point, if he had any comments to offer on BIB–RFE/RL relationships. Roberts produced a carefully drafted document that he proceeded to read. He quoted from the Sparkman letter and from Senator Percy's endorsement of the Sparkman point of view. He then cited Roche's suggestion in the 1977 annual report that corporate directors should be selected by the BIB. Roberts complained that the board had responsibility with no authority.

Senator McGovern then provided the opening for Roberts to make a specific recommendation. "Do you think, Mr. Roberts," the senator asked, "that it makes sense to revise the legislation so that we provide that members of the corporate board could be taken from members of the BIB . . . to eliminate at least some of the confusion as to who is in charge of oversight responsibility?" Roberts had two alternative suggestions: either that the BIB be enlarged by absorbing two, three, or four members of the corporate board, thus eliminating the corporate board and giving the new enlarged BIB responsibility for both functions, or "that the corporation be immediately converted into an advisory board like the U.S.A. Advisory Commission. . . ." It was instantly clear that the subcommittee chairman approved of the suggestion for a single board; he observed that the double layer—of BIB and the corporate board—insulated the BIB from policy decisions being made with reference to Radio operations. There was no doubt either where Senator Pell stood. "If he [the chairman] introduces a Subcommittee report to move along the line we have suggested, I know I would be strongly supportive of it."[14]

It was only days before an amendment to the BIB Act of 1973 that quickly acquired the designation "the Pell Amendment" was attached to the BIB appropriation for fiscal year 1978. It specified that no grant could be made under terms of the act unless the certificate of incorporation of RFE/RL, Inc., were amended to specify that "the Board of Directors of RFE/RL shall consist of members of the Board for International Broadcasting and of no other members," and that such a board should make all major policy decisions governing the operations of the Radios. Passage of the amendment would place corporate board members in the unenviable position of being forced to amend their own charter and promptly resign, once the amendment had been approved. The penalty would be no grant from Congress and thus no funds with which to operate.

The subcommittee approved the amendment and sent it on to the full committee, which likewise approved with no dissent. It was assumed that the House would follow the Senate's lead so that by the end of the summer the

RFE/RL board would cease to exist as an independent entity. The corporation would still nominally hold its charter, but its board would now be identical with the BIB. The BIB would have the authority to appoint and fix the compensation of managerial officers and employees. The staff of BIB would thus be in a position to exercise ultimate managerial responsibility. The president of the United States would appoint members of the enlarged board, subject to Senate confirmation. Thus would "fiduciary responsibility" and "accountability" be clearly established.

The corporate board responded at its May 10 meeting. It passed a resolution pointing out that the determination of an appropriate structure for RFE/RL involved fundamental questions of public policy and the national interest. It urged the Congress, therefore, to take no action on structural changes "until the important public policy questions affecting the operations of the corporation had been fully studied in connection with the Executive Branch, the Board for International Broadcasting, and the Directors of this corporation."[15]

Corporate board members had no doubts that the public interest would be better served by maintaining the Radios at arm's length from government. They were fearful that a centrally directed corporation under the aegis of the presidentially appointed board would suffer a severe loss of credibility in target areas and dilute the impact of broadcasts, changing them from independent and objective views of private citizens to official or at least semiofficial government pronouncements. The considerable success of the Radios over the years, they felt, had derived from the principle of independence from government enunciated by George Kennan in 1948 and 1949 and supported by CIA leadership over the years.

There were elements on the Washington scene favorable to the RFE/RL defense, including Zbigniew Brzezinski, director of the NSC. Abshire's resignation had been prompted by his recognition that the new president would appoint his own man as chairman. The appointment went to John Gronouski.* A combined effort by the White House and the RFE/RL board succeeded in convincing Gronouski that it would be unwise to move toward support of the Pell Amendment before he had an opportunity to observe for himself how well or badly the system was working. He assented and further agreed to urge members of the Congress to withhold support until he had had an opportunity to determine for himself whether or not he could recommend the enactment of such a change in the established structure.

It was Senator Humphrey, however, who saved the day for the private corporation. He had been absent from the Foreign Relations Committee on

---

*He had participated in developing the recommendation that had led to the creation of the BIB and the separate corporate structures in the double-tier relationship that was now the subject of such bitter controversy.

the day that the Pell Amendment had been sent on to the full Senate, but he was determined that it would not pass. On the floor of the Senate he delivered a ringing defense of maintaining the separation between the BIB and RFE/RL, and he won a lopsided victory. The Pell Amendment died, but only for the time being. Gronouski had promised that he would report back to the Senate. If what he observed satisfied him, he presumably would not press for new legislation. However, if problems continued, the Pell Amendment could quickly be revived.

The RFE/RL board responded to the victory on the Senate floor and pressure from Gronouski by adopting an amendment to its corporate documents, placing the BIB chairman on its nominating committee and giving him an absolute right of veto over all nominees. It also made him an *ex officio* member of the board and extended an invitation to him and to Executive Director Roberts to attend all meetings. It later amended its corporate documents again to grant BIB participation in the selection of a broad range of executive personnel. At BIB insistence it moved its executive headquarters from Washington to Munich, thus for the first time since the birth of the two corporations removing its senior executive corps from a U.S. site.

The erosion of the corporation's independence and the corresponding increase of the BIB's power were not enough, however, to satisfy the critics. The two-level structure simply did not look symmetrical to members of Congress or to the transition team that studied the Radios for the new Reagan administration, which took office on January 20, 1981. The BIB staff was still not satisfied that it had sufficient power to maintain "active oversight," and changes in the corporation's articles of incorporation did nothing to satisfy the demands for "fiduciary responsibility." The Reagan administration quickly declared itself in favor of managing the Radios through a single board of directors. Frank Shakespeare, a former USIA director, was appointed the BIB's new chairman, and he campaigned actively for a single board in which all authority would rest.

Senator Pell reintroduced his amendment. It passed the subcommittee without dissent and the full committee sent it on to the Senate. A companion bill proceeded through the House of Representatives with similar ease. RFE/RL directors argued that so important a public policy question should not be enacted into law without public hearings, but their protests were in vain. In the autumn of 1982, six years after the merged corporation had been chartered and organized, the directors were forced to vote for dissolution. The corporations that had been founded more than 30 years earlier with a commitment from government officials to keep them independent of government were no longer independent. They were now responsible to a board appointed by the president—a far cry from the structure that had been recommended by George Kennan in 1949 and maintained by CIA leadership through more than 20 years of cautious oversight that maintained strict budgetary controls in CIA hands but, within only very general policy guidances, left editorial and program responsibility to Radio management.

Cord Meyer, who had been the senior CIA officer overseeing Radio operations for almost two decades starting in 1954, wrote in a syndicated column in November 1981, that the Pell Amendment would not only "vastly increase his [Frank Shakespeare's] own managerial authority over the Radios, but the administration will be extending government control over an institution whose private character is essential to its work. . . . [The] able American professionals who direct the Radio programming in Munich, the brilliant émigré desk chiefs, and many concerned State Department officials are all fearful that the uniquely successful American effort to reach the people behind the iron curtain is now endangered.[16]

Edward W. Barrett, who had been a member of the Free Europe Committee Corporation in 1949 and 1950, assistant secretary of state for public affairs in the early 1950s, a member of the Eisenhower Commission in 1973 and 1974, and had been elected to the Free Europe Board in 1975, was even more blunt in condemning the move. In a column he wrote for the "Op Ed" page of the *New York Times* on July 24, 1982. Barrett wrote:

> A Congressional conference, without benefit of hearings, is rushing headlong into a move—the Pell Amendment—that, despite claims to the contrary, amounts to federalizing those Radios under a Board appointed by the President, a move that would alter the special status that has made them so effective. That amendment would shatter a subtle but vital distinction: that of free radios assisted but not directly run by the government, serving as a surrogate press in which Russian, Polish and other broadcasters provided captive compatriots with domestic news and views otherwise kept from them.[17]

Barrett charged that agitation for change had come from members of the BIB who yearned for a more direct hand in operations and from members of Congress who had said they favored the merger of the Radios into the VOA. He described the proposed Pell Amendment as "an awkwardly drawn piece of legislation that would abolish the independent citizens board and substitute a slightly enlarged Board for International Broadcasting" and added that the legislation would leave "an oversight board in effect to oversee itself."

In an earlier letter to John S. Hayes, who was the chairman of the RFE/RL board at that time, Barrett had insisted that he would resign on the date the Pell Amendment became effective. In that letter he wrote "we come to appreciate, that a vital part of this operation was the preservation of a measure of independence for the broadcaster and a degree of insulation for the White House and the Department of State ensuring that they were not to be held responsible for every word broadcast over the Radios."[18]

Support for the Pell Amendment, however, was so strong and the opposition so scattered that it was quickly enacted into law, and reorganization steps began. President Glenn Ferguson resigned. Executive Vice-President Ralph Walter, who had joined the Free Europe staff in 1951, 31 years earlier, was terminated; former Senator James Buckley of New York was offered and accepted the presidency. Douglas Manship's term as successor to John Hayes as chairman of the RFE/RL Board was terminated on the date that the RFE/RL Board was dissolved. The two-tiered structure had been demolished; there could no longer be questions about "fiduciary responsibility" or "accountability." They were now the sole responsibility of BIB, and "active oversight" was no longer a matter of concern. The BIB staff members were now in a position to manage the Radios directly rather than oversee a separate corporation.

NOTES

1. Letter from David Abshire to Senator John Sparkman, dated September 14, 1976, written on letterhead of BIB. Copy in Archives of the Hoover Institution. 5 pp., copies distributed to members of RFE/RL board by Walter Roberts, executive director, BIB.

2. Letter from Senator John Sparkman to David Abshire, dated September 30, 1976, in reply to letter from Abshire dated September 26, 1976, written on letterhead of United States Senate. Copy in Archives of the Hoover Institution. 2 pp., copies sent to RFE/RL board by Roberts with covering letter dated October 4.

3. Letter from Senator Charles Percy to David Abshire, October 1, 1976. Copy in Archives of the Hoover Institution. 1p.

4. Memorandum from Stuart Philip Ross to Sig Mickelson, October 9, 1976. Copy in Archives of the Hoover Institution. 4 pp.

5. BIB, Minutes of meeting, April 14, 15, 1976, p. 19. Unpublished MS, copy in Archives of the Hoover Institution.

6. BIB, Minutes of meeting, July 7–8, 1976, pp. 5–6. Unpublished MS, copy in Archives of the Hoover Institution.

7. David Binder, "Two U.S.-run Radios Chided on Salary—Report Finds Excessively High Pay Scale in Stations Beamed to Soviet Bloc," *New York Times*, July 2, 1976. p. 4.

8. U.S. Congress, Senate, excerpts from the statements by Senators Pastore and Mansfield, in *Congressional Record* (Senate), S11478. 94th Congress, 2nd Sess., July 2, 1976. These excerpts include the Pastore and Mansfield statements, the David Binder text from the *New York Times* of the same day, and RFE/RL comments. Copy in Archives of the Hoover Institution.

9. David Abshire, informal talk to members of RFE/RL board at Century Association, New York, unpublished copy of rough transcript, dated October 14, 1976, Archives of the Hoover Institution.

10. BIB, *Third Annual Report* (Washington, D.C.: U.S. Government Printing Office, 1976), p. 49.

11. *Ibid.*, p. 44.

12. *Ibid.*, p. 45.

13. Douglas Manship to David Abshire, letter dated February 15, 1977. Copy in Archives of the Hoover Institution. 3 pp.

14. U.S. Congress, Senate, Subcommittee on International Operations, Committee on Foreign Relations, excerpts from testimony, April 1, 1977. 95th Cong., 1st Sess., 1977, p. 47. Archives of Hoover Institution. These excerpts also include full testimony of Walter Roberts.

15. RFE/RL Board of Directors, Minutes of meeting, May 10, 1977, unpublished MS copy in Archives of the Hoover Institution.

16. Cord Meyer, "Bureaucrats Seek Control over Radio Free Europe," *Baltimore Evening Sun*, November 20, 1981, Op Ed page. Copy available in Archives of the Hoover Institution.

17. Edward W. Barrett, "Spoiling Success," *New York Times*, July 24, 1982, Op Ed page. Copy on file in Archives of Hoover Institution.

18. Letter from Edward W. Barrett to John S. Hayes, dated August 17, 1981. Copy in Archives of the Hoover Institution.

21
The 1976 October
Revolution

M OST OF RFE/RL'S problems over the years have been of relatively short
duration. They were hardly ephemeral, but they came and went
within a measurable period of time and, for the most part, the causes, immediate effects, and the eventual solutions can be clearly identified within a given
span of time. Amcomlib's futile efforts to create a Coordinating Center of the
Immigration in 1951 and 1952 gave way to a board decision in 1953 to go
ahead and broadcast as Radio Liberation, with or without the émigrés. Free
Europe's trial by fire during the Polish and Hungarian riots of 1956 ended
abruptly after the Hungarian Service was absolved of the blame for inciting a
revolt, as a result of analytical reports published in the winter of 1957. The
internal rebellion at RFE resulting from dissension in the Czechoslovak Service in 1960 was put down by firm management action within a few weeks.
The *Ramparts* revelation set off a string of exposés of near-disastrous conse-
quences, but theoretically the two Radios could breathe more easily after the
passage of the Board for International Broadcasting Act in 1973. Consolidation and merger were painful and sometimes grim, but eventually the staff
was shrunk by almost 30 percent and the two disparate corporations moved
forward together. In each case, decisive management action or demonstrations of governmental support succeeded in putting to rest the destructive
forces that would have continued to be disruptive or even, as in the case of
the Fulbright hearings, to have caused dissolution of the enterprise.

An internal problem within the Russian Service of RL, however, has been
causing a constant nagging pain and occasional convulsions since the idea of
forming a U.S.-supported council of the emigration was first proposed in the

policy sections of the Departments of Defense and State, the CIA, and the OPC. The fruition of the dream of U.S. planners depended upon obtaining cooperation of the quarrelsome melange of disparate elements among the immigrants from the USSR. Chapter 7 describes how the American management was forced to decide whether to continue the endless charade with the constantly shifting forces of émigrés or simply go ahead to implement their plans with or without support; history shows that they went ahead. However, the squabbling elements continued to squabble. Sargeant throttled the efforts of the NTS to disrupt the project by decreeing that no known NTS personnel could be employed without renouncing NTS objectives and pledging to do no proselytizing on RL premises. Vigorous enforcement of the no-nonsense decree permitted RL to expand its program services, improve quality, and reach for a constantly expanding audience. But the progress that was made was only in spite of continuing undercurrents of dissension among members of the Russian Service.

Russian emigrants as a general rule have left the Soviet Union in waves. The timing of the waves has depended on circumstances in the USSR. A first wave of several hundred thousand anti-Communists fled during the 1917–22 period. Many were intellectuals, academicians, writers, and political leaders who were willing at any cost to avoid living under the Communist regime. The largest number went to Paris; many went to New York. By the late 1940s a considerable percentage had been assimilated into Western life.

Then came the second wave. Shortly after Hitler's invasion of the Soviet Union in 1941, they started passing across the borders into Germany as prisoners of war, slave laborers, displaced persons, and a limited number as escapees. Some prisoners of war joined German units and went back to fight again on Russian soil against their former comrades-in-arms. In all, between 8 and 11 million refugees from the Soviet Union were somewhere in the West shortly after the war had ended. Many were forcibly repatriated, but it was from among those who remained, many of them in Germany, that the American committee tried to create a unified central organization.

The first wave had consisted largely of intellectuals who quarreled with communism and the Communist leadership on rational grounds, but the members of the second wave were soldiers, both officers and enlisted men, laborers, middle-level managers, and their motivations for remaining in the West were more emotional than intellectual. They had lived under Stalin's rule of terror and had observed the brutal tactics of the secret police. They had experienced the insecurity of life in a police state and were accustomed to suspicion, secrecy, stealth, and conspiracy. Among them, however, there was little of the competence and experience in the art of communication that had characterized the first wave. They drifted along with their strong-minded leaders into the various groupings, extending from far right to moderate left, from the NTS through Vlasovites and Malgounites to Mensheviks.

RL was relatively calm through the years from 1954, when management cracked down hard on the NTS, until the late 1960s, when the third wave started, as a trickle at first, turning into a mass movement in the early 1970s. Many of the emigrants in the third wave were Jews who had seized on the opportunity to leave when the Kremlin first loosened the bonds that kept them in the Soviet Union. In this wave there were scientists, authors, professionals, journalists, editors, and people from the theater; many of them were experienced communicators. Their motives for leaving were different from those of both the first and second waves. Many left because they saw what they considered the prospect for a better life outside the Soviet Union. They had lived most or all of their lives under a Communist regime and had learned in some measure to adjust to it, to roll with the punches. Some had achieved positions of prestige and importance in Soviet academe, the theater, or in publishing fields. To a vastly greater extent than the second wave, they had the talent and experience to write, produce, and voice the programs that RL was broadcasting back to the Soviet Union.

The third-wave members had another gift that was lacking in the second wave. They had lived in the Soviet Union long enough and recently enough to understand the people in a 1970s environment, their interests and habits, their patterns of life, and, even more important, their language. Language in any culture changes so rapidly that the diction of two decades earlier may sound stilted and archaic. The newcomers could speak 1970s Russian.

RL management had been desperate for staff renewal for a number of years. There had been some staff accretions through the years but these had been largely through the employment of Russians who had been in the West for some years. What was sought now was new émigrés. Some critics contend that RL grabbed too fast when the management saw the beginning of the third wave appearing in the West. They were fearful that the Kremlin would quickly close the spigot, shutting off the flow of new talent, so they took what was available, not being able to foresee that not only the quantity but the quality of the flow would continue to increase.

The hasty action proved to be a mistake. Although some marginally competent newcomers were added to the staff, their employment quickly stirred the latent prejudices and stimulated a tendency toward disputation among the older employees. The most emotionally charged undercurrent was that the new employees were Jewish, not traditional Russians, practitioners of the Orthodox faith unified by an almost mystical sense of loyalty to Great Russia. They came from what appeared to be a different Russia; they had been Sovietized and even spoke what appeared to be a different language.

There might have been some hope for peaceful assimilation of the newcomers had not crisis intervened on the American side of the Atlantic. It was about the time that the recruits began appearing in substantial numbers that Senator Fulbright opened the 1971 Foreign Relations Committee hearing on the future of both Free Europe and the Radio Liberty Committee. The hearings increased the feeling of insecurity among the Munich staff and aroused further suspicion of the new wave. Subsequent programs to consolidate, reduce staff, and cut expenses produced a pervading sense of doubt, even of doom. The climate was ideal for all the old prejudices to erupt and shake RL's whole organization.

In 1975 the consolidation effort reached a climax. As has been related, the old Radio Liberty Committee in effect ceased to exist as a wholly independent unit, being absorbed into a new conglomerate with RFE. Worse, RL personnel were forced to evacuate their safe cocoon in their headquarters building in Munich and move in with the RFE staff in the Free Europe building—only a mile and a half away in linear measure, but an incalculable distance away in terms of tradition, culture, language, and religion.

It was a difficult move to make. Staff members were uprooted from an environment in which they felt comfortable and thrust into an unfamiliar building that was too small to contain both services without crowding. RL's separate headquarters had served as a protective haven, but now protection was being removed. Even the languages spoken in the corridors would be different. English and the six East European languages would mix with the Russian of RL; the canteen would be shared, as would studios and tape rooms. A combined newsroom was to be divided by a glass wall into RL and RFE sections, the separation serving as a kind of security blanket, until the wall came down a few months later.

The move took place in November 1975. There was an undercurrent of hostility that manifested itself from time to time during the early months of 1976, but no violent outbreak occurred until late summer. Then, in fairly rapid succession, there occurred two incidents that could conceivably have destroyed the service or so crippled it that much of its confidence would have been seriously impaired. Both incidents appeared minor, their significance almost unrecognizable to an outsider. The first occurred in August 1976 at a meeting of the cultural section of the Russian program service. The principal protagonist, from a traditional Great Russian point of view, was Victoria Monditsch Dreving, known to the staff as Vicky Semenova. Monditsch Dreving had been removed by German army personnel from her home in Rostov Don as a teenager early in the war. She was one of the first to join the Russian service staff at RL in 1952, one year before its first broadcast. Her role was to serve as an announcer. Although she had not been in the USSR since the early 1940s, she embodied all the attitudes that make up the Russian mystique, including support for Russianism and the Orthodox church.

The chief target of Monditsch Dreving's ire, because he so neatly represented the characteristics of the third wave of emigration, was Vladimir Matusevitch. Matusevitch was Jewish. He possessed a doctoral degree from the University of Moscow, specializing in Russian culture, on which topic he had written extensively for Soviet journals, and he had held a high position in government-supported cultural activities. Only in the fact that he was not an émigré, but rather a defector, was he nonrepresentative. While on a cultural mission to Norway in 1968, he made a calculated decision not to return to a nation for which he held no respect. Obtaining permission to remain in the West was not difficult, since he was able to claim U.S. citizenship through the fact that he was born in New York in 1936 when his father was serving as a U.S. representative for Amtorg, the Soviet trading agency. After his defection, Matusevitch spent some time as a Scandinavian correspondent for RL in Copenhagen and moved to Munich in 1973. In 1974 he was promoted to managing editor of the Russian program service.

The new appointment placed him squarely in Monditsch Dreving's line of fire. The Russian traditionalists were suspicious of the newcomers for a variety of reasons. The new wave, they felt, had been Sovietized by living under the Kremlin regime. They had left the Soviet Union, not out of idealistic motives, but to find what they considered a better life in the West. Some, including Matusevitch, had served the Kremlin. Finally, many were Jewish, not worshippers in the traditional Russian Orthodox Christian church.

Monditsch Dreving began to complain at staff meetings that RL's Russian service lacked a "Russian spirit." In her complaints she had strong support from many others who felt the same way, including members of the influential NTS. At the critical August 1975 meeting of the cultural staff of the Russian service she repeated her complaint concerning the "Russian spirit." Matusevitch answered, according to reports circulating after the meeting, that "our broadcasts are not for the Russian people, but for the Soviet people . . . in the Russian language." He could not have struck a more sensitive nerve. His callous putdown of the "Russian spirit" infuriated the traditionalists and narrowed the focus on the troublesome issues dividing the two factions in the Russian service.

Monditsch Dreving immediately took the offensive, sending off a vigorous memorandum to members of Congress, the BIB, the RL board, and senior corporate executives. Munich executives reprimanded her lightly for carrying her personal vendetta to such lengths, but they took no definitive action.

The badly divided staff continued to turn out broadcasts, but in a hostile environment that showed no signs of moderating. The NTS publication *Possev* reported approvingly on Monditsch Dreving's memorandum, which in essence was deeply critical of RL. The Radio's Munich management then warned Monditsch Dreving again that unless she were to "cease and desist," she would either be transferred out of Munich or fired altogether.

RL management finally took firm action in late October 1976, but it was not what might have been expected. Matusevitch was removed from his post as managing editor. A cosmetic change in staff organization consolidated the previously separate news and feature sections and the Russian program department under common American leadership. Members of the dissident group protested loudly, calling the changes the "October Revolution of 1976." Matusevitch, who on occasion had protested that he would prefer not to be an executive, complained now that he was a victim of anti-Semitism. He charged that the NTS was behind a letter-writing campaign that was continuing to inflame the staff and that it aimed to convert RL into a mouthpiece of Russian nationalism. He wrote to RL Executive Director Francis F. Ronalds, Jr.: "You have created a situation in which the organizers . . . of a chauvinistic and anti-Semitic campaign are celebrating a victory."

The corridors were beginning to quiet down when another incident, in January 1977, reinflamed all the old passions. An RL staff member had invited Leonid Plyusch, a recent Soviet émigré and widely known scientist, to meet with a group of RL employees. In the course of the discussion, Plyusch quoted a Soviet citizen as having said, "Jews are the entropy of Europe." A member of RL's Armenian staff who was in attendance observed that the statement was not necessarily pejorative. That was all it took to fan the sparks into another flaming controversy.

The Armenian, Eduard Oganessian, was a cyberneticist with excellent credentials. Following the statement he was promptly denounced as anti-Semitic. This time, Jewish staff members took the offensive. They condemned management's failure to take action against alleged mistreatment of Plyusch and identified Oganessian and Monditsch Dreving as the culprits. Oganessian apologized, but memoranda from Jewish staff members critical of him started circulating widely, repeating charges of anti-Semitism. This aroused the traditionalists to action. Some 70 staff members signed a statement accusing the leadership of the complaining element of inciting national hatred. The accused then took the matter to court, filing libel suits against 12 of the signers of the petition.

Eventually the repercussions from this incident, too, began to fade, but the strong undercurrents of rancor remained. A new manager for the Russian service was employed, but he failed to restore harmony. Efforts to encourage a lasting truce were unavailing. The two camps remained ideologically as far apart and emotionally as malevolent as when the third-wave personnel had begun to make inroads into leadership positions.

Management was concerned not only about keeping employees from each other's throats in Munich but also about the possibility that scripts might begin to reflect the hardening points of view. There was also considerable anxiety that the increasing intensity of the charges of anti-Semitism might begin to affect congressional attitudes, which in turn would impinge on the RFE/RL budget. Surveillance by management over broadcast output was intensified. Incidents that might inflame the old passions were avoided as effectively as possible, and Russian-speaking American leadership maintained close contact with the program producers, writers, and editors.

BIB staff members were concerned, however, that scripts were beginning to reflect some of the prejudices that permeated the two factions. The BIB staff program specialist, James Critchlow, who was also a Russian-speaking former RL executive, made a clandestine trip to Munich in early 1981 to monitor broadcasts and examine scripts. Excerpts from Critchlow's report appeared in the press before Radio executives had been informed that the report existed, and this infuriated RFE/RL leadership. Critchlow condemned management for failure to control effectively the broadcasts of its Russian service: "Evidence was found of serious policy violations, including anti-democratic, anti-Western, anti-Polish, and anti-Catholic references, as well as material potentially offensive to non-Russian nationalities of the Soviet Union. . . . [While] I found no overt evidence of anti-Semitism, there were anti-Semitic overtones in some broadcasts." Critchlow's strongest complaint was that "a common thread running through the violations is the expression of Russian nationalistic and xenophobic views." The implication was plain that the Russophiles, those most emotionally attuned to propagating the "Russian spirit" were, if not in firm command, at least in position to make their point of view heard in RL broadcasts. In summary, Critchlow wrote that "RFE/RL management has lost control of the RL Russian output."[1]

President Glenn Ferguson of RFE/RL responded, but not before mid-April, ten weeks after the issuance of the original report. The response was delayed by the bomb explosion that shattered parts of the RFE/RL headquarters building in Munich shortly after the Critchlow report was released. Ferguson did not claim infallibility for management or for the service, but he cited the paucity of Critchlow's evidence and the limited number of programs he had analyzed.[2] Before Ferguson's comments had been circulated, however, Drew Pearson got access to the Critchlow report and proceeded to castigate RL in terms familiar to Pearson's readers. "Incredibly," he wrote, "Radio Liberty has been beaming religious and historical programs in the Russian language that parrot Radio Moscow. The U.S. station has even sided with the Kremlin on Polish issues." He commented, "[W]hether these broadcasts are the result of sabotage or merely stupidity is not clear." Finally, he quoted the Critchlow report to the effect that "American management has lost effective control."[3]

Pearson's charges were exaggerated, however. Critchlow had obtained some of his evidence from members of the third-wave faction who had been most articulate and outspoken in criticizing the Russian traditionalists of the second wave (in fact, some American executives in Munich contend that Matusevitch was a major source of evidence for Critchlow's research). At any rate, palliative measures to restore harmony resulted only in an uneasy truce.

At this writing the smoldering embers of animosity still underlie the Russian service and may, from time to time, burst again into flame.

The question the RFE/RL management now has to face is how long the uncertain truce will persist and how violent the next upheaval will be. The long-term prognosis is favorable. Russian emigration continues to flow to the West in a measurable tide. As long as it continues to flow, RL will have a constantly enlarging pool of human resources from which to draw in order to refresh and reinvigorate its aging staff. It is anticipated the new emigrants will not carry with them the same baggage of hard prejudices that have torn the service so badly in the past. Until the last vestiges of the old antagonisms are removed by time, however, it appears that RL will have to contend with frequent recurrences of the bad blood between the contesting elements in its workforce.

NOTES

1. James Critchlow, Memorandum for the Board for International Broadcasting, "Review of Radio Liberty Russian Service Broadcasts," 28 pp. and exhibits, January 29, 1980. Unpublished MS, copy in Archives of Hoover Institution. (The 1980 date is an error. The report quotes programs broadcast in January 1981. The date of submission should read January 27, 1981.)

2. Glenn W. Ferguson, Memorandum to Board of Directors Radio Free Europe/Radio Liberty," 9 pp. and attachments, April 13, 1981. Unpublished MS in Archives of the Hoover Institution.

3. Drew Pearson, "Radio Liberty Making Statement on the Air," *Washington Post*, April 14, 1981, p. B15.

22
Was It Worth the Cost?

IT WAS INEVITABLE that when RFE and RL came out from under the CIA's fraying cover between 1967 and 1971 influential citizens, particularly members of Congress, would begin to question the government's wisdom in the ways it spent its money. Putting a dollar value on an international propaganda enterprise, however, is an exercise of dubious merit. There are simply no gauges, dials, or pricing mechanisms that furnish readings accurate enough to convert opinions into figures for a profit and loss statement or a balance sheet. Any attempt to arrive at a bottom line would be futile. Furthermore, the fabric of human experience in the target areas is too complex to assume that any one stimulus, such as an RFE or RL broadcast schedule, would create an easily trackable effect. Public opinion is more likely to be moved, if it is moved at all, at an almost imperceptible pace by a constant flow of information following a consistent pattern. Hopes for sudden shifts or cataclysmic results represent wishful thinking. A gradual modification of the climate of opinion in which leaderships exercise their decision-making role is about the best that can be hoped for.

It is possible, however, to search in three discrete areas for clues that can help provide answers to the questions posed by legislators and government executives regarding the worth of the two Radios to U.S. taxpayers. The first lies in the actions taken by East European leaders to distort or blot out the radio signals. The second may be found in such positive information as may be unearthed regarding the degree and intensity of listenership and in overt responses to selected broadcasts. And the third lies in the relative intensity of attacks launched by Communist leaders, either verbally, by seeking support in international bodies to legislate them out of existence, or by terror, assassinations, or bombings.

The highest compliment Eastern leaders have paid the two Radios is their unmitigating, sometimes violent, opposition. Almost from the very first broadcasts, Soviet and East European media have been condemning the stations as "mouthpieces of the cold war," "fascist cut-throats," "parrots of the ether," "slanderers by radio," "lie mills," "dregs of humanity" and "servants of the CIA." In a lengthier burst of venom, Tass once labeled RFE and RL as "the gathering place of renegades and former Nazis who are shedding crocodile tears about alleged violations of human rights in the Soviet Union." Satellite media have followed with language no less bombastic.

Nor have attacks been limited to words. Previous reference has been made to bombing, assassinations, beatings, and heavy-handed attempts supported by threats to encourage redefection.*

Bluster and terror reflect the intensity of Communist opposition and the depth of the animosity that motivates it, but they have done little to diminish effectiveness. Two other courses of action, though, do pose greater hazards. The first, electronic jamming to render the radio signal either totally unintelligible or so obnoxious that only the most avid listeners are willing to suffer with headsets in place, stands the best chance of rendering the Radios impotent. The second course, imposing international political pressures either directly on governments that are host to RFE or RL facilities or through international bodies, has not so far succeeded, but theoretically, given the right set of conditions, it could succeed in the future. The objective would be to bring about the cancellations of licenses and leases, thus depriving the Radios of the right to broadcast.

There is really no way other than jamming to stop shortwave signals from reaching listeners. Medium-wave, long-wave, and television signals are limited in the distances they can travel and are more easily jammed than shortwave. Newspapers, magazines, books, video tapes, audio tapes, and any hand-carried printed or written materials can be confiscated by customs inspectors at national borders. Telephone lines can be blocked or conversations monitored, as can teletype lines or telegraph circuits. Under present international regulations satellite signals crossing international borders, except for unavoidable "spill-over," must be received by officially authorized ground stations functioning as common carriers, and in Eastern Europe and the Soviet Union the ground stations are operated by governments. Only the shortwave signal is wholly impervious to defensive action (except for jamming). So

---

*The bombing of RFE/RL headquarters in Munich, as described in Chapter 1, while it has not been finally proved to be the work of Eastern agents, brought the campaign of vilification to a smashing climax. Bavarian police continue to believe that responsibility lies somewhere in Eastern Europe, and subsequent information concerning the alleged participation of Bulgarian agents in the assassination attempt on Pope John Paul II tends to confirm the theory. It is clear that Communist leaders do not blink at terror if terror promises results they consider to be in their best interests.

the Soviets and their allies use the only process available to block it out, distort it, or convert it into a meaningless jumble of sound, by flooding the airwaves with electronically generated shrieks, whistles, roars, screeches, howls, and wails. They can do this either by broadcasting a variety of obnoxious noises on the same channel as that being used by the original broadcaster or by propagating loud sounds on an immediately adjacent channel. The cost is high, and the drain on manpower and facilities considerable, but it is evident the Communist leadership finds the maintenance of tight information controls to be of sufficient value to justify the effort.

There are two ways to jam an unwanted signal, both of them involving the use of shortwave radio transmitters. The first, called "sky-wave" jamming, uses high-powered shortwave broadcasting stations situated a long distance back from the target areas, usually between 1500 and 2000 miles, the same distance from the targets as the original program transmitters, taking advantage of the fact that the shortwave signal is most effective at this range. The targets thus lie halfway between the RFE and RL main transmitters and the sky-wave jammers. The two signals—one from the program transmitter, the other from the jammer—rise to the ionosphere and are reflected back to earth, where they collide, creating the howling and screeching sounds that block out the program signal. The other system, called "local," or "ground wave" jamming, involves the use of scores of smaller, low-power, short-range transmitters in tall buildings, even in some church steeples, in the area in which the signal is to be blotted out.

Virtually every community in Eastern Europe and the Soviet Union, except for Hungary and Romania and to some extent Poland, is heavily jammed. This means not only that there is an extensive array of powerful sky-wave jammers stationed somewhere in Eastern Russia or Soviet Central Asia, but also that smaller jamming transmitters are strategically placed within the environs of all the major cities. KOL Israel, Radio Peking, and Radio Albania are also jammed, and sometimes the jamming is also applied to the VOA, the BBC, and Deutsche Welle, but RFE and RL have consistently been the main targets. RFE/RL engineers estimate that the entire Soviet jamming network requires a total of between 2000 and 2100 transmitters of various sizes located at 13 sky-wave jamming centers and 95 local jamming centers. A report written by the corporation's engineering staff in the winter of 1978 reveals the following:

> Each city with a population of over 250,000 has its own local jamming station. In general, jamming stations have about 15 jamming transmitters, each with a power of from 5 to 20 kilowatts. Each local jamming station has associated with it a control and monitoring station, located about 15 miles from the jamming station. Local jamming and control/monitoring stations are connected by phone lines. The latter monitors the frequencies to be jammed, and oversees the operations of the jamming station.

Both the jamming station and the control/monitoring station operate around-the-clock. Both have at least two people per shift.

Each control/monitoring station reports to a larger regional control/monitoring station periodically. The regional station can call in additional (sky wave) jammers if the local jammer station is overloaded (if there are more than 15 frequencies to be jammed).

Periodically, each local jammer station is provided with a schedule of frequencies to be jammed.

Although the "average" jammer station has 15 jamming transmitters, large population centers like Moscow and Leningrad have considerably more transmitters available. Moscow probably has three or four separately located jammer stations, each operating on its own schedule of frequencies.

The surprising fact, however, is that even such varied cities as Tallinn in Estonia, Riga in Latvia, Yerevan in Armenia, Alma Ata in Kazakstan, and Samarkand in Uzbekistan, are also heavily jammed.

The engineers estimate that about 5000 people, many technically trained and skilled, are required to operate this web of irritating noise makers. This contrasts with the 1765 employed at RFE and RL combined. A most conservative estimate of annual Soviet costs was pegged at approximately $135 million. Capital costs required to establish the network are estimated to have totaled approximately a quarter of a billion dollars. The complex system requires 24-hour-a-day manning, constant maintenance, and split-second shifts of frequencies. It demands swift communications, instant decisions, careful coordination, and constant monitoring in order to block those programs they consider most objectionable to their own interests.

It is censorship of the most virulent kind, unselectively blotting out whole programs, not words or paragraphs. It seeks to wipe out the entire service without any consideration of specific content; it denies to its citizens any ideas, information, and news that can upset the carefully preordained diet prescribed by the leadership. Western nations argue that jamming is clearly illegal. They point to Article 35 of the Montreux International Telecommunications convention—"All stations, whatever their purpose, must be established and operated in such a manner as not to result in harmful interference to radio services or communications of other members or associate members"—and to other similar references in other international telecommunications accords. They also cite the Universal Declaration of Human Rights, which includes the right to "seek, receive and impart information and ideas . . . regardless of frontiers."

The Soviets and their allies, however, read the documents differently. As in so many cases of East–West relations there is no common understanding of the written word, whether by semantic misperception or willful distortion. What seems to mean "white" in the West may be interpreted to mean "black" in the East, and vice versa. The clause in the Montreux convention that seems to outlaw harmful interference to radio services of other members seems clear enough on the surface. Similar apparently forthright condemnations of jamming have been recorded in a number of other international telecommunications conventions but they have little effect on nations that do not intend to be tied down by them. A UN General Assembly resolution adopted by a 49-to-5 vote in December 1950 condemned jamming as "a violation of the accepted principle of freedom of information and as a denial of the rights of all persons to be fully informed."[1] The resolution, however, provides a wide-open escape clause for any nation that sees fit to exercise a little freedom in interpretation. It invites all governments to "refrain from all broadcasts that would mean unfair attacks against other peoples anywhere." It is easy to go on from that point to develop the theory "that while the ether is free and jamming in principle is condemned, it is permitted if required to exclude hostile propaganda."[2] So what may seem perfectly clear in an open society appears as something entirely different in a closed society. As Whitton and Larson put it, "the legality of jamming is essentially a problem of treaty interpretation, not of international law."[3]

This is all the opening that the Soviets and their East European allies need. They can simply claim that the foreign broadcasts they jam are incitements, provocations, slanders, interference in their internal affairs, or hostile acts, even, if they want to stretch the point a bit, "hostile acts leading to war." With the appearance of utter innocence, they can charge that it is the staffs of RFE and RL who are the provocateurs and aggressors and that they have every right under international law to jam. There seems no solution, no way of finding common ground. As Whitton and Larson put it, "What Washington considers the simple truth may become in the eyes of Moscow harmful propaganda."[4]

So the jamming against the Radios continues growing in intensity in an almost constant ratio. In 1977 John Gronouski, then BIB chairman, made a grandstand play to put an end to jamming when he announced that he would grant the Soviets a right of reply, à la FCC rules in the United States, to any broadcasts that were found to be demonstrably false or defamatory. The Soviets did not deign to pay attention to the offer, which was just as well, since it would have been difficult to find an international FCC with the power to adjudicate fairness claims. Moreover Gronouski would have been guilty of encroaching on Radio managements if he had overstepped the BIB's oversight function by directly interfering in program matters.

The battle against the jammers, however, is not a total failure. Millions of East European and Soviet listeners either find methods of avoiding the worst of the jamming or tolerate the screeches and howls while they remain tuned. And hard evidence from a variety of sources indicates that signals do reach eager listeners in surprisingly high volume. The fact is, a fool-proof jamming system has yet to be designed. Sky-wave jammers are at best limited in their effectiveness and quite ineffective for two or three hours a day during a period described by engineers as "twilight immunity," when darkness has already covered the area in which the jamming transmitters are located but it is still light in Germany, Spain, and Portugal where the broadcast signal originates. The jamming signal during this period of "twilight immunity" penetrates through the ionosphere rather than reflecting from it, so it is lost in space or diverted.

The range of the local jammer is so limited that it is rarely effective outside the confines of the metropolitan area in which it operates. There are now a sufficient number of motor cars in major Soviet and East European cities to make it possible for thousands of interested citizens to drive to the country to pick up their favorite broadcasts, and a sufficient number have access to *dachas* (weekend cottages) in the country where they can go to listen to a relatively clear signal. It has also been discovered that jamming is negligible near airports, where the jamming signal might interfere with air-traffic communications.

The evidence is conclusive: jamming or no jamming, signals do get through to their intended audiences. Obtaining audience "ratings" is accomplished by adaptation of processes used in the West—no mean feat in countries where Western poll takers have access neither to doorbells nor to telephones, not even to the mails, and where a Nielsen audimeter would be as unlikely a device as a multiparty voting machine. RFE and RL have, however, each set up audience-measurement machinery, each in its own way and each conducted from outside the geographical area being surveyed, and enough data are available to give programmers valuable guidance in program production and schedule building.

RFE was first to establish audience-research facilities. Since research directors could not send interviewers into Poland or Czechoslovakia or Hungary, they did the next best thing: they arranged to have the Poles, Czechs and Slovaks, and Hungarians interviewed when they left their homelands on holidays or business trips. They soon discovered that travelers visited the West in rough proportion to their demographic breakdowns at home. The percentage of blue-collar workers of the traveling public was of relatively the same portion as that proportion of blue-collar workers to the total population, and so it went with students, farmers, shopkeepers, professional personnel, academics, and managers. This meant that carefully selected samples were possible. There were so many dangers involved in having RFE personnel doing the interviewing that the decision was quickly made to go to outside poll-taking agencies. By this process, RFE's research department was able to retain the services of trained professional interviewers, avoiding the danger that results could be skewed to obtain answers desired by RFE management and also, perhaps more important, avoiding charges of using the interview process as a method of spying. Fortunately, there is a plenitude of European research institutes comparable to the Gallups, Ropers, Harrises, Nielsens, ARBs and the like in the United States. RFE questionnaires, let out under contract to established research institutes, enabled RFE assignments to be merged with orders from other clients, and any identification with RFE in the minds of the respondents would be buried deeply. The procedure is still followed today.

RFE personnel decide on the topics to be researched, write the questionnaires, tabulate the results, and analyze the data. Professional personnel employed by the research institutes conduct the interviews, record the results, and transmit the data to RFE headquarters at Munich. There are not enough respondents available at any given time to obtain a sample large enough to yield valid results, so data are retained until an adequate number of responses is on record to justify confidence in the validity of the data.

Interviewers armed with questionnaires intercept travelers at railroad stations, airports, and bus depots, mostly in the major cities along the East European border: Vienna, Munich, Frankfurt, Hamburg, Copenhagen, Stockholm, and Helsinki, and in Paris and London. Remarkably little hostility has been noted among the East European travelers. Most yield willingly to requests for interviews. Because the identity of the client for whom the survey is being made is never revealed, there is little or no effort to reply in a manner calculated to furnish the response most likely to be favorable to the client. Elaborate checks are applied to assure the validity of the responses and to eliminate potential errors. Henry Hart, Director of RFE's Audience and Public Opinion Research Department, insists that he constantly achieves a confidence level of 3.5 percent plus or minus, which would make RFE polls about as accurate as the Gallup and Roper polls in the United States except that they measure results over a period of weeks or months, not days or hours. Only regarding the Bulgarian returns is RFE management uncertain. Fewer Bulgarians travel, particularly to the West, so samples are smaller and data somewhat shaky.

The results, which have been relatively constant over the years, indicate that RFE's largest audiences are in Poland and Romania, with Hungary following closely and both Czechoslovakia and Bulgaria substantially lower in the rating scale. More than 50 percent of Poles are regular listeners. During the crisis following the declaration of martial law in 1981, the figure rose to 70 percent for several weeks before settling back somewhat; this record was achieved in spite of severe jamming particularly in the major cities. Hungary and Romania do not jam, so the RFE signal is able to compete freely with local government radio. In Hungary the competition is stiff. The Hungarians have proved flexible and quick to adapt Western methods of building attractive program schedules, forcing the RFE Hungarian service to innovate constantly to stay in competition. Romanian radio, according to RFE management, is drab, colorless, slow in reaction time, and unimaginative, furnishing the ideal opening for an aggressive Free Europe Romanian staff. In both Czechoslovakia and Bulgaria jamming is loud, protracted, and all-pervasive. Listening in almost all areas is complicated by whistles, howls, and screeches. But even with all the attention given to the Free Europe signal by the Czechoslovak jammers, more than 35 percent of all Czechs and Slovaks are counted as regular listeners.

Some program executives, who at first regarded audience data as a novelty with little practical value, have come to rely on it for guidance in scheduling and program production. News is consistently the highest-rated item in audience-preference scales, and all five RFE services begin each hour with ten minutes of news. Compilations of editorial comment from major metropolitan dailies throughout the West also rank high, as do magazine-type programs dealing with public affairs topics.

RL's efforts to develop useful audience research data had to overcome vastly greater handicaps. While traveling in the West is common among East Europeans of all stations in life, it is sharply restricted for citizens of the Soviet Union. East European travelers are relatively free to move about on their own, meet local people, visit local restaurants and coffee shops, and meet with friends and relatives. Soviet travelers, on the other hand, are carefully selected before being granted visas, usually travel in groups under surveillance, have little freedom to make local contacts, and are generally discouraged from mixing freely. For the most part, they are selected from privileged classes and have earned the right to travel by faithful service to the party or government. Few except for faithful party members and academics are fluent in languages other than Russian, and to them Western Europe is a distant land, culturally quite unlike the homeland. (This is in contrast to East European countries, which have common borders to the West and well-established cultural affinities.)

To make the best of a highly complex situation, RL's director of audience research, Max Ralis, developed a system designed to obtain the maximum results from the meager crop of potential respondents. It was clearly understood in advance that the number of Soviet citizens who could be interviewed would constitute only a fraction of the number available to RFE, that in no way could they be described as a cross-section of Soviet society, and that casual interviews could not be set up in railroad stations or airports as they could with the East Europeans. The system designed by Ralis and his assistants depended on lengthy and casual conversations in restaurants, coffee shops, or bars, with no notes taken. Interviewers recorded the data only after returning to their hotel rooms or offices. It was crucial to maintain the atmosphere of a congenial meeting of friends and to let the conversation ramble and drift. Helsinki has turned out to be, as expected, the most productive interviewing center, but Paris and London yield some results, as do Vienna, Rome, and other international ports of call.

Since only 1000 to 1400 interviews can be obtained annually by this process, there is no semblance of a scientifically selected sample. Computer simulation was required to convert the raw data into a model of the entire Soviet Union. Ralis and his associates worked with social science researchers at the Massachusetts Institute of Technology, including most notably Ithiel de Sola Poole, in creating the model they used. The confidence factor is considerably lower than RFE's (only about 18 percent plus or minus), but in the case of broad, uncomplicated cuts of the population, Ralis and his associates feel this is adequate to furnish clues as to audience preferences. The statistical data can be used to furnish guidance as to listening patterns among men versus women, urban residents versus rural, and well-educated versus those with meager education, but it can hardly pinpoint preferences for specific programs or listening patterns during specific times of the day or obtain meaningful data concerning the remote geographical areas of central Asia. The usual pattern is to complete a statistical analysis every two years. This furnishes a data base of between 2000 and 2800, adequate to furnish the sketchy results described above. Bigger budgets might conceivably yield more frequent returns, but a high confidence level seems a remote possibility.

USSR audience levels are appreciably lower than those in East Europe; this is attributable in part to the vigorous jamming in all parts of the Soviet Union, and in part to the greater insularity of Soviet citizens. Approximately 3.2 million Soviets are believed to listen to RL each day, or about 10.1 million each week.[5] VOA and BBC external services have consistently registered higher audience levels, at least in part because they have generally been exempt, except in rare circumstances, from the rigorous jamming that greets all RL signals. Jamming also skews the audience to the better-educated urban dwellers who are sufficiently interested in public affairs to suffer the pains of the noises furnished by the jammers and have both the cars and portable receivers to drive out of Moscow to *dachas* or secluded spots, many of them near airports, where they can listen out of range of the most pervasive of the jamming.

Audience research at both Radios demonstrates that there is listenership: intensive in the case of most of Eastern Europe; moderate, but enough to be influential, in the Soviet Union. But the available data give no clue as to whether the listenership is passive, permitting the signal to pass through the mind without leaving an imprint, or whether the broadcasts contribute to an environment that may eventually lead to demands for modification of government structures and processes. Will it eventually create among the public such a demand for free communications that public pressure will force leaderships to yield by modifying or eliminating censorship?

There are scattered bits and pieces of evidence to indicate that not all the listening is passive, that reactions are sometimes intense and enthusiastic, that listeners are loyal and consistent, and that the service from Munich is a critically important element in the lives of the listeners, furnishing them a source of information concerning not only the outside world but in many cases significant events taking place in their own areas—events of which knowledge is restricted because of censorship or the inattention of local news-gathering agencies.

Andre Sakharov, for example, who was not permitted to leave the Soviet Union to accept the Nobel Peace Prize in Oslo, listened to his wife's acceptance speech over RL facilities. His daughter, in a different part of the USSR, likewise heard the speech. Alexander Solzhenitsyn once said in an interview in Moscow, "If we hear anything about events in this country, it is through their—the Radio Liberty—broadcasts."

The most spirited responses, however, come from Eastern Europe, where RFE's listenership ratings are higher and listening is easier. Two events, in particular, illustrate the influence that RFE is able to exert in periods of crises.

When the Polish government declared martial law on December 13, 1981, and imprisoned many of the leaders of the Solidarity Union, it imposed a communications blackout unprecedented in its scope. Not only were international communications channels cut totally, but even domestic telephone, telegraph, and postal services were suspended. It was almost as if Poland had returned suddenly to the Dark Ages. The purpose was clearly to prevent any communication from being heard among Solidarity members or their leaders. The government did not relish the fact that RFE's Polish service had been a critically important source of information for the Polish people in general and Solidarity in particular, since the advent of the Solidarity movement in the summer of 1980. Solidarity leaders had been knowledgeable enough about communications processes to recognize that information released to a Western wire-service reporter or a metropolitan newspaper correspondent in Warsaw, Gdansk, or Czestochowa would find its way back into Poland, sometimes in minutes, by way of an RFE broadcast. Regular listenership to RFE in Poland boomed upward to the 70-percent level during the height of the crisis. When the communcations blackout was imposed, the sources of information used by RFE were cut off along with all other dispatches from that country. Western press agencies and newspapers no longer had access to telephone, telex services, or the mails. Information from inside the country came only from travelers who were able to slip across the carefully guarded frontiers, but this was meager at best. RFE was thus limited to picking up what morsels of information it could in Western capitals and from cities at or near the Polish frontier, supplemented by conversations with travelers after the flow started to trickle out, principally through Vienna.

On the day after the nearly impenetrable blackout curtain descended on Poland, RFE's Polish service began to get calls from Poles in the West, inquiring about relatives caught up in the silent cavern that Poland had become. A younger staff member on the Polish desk suggested using a time period to relay some of these calls so that they might be heard by listeners in Poland. He was quickly authorized to prepare a program for airing as soon as possible. At this point, the Polish service made excellent use of the medium-wave transmitter at Holzkirchen. Germans and Austrians could listen regularly to the signal from that transmitter. Poles living or visiting in those countries made it a point to do so regularly. Many in West Germany were tuned in when this first program to send messages to individuals in Poland was transmitted. In addition to broadcasting the messages, the announcers on the program invited additional communications to be relayed to Poland and on several occasions repeated the telephone number of the Polish service in Munich.

A substantial response was expected, but not the avalanche of calls that followed. The switchboard was deluged. One short program was clearly not sufficient, so it was decided to create a new series at a regularly established time and to promote it extensively. The title selected was a variation on the descriptive term used for the Berlin airlift, "The Bridge to Berlin"; the new program was called "The Telephone Bridge to Poland." Jan Tyszkiewicz, a veteran producer who was on vacation in Florida when martial law was declared, rushed back to Munich and within 48 hours was on the job. He was assigned the producer's role.

A program that had started as a one-time experiment quickly expanded to two periods daily of 50 minutes each and then to three. Extra phones were installed as the few available lines were swamped. When possible, messages broadcast to Poland were held to no more than 30 seconds in an effort to get as many as 100 into each 50-minute period. Representatives of newspapers, wire services, radio, and television quickly caught on to a story with all the elements of high drama: pathos, compassion, grief, tenderness, and relief on the part of both senders and listeners when they found it possible to communicate again to friends and relatives. Tyszkiewicz says that he and his staff could hardly find a quiet spot to prepare the program as they were constantly "chased by journalists, television cameramen, and photographers."

A father and son had left Poland on December 12, the day before martial law was declared, on a Danish ferry bound for Copenhagen. The father died on shipboard. Since all communication with Poland had been cut, there was no way the son could get word of his father's death back to family members in Poland. In Copenhagen he learned of "The Bridge" and sent a message in Polish to Munich; it was quickly relayed by "The Bridge" staff.

A Polish mother left her sick child with a neighbor while she made a brief trip to Germany. When the border was closed she was frantic to get information back to the neighbor concerning vital antiallergy medication that was necessary to keep the child alive. "The Bridge" relayed the message, including full instructions concerning dosages and time for medication.

A Pole in his twenties, visiting in Germany, had a different kind of problem. He wanted to marry in Germany the daughter of Polish parents but was told he could not do so without formally requesting of the parents the daughter's hand in marriage. The Polish service relayed the message, and while an answer was out of the question as long as communications were blocked, the fact that the parents had been informed was assumed to be an adequate gesture under the circumstances. The marriage vows were consummated.

There was soon evidence of reaction behind Poland's sealed borders. Polish youth formed listener groups that monitored broadcasts, recorded the messages, and delivered them personally in the event that they had been missed by the persons to whom they were addressed. "The Bridge" almost overnight had become a major factor in easing the tensions brought on by the blackout. The success of "The Bridge" at both the sending and receiving ends is hardly a reflection of the influence of RFE on public policy formulation, but it demonstrates the power of Western shortwave radio to penetrate communications barriers and to force government officials to take notice.

Requests for broadcasting messages came from all over Western Europe, North America, and even from ships at sea. RFE handled as many as 500 messages a day, seven days a week, for a total of 3500 weekly. This went on from mid-December well into the spring. As Polish censorship softened, letters from Poland began to reach Munich, making "The Bridge" no longer solely a one-way communications link, but rather giving it a two-way dimension.

By spring RFE, believing the crisis was weakening and that "The Bridge" was consuming valuable time that now could better be devoted to other types of information, began to cut back, first to twice weekly and then finally to once a week on Saturday afternoons. But it was evident that RFE had discovered that it could fill a basic human need in a period of tension and despair. It could furnish a mechanism to enable people separated by government edict to communicate in a warm-hearted way calculated to ease their tensions in a period of great uncertainty.

Some four and a half years earlier in 1977, RFE's Romanian service had filled a somewhat similar role. Early one Saturday evening in early March large areas of Romania were devastated by a severe earthquake registering 7.2 on the Richter scale. Bucharest, the capital and largest city, was hardest hit. Buildings collapsed, hundreds were injured, and scores died. Transportation facilities were shattered.

The director of RFE's Romanian service, Noel Bernard, received a cryptic call, from the RFE Romanian monitoring service at his home at about 8:00 P.M., reporting that the monitor could not find any trace of a signal from Romanian radio on any frequency. Bernard reacted instantly. He had thought for some time that if any coup were ever going to take place in Romania it would be while Ceausescu was absent from the country. On this March night, the Romanian president was visiting in Africa, so the conditions, Bernard felt, were as favorable as they ever would be for an overthrow of the government, and one of the first signs would be silence on the radio frequencies. He gave the order "keep in touch" and sat down to wait it out. A half hour later, RFE's central news department called to advise him that the U.S. monitoring station in Boulder, Colorado, was reporting that a large seismic event had been observed in the vicinity of Bucharest. "At that point," Bernard says, "the adrenalin started flowing. I started for the office." By the time he arrived, it was clear that a major tremor had severely shaken the Bucharest area.

The skeleton staff broadcast what information was available while Bernard called the technical operations office to request overnight transmitter time and 24-hour access to a studio. Reports coming out of Bucharest were meager, but the Romanian staff relayed what they had available from wire service reports and earthquake monitoring stations outside Romania. After approximately an hour and a half, Bucharest radio came back on the air with a combination of music and public service announcements. They were furnishing basic facts to Bucharest citizens, such as where to find a pharmacy, where to call for urgent assistance, and how to find transportation to leave the area. In Munich, the Romanian service recorded the announcements and quickly rebroadcast them back to Romania. Soon, calls started coming in from listeners in Germany and Austria, asking RFE to relay messages to friends and relatives in Romania. They had been following the RFE broadcast on the Holzkirchen medium-wave transmitter.

That triggered a surprising response from Romania. Calls started coming from Bucharest to RFE headquarters in Munich, responding to queries from the West. RFE put on additional operators to handle the deluge. There were occasions when the Bucharest operator would break in, at the conclusion of a call, to say, "Hello, RFE. Hello, RFE. I have another call for you. Please stand by." Some 135 to 150 calls were accepted and answered during a two-day period immediately following the quake. As in Poland four and a half years later, listener clubs, formed in the heat of the emergency, organized to monitor all RFE broadcasts in the Romanian service, write down messages, and use motorcycles or bicycles to deliver the messages to the persons addressed.

Audience-measurement statistics, compiled later, showed that the audience soared. American correspondents reported that Romanians took to calling RFE "Bucharest IV" giving it status along with the government's stations, Bucharest I, II, and III. The Romanian government made no effort to restrict communication with Munich, apparently because to do so would have led to incalculable repercussions.

The episodes in Poland and Romania, backed up by audience-measurement statistics, are resoundingly clear evidence that the Radios reach large audiences. The reluctance of Romanian authorities to sever communications links with Munich during the height of the emergency indicates their concern that such a measure might have triggered a violent reaction. The drastic processes employed generally across Eastern Europe and the Soviet Union, including jamming and efforts to shut down transmitters, clearly reflect Communist concern regarding their ability to maintain an airtight information vacuum. Such measures suggest that the Radios might be more than simply irritating pests. They might, conceivably, lead citizens of the affected countries to demand elimination of restrictions on the flow of information and even modification of harsh policies. An East European or Soviet leader could certainly sleep more soundly and breathe more easily if he did not have to be concerned that his carefully controlled information monopoly might be penetrated by irreverent outsiders.

NOTES

1. John B. Whitton and Arthur Larson, *Propaganda* (Dobbs Ferry, N.Y.: Oceana, 1964), p. 211.

2. *Ibid.*, pp. 214–15. Whitton and Larson cite a number of cases where jamming had been justified as self defense.

3. *Ibid.*, p. 216.

4. *Ibid.*, p. 219.

5. Audience data are derived from BIB, Seventh Annual Report (Washington, D.C.: U.S. Government Printing Office, 1981), p. 19.

23
A Glimpse into the Future

CONTRARY TO EXPECTATIONS when they were founded, the Radios have endured through more than three decades. Theirs has not been a tranquil existence. There has been barely a moment free of some crisis, external or internal, political or emotional, financial or managerial. Although several times on the brink of an abyss, they have always managed to escape to more solid ground. The operation now looks, at least superficially, more stable than it has in years. Management and administrative procedures and relationships to government have been simplified—whether to the advantage of the Radios' independence and capability to carry out their delicate and intricate missions, it remains to be seen. Conflicts between the government oversight board and the independent corporate board have been mitigated by the simple procedure of eliminating by legislation the corporate board and giving the responsibility of both functions to the same presidentially appointed body.

Now, what of the future? The common assumption in the early 1950s was that neither Free Europe nor Amcomlib would be needed for more than a few years, but after the abortive Hungarian Revolution in 1956, all that changed. Now there seems to be no discernible point in the future when it will be possible to say, "The job is done. It is time to dismantle the machinery and shut down the transmitters."

Radio management has consistently taken the position that its goal should be to open communications channels in the East and to breach the censorship barriers effectively enough so that leadership in the target countries would be encouraged to open up communications channels and create a new, uncontrolled information environment. The freer environment would replace the rigid censorship, clogged information channels, and tightly controlled media responsive only to the desires of government leadership. When East European and Soviet communications are as free as those in the West, there will no longer be a need for the type of services that the Radios furnish. All of this will be available from local domestic media. But how soon will that state of blissful freedom be attained? The best guess is that it is a very, very long time away and could very well come as a defensive measure, a response to the plain fact that information is available from the West despite censorship. At that point, with uncensored information inundating the environment, leaderships might decide that maintaining censorship is a futile exercise.

International shortwave broadcasting will never lead to massive shifts in public attitudes. The process of public opinion formulation is usually exceedingly slow. A number of years ago, the BBC's director of external services at the time wrote that the effect of international broadcasting is "diffuse rather than direct or immediate. It tends to affect the climate of opinion in which political leaders make decisions rather than the immediate decisions themselves."

It is quite possible that the Polish opposition to that country's ruling powers in 1956, 1970, 1976, and again with the rise of Solidarity in 1980 may have been inspired by news of what Poles regarded as a freer and better world outside. And they were likely emboldened by a feeling of solidarity with the democratic West. But it is now clear that that is not enough. No such message had won over the leadership of the Kremlin, which refused to tolerate insubordination in a satellite state and demanded the imposition of martial law to maintain a closed society. So it was in Czechoslovakia in 1968 and in Hungary in 1956. The majority of the Poles, Hungarians, and Czechs and Slovaks may have been ready for a free society, but the Kremlin was not, and East European leaders lacked the muscle for a dispute with Moscow. It should be apparent now that freedom in Eastern Europe cannot come without the acquiescence of the Kremlin, and that can occur only after the climate of opinion in the Soviet Union has changed so drastically that the leadership will have to make concessions to it. In all probability, that is still many years and countless hours of broadcasting in the future.

If RFE and RL are to continue functioning into the indeterminate future with any moderate degree of efficiency and effectiveness, something will have to be done quickly to give them tools to carry out their mission. As a Heritage Foundation analysis in 1981 pointed out, they "still lack the resources to finish replacing 1950's vacuum tube equipment."[1] Maintenance of equipment in the crisis years since 1971 has been reduced to the bare minimum required to keep the machinery functioning. Studios, for the most part, still lack state-of-the-art transistorized microphones and recording and communications devices.[2] Progress has been made, however: in 1975 and 1976, ten new 100-kilowatt transmitters were installed at Biblis and Lampertheim in Germany; in 1978 and 1979, eleven new 250-kilowatt units at Gloria and Holzkirchen. But both Radios are still underpowered compared to their East European and Soviet counterparts. They lack the power to overcome jamming, and they lack both power and transmitter sites to put an acceptable signal into Soviet central Asia. Transmission to the Soviet maritime provinces and eastern Siberia, carried out from Taiwan, was discontinued as an economy measure in 1971.

Soviet central Asia is a particularly critical area. There are now almost as many non-Russians as Russians in the Soviet Union, and the fastest growing single element is the Muslims in the central Asian republics. The January 1979 census of the USSR shows that 16.4 percent of the entire population was made up of Soviet Muslims, an increase of more than 2 percent in the nine years since 1970, when the figure was 14.3 percent. The combined population growth of the Muslims in the nine-year period exceeded 25 percent, in contrast to only a 6.5 percent growth in the non-Muslim population. The implications for the future are staggering. Will a labor shortage in European Russia be made up by moving Muslim laborers to the factories or by relocating the factories in central Asia? Will Muslims be integrated into military units led by Russians, or will they form all-Muslim units? Since most of the Muslims live in areas contiguous with the Muslim countries of Asia and the Middle East, how will they react to successive Middle Eastern crises? RL's audience research department shows some evidence of limited listenership in the area, but power is too limited to achieve any degree of consistency. Greater power, the availability of more frequencies, and more favorable transmitter sites would permit RL to reach the Soviet Union at a particularly vulnerable point.

Jamming is the problem that gives Radio personnel the deepest concern. It is so overwhelming and all pervasive that there is no city in the Soviet Union of more than 250,000 population that is free of it. Higher power and the use of more frequencies are the only sure-fire remedies. But achieving greater power will be costly: there must be capital outlays for new equipment, installation costs, and sharply increased electric power costs. Congress will have to appropriate the funds, and the White House, through the OMB, approve the appropriations. Acquiring more frequencies presents a more complicated problem. Frequencies are allocated by the International Telecommunications Union (ITU), the UN-related agency based in Geneva. Any application for additional frequencies is subjected to international scrutiny and frequently depends on political tradeoffs. In addition, the electronic spectrum is already overcrowded. Forcing more frequencies into the already jam-packed bands only denigrates the signals being broadcast, causes interference, and reduces clarity of output to the point, on occasion, of almost total unintelligibility.

The simple solution to all the problems of increasing transmitter sites, acquiring new and more powerful transmitters, constructing higher gain and more efficient antennas, and mitigating or virtually eliminating the impact of jamming would be to convert to satellite transmission. Just take some of the satellite makers' magic elixir and all aches and pains will vanish in moments.

But as is the case with so many nostrums, there is no guarantee that the potion will work. Even if adequate transponder space could be obtained for a reasonable fee (one comparable to the cost of terrestrial broadcasting, for example), licenses would still have to be obtained from the ITU for the frequencies to be used. The entrepreneur, whether private or governmental, whose satellite transponders would retransmit RFE and RL signals would have to go to the ITU to obtain "parking space" in the geostationary orbit from which the satellite could "see" a large enough part of the Soviet Union or Eastern Europe or both for the signal to reach the target areas. Potential listeners would need receiving antennas and home terminal units to convert the signal received from the satellite to a frequency that would fall within the range of frequencies in which the receiver is capable of accepting the signal. In view of the Soviet Union's belligerent, even saber-rattling attitude toward any satellite signals that might infringe on USSR territory, it seems unlikely that the ITU would be able to grant the necessary licenses and permissions. In one blustery speech to the United Nations in the early 1970s USSR Foreign Minister Andrei Gromyko threatened that the Soviets would shoot down any hostile satellite that included the Soviet Union within the footprint of its antenna patterns. In the Soviet view, unwanted information is hostile. Unavoidable spillover of a satellite signal crossing over international borders probably will not occasion reprisal, but planned invasion of the air space of a sovereign state by broadcasting can be undertaken, according to theories expressed in international bodies, only with the expressed approval of the receiving state—"prior consent" as such approvals have come to be known.

International procedures and codes of conduct may yet be modified before they are frozen into international law, and "spillover" may be generally condoned, but it is difficult to foresee the Soviet Union or one of the East European nations within its sphere of influence looking benignly on a deliberate attempt to use space as a means of broadcasting within their borders material that is offensive to them. Even now, the Soviets charge constantly that the Radios' signals constitute "interference in the internal affairs of participating states." Permitting broadcasts by satellite into their territory would run completely counter to the whole Soviet program of support for "balanced flow of information" and "prior consent" before permitting any broadcast material to cross international borders.

Broadcasting by international shortwave across international borders is just as offensive to the Soviet Union as broadcasts from satellites would be, but shortwave has been accepted by most of the nations of the world as a permissible, if not always an approved, practice. And the Soviet Union itself is its most prolific practitioner: some 2000 hours weekly, as against between 1800 and 1900 for the three American services combined. No matter how hard the Soviets and their friends try to establish legal grounds for international communications control, it would be difficult to apply it to a medium in which so many nations are participating. But a new distribution methodology involving satellites is an entirely different matter. There, the votes may be at hand in international bodies to outlaw the process.

The only viable alternative is beefing up the terrestrial facilities: adding high-powered transmitters, new high-gain antennas, employing more effective microphones, and acquiring higher-quality recording facilities and filtering processes to improve signal quality, thus making it more likely that a marginally listenable signal will slip through the heavy jamming. Money will buy all except for new transmitter sites. Only through determined political negotiation and the application of whatever leverage, delicate or heavy-handed, that is available to the U.S. government will we succeed in freeing up sites suitable for new operating bases with a reasonable chance of putting an acceptable signal on a consistent basis into the target areas. This is particularly true of broadcasts into Soviet central Asia.

There are other acceptable sites in Spain in addition to the Playa de Pals, but if the Spanish government is even unwilling to extend a lease on the Pals property, which expired in 1976, it is highly unlikely that it will accede to requests that the United States be given permission to extend its operations from that country. This would apply to the Balearic Islands as well as to mainland Spain. An operating base in the Middle East would offer new opportunities to pump strong signals into Soviet central Asia, but until the political turmoil simmers down and more stability replaces it, Middle Eastern sites look like sorry prospects indeed. Israel would be the most likely possibility, but building a base there, if all the necessary permissions were granted, could bring on a rash of additional Middle Eastern tensions. The VOA has an efficient operating base in Kefala in northern Greece that would serve RL interests well, but permitting the RL to broadcast signals from Kefala would almost certainly bring down the full wrath of the Soviet jammers on the VOA signal, as well as on RL's. With sufficient funding from Congress, RFE/RL might renew its lease with the Republic of China government for facilities on Taiwan. The government in Taiwan would probably be cooperative as they have been before, but U.S. negotiators would have to decide whether such an agreement would incur risks affecting the future of our relationships with the government of mainland China that would outweigh the advantages.

In short, prospects look bleak for finding sites to increase substantially the signal power other than by replacing lower-power facilities of the bases now operated with newer and more powerful equipment. Broadcasting from U.S. soil sounds alluring, but in order to make it feasible the physical nature of the shortwave signal would have to be altered, and that seems beyond the capability of physicists or electrical and electronic engineers. Sharply higher budgets to improve the current facilities and replace the weaker transmitters apparently constitute the only reasonable course open.

The weakness of signal strengths and the lack of capability of overcoming jamming are the most obvious of RFE/RL's shortcomings, but there are others. The whole organization needs a transfusion of new blood. The staffs are aging, becoming more and more removed from the countries into which they broadcast and the people who constitute their audiences. Staff rejuvenation received a severe blow in the middle 1970s when the newest and youngest employees had to be terminated during the meat-axe staff reductions. Monetary resources have been so skimpy since that time that it has been impossible to undertake a carefully crafted, intensively planned campaign to bring in fresh faces, new skills, and new approaches better attuned to the changes that have been taking place in Eastern Europe and the Soviet Union.

Self-serving political interference from members of the Congress began to surface when the CIA ceased to serve as a buffer between Capitol Hill and the Radios. Radio executives in the future could find themselves in the position where they devote an inordinate share of their time to protecting themselves from ill-informed attacks from individual congressmen or in seeking evidence to reply to petty, politically motivated questions. Serving under a board of directors appointed by the president could conceivably lead to political pressures and encouragement to alter policy to conform to the political interests of the party in power in the White House.

There will almost inevitably continue to be questions asked about the very existence of the Radio. A new surge of the spirit of détente that induced Senator Fulbright in the early 1970s to condemn the Radios as "needless irritants" and "outworn relics of the cold war" could inspire a new wave of similar criticism. Mounting costs that will be an essential element in strengthening the broadcast output will inevitably stimulate more demands for economy. Politicians of the right will continue to demand that the Radios take a tougher stance, strike back at the Soviets in the same tone that they strike at us. Partisans of the left will almost certainly echo the Fulbright line and demand termination of the entire effort. Memory of the CIA connection may never be totally erased. When intelligence agencies of the U.S. government are in disfavor, some of the hostility toward them will continue to rub off on the Radios, particulary RFE. The suspicion that RFE may have contributed to the deaths of many Hungarian insurgents in 1956 may never be lost. And as long as the broadcast efforts continue, the East European states and the Soviet Union will continue to snipe at the Radios in their own media, in international organizations, and in direct pressure on the governments that make facilities or licenses available to them. The bombing of 1981 and the assassination of Georgi Markhov, moreover, may not be the last efforts at intimidation by terror.

In all probability, the Radios will continue to lead a stormy life, buffeted by political and economic pressures at home and forced to stave off continuing hazards abroad. But into the foreseeable future some kind of continuation seems secure and a gradual softening of hard-line Communist attitudes, stimulated in part by the RFE and RL broadcasts, seems a likely possibility.

The greatest danger the Radios may face is that their supporters will demand too much too soon. They can aid in creating a climate that is receptive to change. They can assist in accelerating movement toward change. They can mobilize support for new, more moderate policies. But they would surely lose their credibility and thus the basic source of their strength if they rashly encouraged risky insubordination or foolhardy action that would put the cause of freedom in jeopardy. Credibility and trust come first. Then informed and sympathetic listenership will most certainly follow. That is about the most we can ask, but if we can achieve even the minimum objective, the possibilities for a continuing world peace will seem just a little brighter.

NOTES

1. Gerald Mansell, "Information Without Frontiers," in *Issues in Communications* (London: International Institute of Communications, 1977, No. 1), p. 40.

2. The Heritage Foundation, "Mobilizing the Airwaves: The Challenge to the Voice of America and RFE/RL " (Washington, D.C.: The Foundation, November 1981), p. 13.

Notes on Sources

Interviews, nearly 100 of them, constituted the single most valuable source of information out of which this story of Radio Free Europe and Radio Liberty was reconstructed. The interviewees were a variegated set of individuals each of whom had had some personal contact with an aspect of the Radios' history, including former senior officials of the OPC and the CIA, executives of the Radios throughout their histories, émigré employees of various language services, members of boards of directors past and present, both of the corporations and of the BIB, and production personnel who had been involved in one or the other of Radios from the early days of the projects.

More than 70 of these interviews are recorded on tape cassettes and are filed in the archives of the Hoover Institution on the Leland Stanford University campus in Palo Alto. Each adds to our understanding of a facet of the RFE/RL story in a highly personal way.

The interviews are supported by my own personal recollection of direct and indirect contacts with Free Europe over a period of more than three decades of its existence and my services as president of both Radios and the merged RFE/RL, Inc., for three years, from 1975 to 1978. These recollections are backed up by memoranda, reports, analyses, briefing books for use in congressional hearings, minutes of board meetings of the two corporations, their merged successor, the Radio Free Europe Fund Incorporated, and the Board for International Broadcasting, of which I was an *ex officio* member.

Many magazine articles have been written about RFE and RL and their parent corporations and published in scholarly journals, but they deal almost entirely with analytical questions involved in East–West relations, not with details regarding the origin, early growth, and maturation of the Free Europe Committee and Amcomlib. Consequently, there is very little in periodical literature out of which it would be possible to construct an account of the Radios' development and, except for RFE's indiscretions in the Hungarian Revolution and its problems following the revelation of the CIA backing, little detail about their methods of operation. Newspapers, notably the *New York Times* and *Washington Post*, have from time to time reported on Radio affairs, but for the most part such reports were carried only during crisis periods or on the occasion of such staged events as the massive Crusade for Freedom drive launched in 1950 and 1951.

Only two books have been published on RFE and none about RL. The most recent volume on RFE was Allan Michie's *Voices Through the Iron Curtain*, published in 1963. While it gives detailed and colorful accounts of the Polish and Hungarian revolutions, it lacks any critical appraisal of the output of the Radios and any reference to activities of the intelligence community. Michie wrote as a former deputy European director of RFE stationed in Munich and was obviously constrained from telling all he knew.

The other volume, by Robert T. Holt, entitled *Radio Free Europe*, was published four years earlier, in 1959. It was a revised version of his doctoral dissertation submitted to the Graduate School at Princeton University a year earlier. Holt hinted at the intelligence community's involvement when he wrote that Free Europe could not possibly exist on the financing it obtained from private sources. "Obviously," he observed, "any financial relationships that might exist between Washington and Radio Free Europe can not be discussed in this volume." In so writing, Holt missed the crux of a unique and fascinating experience in international political communication.

Like the Michie book, Holt is valuable on the Polish and Hungarian episodes and on structural and organizational questions, but the account is notably threadbare and lacks a discussion of the OPC/CIA element. (Of course, in 1959 RFE had been in existence for only 10 years and RL for only eight.)

One invaluable source that only recently became available was the papers of Frank Altschul, one of the original Free Europe directors, its treasurer and head of its radio division during the first two years of its existence. These papers, now deposited in the Lehman collection at Columbia University, furnished invaluable clues as to the personalities who wielded the real power in the early days, the relationships to the Intelligence Community, the internal policy disputes within the board and executive staff, and the evolution of policy. They also furnished valuable hints as to where to look for additional details.

Other pertinent matter proving useful included the *Congressional Record,* reports of congressional committees, the annual reports of the BIB, the minutes of the boards of directors of both Radios and of the BIB after its creation, and finally the Eisenhower Commission's report entitled "The Right to Know."

Reconstructing the beginnings of both the Free Europe Committee and the American Committee for the Freedom of the Peoples of Russia Incorporated, as it was first known, was the most difficult problem. Interviews with Thomas W. Braden and Cord Meyer, who were the CIA contacts for the Radios for more than two decades, furnished some clues as did the Altschul papers. Books on the Dulles family by Mosely (Leonard Mosley, *Dulles*, New York, The Dial Press/James Wade, 1978), and by Ray Cline on the CIA (*The CIA under Reagan, Bush and Casey*) corroborated the findings. Oliver J. Frederickson's unpublished manuscript prepared for the Radio Liberty Committee, "Fifty Years of the Soviet Political Emigration: 1917 to 1967," recounting the efforts to create a unified council of the Soviet emigration, provided a rich account of Amcomlib's struggle to create a unified council that would assume broadcasting responsibility. The most valuable single source on this period, however, was Book IV of the Final Report of the Select Committee to Study Governmental Operations With Respect to Intelligence Activities by the U.S. Senate, published by the U.S. Government Printing Office in 1976. This report by the so-called Church Committee furnishes a detailed account of the international relations problems facing the U.S. government in the postwar period and of the political climate of the period during which Free Europe and Amcomlib were conceived and nurtured into functioning organizations. It provided a framework into which personal accounts of some of the intelligence personnel who had created the Radios could be fitted.

The reports and analyses of the Radios prepared by the GAO, the first requested by Senator Fulbright and delivered in May 1972, and the next two by the BIB, submitted in 1976 and 1981, provided a nuts-and-bolts description of operations and recommendations for improvement in areas that GAO describes as weaknesses. Two reports, one on each corporation, requested by Senator Fulbright and prepared by the Congressional Research Service of the Library of Congress, are a little heavier on the substantive side than the GAO volumes and furnish useful background particularly on the evolution of policy.

CHAPTER 1: A Quiet Night in Munich

The story of the bombing of RFE/RL headquarters in Munich was developed almost entirely through interviews with RFE/RL executives in Munich who were on the scene within minutes after the event and with one of the injured, Ingeborg Eberl, the telephone operator who sat within just a few feet of the point of impact. The greatest volume of detail came from Earnal Campbell, the vice president for engineering operations; Richard Cummings, security director; and A. Russell Poole, director of administration. The atropine incident was covered in the *New York Times* shortly after it occurred and is alluded to in Allan Michie's volume, but the best account I discovered is in the BBC's weekly publication, *The Listener*, of April 12, 1979. The same issue of *The Listener* also carries an account of the Markhov incident, including the conclusions reached by the British police concerning the implication of the Bulgarian secret police in the assassination. The Karas and Fatalibey assassinations are described in detail in an Amcomlib publication issued in 1957.

CHAPTER 2: Our Friends in the South

Assembling the facts required to tell the story of the origins of RFE and RL can only be accomplished on the basis of what might be described as investigative reporting. It involved checking and cross-checking, discovering leads and following them up with reliable sources, and matching published accounts against the verbal accounts given in the interviews. It was obvious that published accounts in the Michie and Holt books told only a part of the story. The Altschul papers indicated the importance of Frank Wisner in the creation of the Radios, and an interview with Thomas Braden confirmed it. Interviews with Lawrence Houston, one of the drafters of the National Security Act of 1947 and for a number of years general counsel for the CIA, Walter Pforzheimer, legislative counsel to the CIA, and Ray Cline, a former deputy director of the agency, were invaluable in filling in details. Book IV of the select Senate committee's report put the whole story into perspective and created a framework in which the more personalized accounts developed through the interviews could be put in place. The role of the OPC, for example, was apparently unknown even to long-time veterans of the Free Europe staff who had been made "witting."

CHAPTER 3: You Can't Dream Big Enough

The Altschul papers and a lengthy interview with Radio Free Europe's first director, Robert E. Lang, furnished much of the raw material for this chapter. The minutes of the meetings of the NCFE board, later changed to Free Europe Committee, established the chronology and added documentation, as did memoranda in the Free Europe Committee files and annual reports of the corporation.

CHAPTER 4: We Enter This Fight with Bare Fists

As in Chapter 3, the Altschul papers were an invaluable source. Additional detail was furnished through interviews with Lang, Braden, Meyer, and Paul Henze, who served for several years as deputy policy advisor to the European director of RFE and during the Carter administration was a member of the National Security Council staff at the White House. William Griffith, the policy advisor to the European director from 1951 to 1959, also added significant detail, as did Jan Nowak, who joined the staff early as director of the Polish service in Munich.

CHAPTER 5: Contract Approved. Salazar

The two key participants in RFE's efforts to establish an operation in Portugal furnished a wealth of detail out of which it was possible to piece together the story of RARET and Gloria. H. Gregory Thomas recounted his critically important portion of the story with gusto, humor, and infinite detail. Manuel Bivar, the Portuguese engineer assigned by President Salazar to work with Thomas, was almost equally fluent in recounting the events from the Portuguese point of view. Additional detail was supplied by Tomas Pinto Basto, who was requested by the Portuguese president to serve on the RARET board, and by Carmen da Costa Perreira, who started as a secretary in Thomas's office in Lisbon during negotiations with the Portuguese Government and by 1975 had become RARET manager. Horacio Neto, RARET's chief engineer, who was one of the first Portuguese employees, described the construction process, the installation of broadcast equipment, and the reaction of the residents of the remote village where the base was built. Minutes of the Free Europe board and annual reports of the corporation substantiated the accounts given by the participants.

CHAPTER 6: Building the Cover

The story of the Crusade for Freedom was developed in great measure by the lively recollections of Abbott Washburn, who planned and executed the first massive campaign. Washburn's account is supplemented by a record of the creation and dedication of the Freedom Bell, given in a booklet published in 1950 by the Free Europe Committee, "The Story of the Freedom Bell." Washburn also furnished a description of the first balloon launching. Additional information was derived from minutes of meetings of the Free Europe board, the GAO report of 1971, and a summary of Crusade for Freedom and Free Europe Fund activities available in the RFE/RL files.

CHAPTER 7: The Stalin Era is Coming to a Close

The story of the origins of RL was even more complicated than that of RFE. Virtually nothing has been written about RL. Secrecy about its funding and early activity was a firm policy of the OPC and the CIA. The first real clue about its origins was found in the minutes of a "pre-incorporation meeting of members of the board of the American Committee for Freedom of the Peoples of Russia, Inc." that took place on January 10, 1951. Reference was made to the fact that money had been sent to the committee's European representative the previous summer. This was clear evidence that the creation of the corporation did not mark the beginning of the effort, and the inference had to be drawn that, as in the case of Free Europe, the OPC was responsible. A fuller account was developed in interviews with Franklin A. Lindsay, the OPC senior officer assigned by Frank Wisner to stimulate the creation of what became RL; John F. B. Mitchell, Jr., who drafted its bylaws and articles of incorporation; and by Allen Grover, who called the first meeting of the board in its pre-incorporation meeting. Oliver J. Frederickson's unpublished report on the Soviet emigration and Gene Sosin's personal account of his experiences with the Institute for the Study of the USSR added detail, as did Peter Khruzhin's recollections of his participation in émigré meetings as a representative of the Vlasovite group. Howland Sargeant, later to become the Radio's president, filled in details with an account of his invitation to accept the presidency, his assessment of the Radio's problems, his reflections on his first years as chief executive in which it was necessary to bring RL from a floundering, dissension-wracked group to a unified organization with a sense of mission. Francis Ronalds, Jr., who later became executive director of RL in Munich, added notes concerning his experiences as the first news director in Munich.

CHAPTER 8: Franco Pays Off

Much of Chapter 8 is based on Sargeant's recollections of his negotiations in Spain in June and July of 1955 and Ernesto Marrero's parallel account on his participation as a representative of the Spanish government in the search for an operating base. Additional detail was obtained in a day-long interview in 1981 with six veteran department heads at the Playa de Pals base, some of whom had been on the Amcomlib payroll from the establishment of the first outpost at Pals. George Dennis, current representative of RL in Madrid, furnished a briefing paper with historical details and participated with Marrero in a lengthy interview.

CHAPTER 9: Years of Transition

Cord Meyer's book, *Facing Reality,* published in 1980, is particularly valuable in tracing the softening of Radio policy during the period of the mid-1950s. He also furnished a particularly graphic account of the Swiatlo incident. A CRS report, written by James Robert Price and delivered to the Fulbright committee in 1972, devoted a substantial section to policy modification. Interviews with Francis F. Ronalds, Jr., former program director and executive director of RL; with Robert Tuck, who joined RL in a policy role and later became director of the Russian service; and with Meyer contributed to fleshing out the account.

CHAPTER 10: An Excess of Exuberance

Interviews with William Griffith, Paul Henze, and Cord Meyer contributed enormously to this chapter. Both Michie and Holt carry detailed accounts of the events in

Poland and Hungary as they unfolded during the summer and fall of 1956 and of the reaction at RFE. Meyer's book, *Facing Reality*, also devotes a good deal of attention to RFE's reporting of the events, including the specific episodes that gave rise to later criticism. American newspapers, including notably the *New York Times* and the *Washington Post*, also devoted attention to RFE's troubles following the Hungarian Revolution, including the complaints and the results of the analyses of performance.

CHAPTER 11: The Implacable Struggle

Most of the evidence forming the basis for this chapter is pieced together from corporate minutes, annual reports, Amcomlib promotional publications, the Congressional Research Service report of March 1972, and interviews with Sargeant; Ronalds; Tuck; Jon Lodeesen, who joined the staff later in a policy capacity; and Robert Redlich, director of public affairs in Munich.

CHAPTER 12: The End of Jiggery-Pokery

Interviews with key participants contributed the bulk of the detail making up this chapter. Lewis Sebesta, now a member of the Czechoslovak service staff in New York, but assigned to Munich in 1960, described the turmoil in the Czechoslovak service that broke out in the fall of 1960. General Smith added detail on the remedial measures he imposed and the overall change in direction that resulted. James Edwards, current news chief, added a complete account of the transformation of the news department. An overall assessment of the importance of the evolving changes was furnished by James F. Brown, who later became director of research and then director of RFE. My own involvement with Free Europe management in New York and with Allen Dulles with respect to the possibility of assuming the directorship of RFE in Munich added perspective.

CHAPTER 13: The Security Blanket Begins to Unravel

An article in *Ramparts* in March 1967 opened the first tear in the Radios' security blanket. The unfolding story of CIA participation in funding can be found in the American press, notably the *New York Times* and the *Washington Post*, and in a CBS documentary broadcast in March 1967, a copy of the script for which can be found in the Hoover Institution files in Palo Alto. Sargeant, Meyer, and Allen Hovey and John Dunning (senior executives of Free Europe in New York) furnished details on the reaction at the Radio headquarters and the CIA. Scores of editorials retained in the Free Europe files suggest the depth of the national reaction.

CHAPTER 14: The Patient Looks Awful, Awful Sick

Details of the unfolding story of the crisis faced by the Radios can be found in the *Congressional Record*, reports issued by the Foreign Relations Committee of the Senate and the Foreign Affairs Committee of the House, and in the nation's press. David

M. Abshire, then assistant secretary of state for congressional relations and later chairman of the BIB, added depth and detail to the story in a lengthy interview. He was particularly effective in the telling the behind-the-scenes story of the maneuvering that led to passage of an appropriations bill that kept the Radios alive when hope seemed to have expired. John Baker, a Department of State officer assigned responsibility for overseeing the Radios, also added helpful detail, as did Sargeant, Hovey, and Dunning.

CHAPTER 15: I Shall Raise My Voice a Little

Congressional documents, as in the case of Chapter 14, form a solid base for this chapter. Per Federspiel, a long-time member of the West European Advisory Committee for Free Europe, a former member of the Danish parliament, and a prestigious Danish lawyer heavily involved in international organizations, furnished a graphic account of the reaction of WEAC members to the disclosures concerning funding and Chairman Fulbright's complaints. Sir Frank Roberts, the United Kingdom representative on WEAC, amplified on this facet of the story, and Pieter J. W. DeBrauw, a Dutch attorney, described the process of forming a Dutch foundation that would be in a legal position to seek European financial support for the Radios. These interviews were supplemented by examination of a detailed report of the history of WEAC in the Free Europe files.

CHAPTER 16: Not Inconsistent with Broad U.S. Foreign Policy

Details regarding the organization and recognition of unions in RFE headquarters in Munich were obtained from the minutes of the Free Europe Corporation board meetings and interviews with Free Europe employees who were active in union activities at English Garden headquarters in Munich. In taped interviews, Evdokim Evdokimov and David Taylor of the American Newspaper Guild and Erwin Schulz of the German Union of Employees (DAG) described the organizing process and the reasons underlying the enthusiasm for unions. The best account of the work of the Eisenhower Commission may be found in its report published as *The Right to Know* issued on February 5, 1973. Edward W. Barrett, a member of the Commission, filled in details and added a human element to the report. The report of the Senate Foreign Relations Committee concerning its hearings of June 12 and June 23, 1973, graphically depicts the concerns of members of the Senate and the growing support for the Radios over Senator Fulbright's opposition. An affirmative report of the Committee on legislation creating a Board for International Broadcasting furnishes the raw material to conclude this chapter.

CHAPTER 17: What We Need Most is a Period of Tranquility

The GAO report of May 1972 was an important takeoff point for this chapter. Briefing books, prepared by the staffs of both Radios for use by Radio presidents at congressional hearings, furnish details concerning staff reduction and consolidation plans.

The first and second annual reports of the BIB to the President of the United States describe BIB activities, decisions, and recommendations. Full details regarding lease negotiations for Spanish and Portuguese bases are available in the Radio files. A lengthy memo from Ronalds describes the consolidation process at RL and complains about its potentially damaging side effects.

CHAPTER 18: 88 Million Eastern Europeans Can't Protest but We Can

The RFE files contain a blow-by-blow account of the events and exchanges of memoranda and correspondence leading up to a strike vote by the unions at RFE in June 1975. A lengthy interview with David Taylor, a member of the news staff, of the RFE Works Council, and an enthusiast for the American Newspaper Guild, added the personal touch and fascinating descriptions of union planning and operations. Evdokimov also contributed to rounding out the story, as did Schulz of the DAG. Recollections of my own role were not an inconsiderable factor in reconstructing the events.

CHAPTER 19: External Problems Divert Attention

Detailed accounts of the problems involved in renegotiating leases for transmitter bases in Spain and Portugal may be found in the RFE/RL files and in the minutes of meetings of the BIB, in its annual reports, and in the minutes of the meetings of the RFE/RL board. Reports in the same files carry considerable detail on Pavel Minarik's return to Czechoslovakia, with the attendant propaganda barrage from that country. A full account of RFE's and RL's relations with the International Olympic Committee, dating back to 1956, and culminating in a vote to grant permission to the Radios to cover the 1976 Olympics in Montreal, can be found in a detailed report prepared by the RFE/RL executive staff in the winter of 1977.

CHAPTER 20: Accountability, Nexus, and Fiduciary Responsibility

Primary sources for this chapter include BIB annual reports, BIB minutes, minutes of the RFE/RL board and executive committee, and internal memos in the RFE/RL files. Copies of the letters included in the exchanges involving Abshire, Sparkman, and Percy are available in the RFE/RL files. The report of the subcommittee of the Senate Foreign Relations Committee, headed by Senator McGovern, carries the text of Roberts' testimony and Senator Pell's response.

CHAPTER 21: The 1976 October Revolution

Memos and documents in the files of the Radios and the BIB are supplemented by lengthy interviews with Victoria Monditsch Dreving, Vladimir Matusevitch, and Gleb Rahr of the staff of the Russian service of RL. The RFE/RL files contain details concerning the incidents described and the Critchlow report is available either from BIB or RFE/RL, as is the Drew Pearson column.

CHAPTER 22: Was It Worth the Cost?

The section on jamming relies on various reports to the RFE/RL management from its engineering staff, from monitoring reports gathered from the fringes of Eastern Europe and the Soviet Union, and from analyses based on data derived from a variety of sources and analyzed by the Radio's engineering staff. A book by John B. Whitton and Arthur Larson, published in 1964 by Oceana, Dobbs Ferry, New York, analyzes the legal basis for jamming and for outlawing it and the arguments used by proponents and opponents. The analysis of procedures used to obtain audience ratings was obtained from printed descriptions of the methodology used by both RFE and RL issued by the RFE/RL research department and through exhaustive formal interviews with Henry Hart, director of RFE audience research, and Max Ralis, then director of RL audience research. Much of the background was assimilated over the years in which I served as the Radios' chief executive. The story of the "Bridge to Poland" first came to my attention in newspaper reports. These were amplified by clippings sent out from RFE/RL headquarters in Munich. I then followed up with an extensive interview with Jan Tyszkiewicz of the Polish staff of RFE, who produced the program. The Romanian earthquake story was intensively reported by the press at the time it occurred in 1976. Subsequently, RFE/RL staff in Washington prepared an extensive analysis of the coverage by the Romanian service. Noel Bernard, chief of the Romanian service when the quake occurred, expanded on the account in a detailed interview.

CHAPTER 23: A Glimpse into the Future

A useful and carefully developed argument for further support for RFE/RL may be found in the report issued by the Heritage Foundation published November 13, 1981. Otherwise, conclusions reached in this chapter are mainly the product of my own experience with RFE/RL and the background acquired in my role as president.

Chronology

1947

July   Congress passes and the president signs the National Security Act of 1947, designed primarily to coordinate the military services into a Department of Defense; at the same time it converts the rather weak central intelligence group into a Central Intelligence Agency and gives it a clandestine intelligence-gathering capability.

The Department of State and the new Department of Defense again enter departmental meetings to discuss the problems of the refugees from the Soviet Union and Eastern Europe, now congregating largely in West Germany, and to consider their possible use as propagandists for the democratic method of government. Two persons particularly concerned are Secretary of Defense James V. Forrestal and the policy advisor for the State Department, Robert Joyce.

Frank Wisner, the former OSS chief for Southeastern Europe and the Balkans, leaves the Carter, Ledyard and Milburn law office in New York to accept appointment as deputy assistant secretary of state for the occupied countries.

December 14   NSC 4/A gives CIA responsibility for covert psychological operations.

December 22   A Special Procedures Group is established within the CIA's Office of Special Operations to carry out psychological operations. The CIA simultaneously was given the responsibility for covert intelligence activities.

1948

February   The democratic government of Czechoslovakia falls to the Communists. It is feared in government circles that an election scheduled for Italy in March 1948 might result in a similar Communist victory.

The Special Procedures Group set up in December 1947, with assistance from other government agencies, uses every available device and lavish expenditure of funds to see to it that the Christian Democratic party succeeds in winning the election. During this same period, this SPG acquires a radio transmitter and a secret propaganda printing plant and has begun assembling "freedom balloons," all to deliver propaganda from Western Europe into the countries of Eastern Europe.

George Kennan, the policy planning advisor to the secretary of state, advocates the development of a covert political action committee. By political action, he means direct intervention in the electoral process in West European countries threatened by losses to Communists, this intervention to be designed to influence public opinion through the media.

Kennan also proposes that the policy planning staff have a directorate for overt and covert political warfare. This group would be under a special studies group reporting to the Department of State, but it would not be formally associated with the department, its funds would be concealed, and its personnel formally carried on nongovernment payroll.

The National Security Council, established under the National Security Act, endorses a dramatic increase in covert operations directed against the USSR, including political and economic warfare and paramilitary activities. At the same time, it establishes an Office of Special Projects. (A month later, it is renamed the Office of Policy Coordination.)

September 1   Kennan, acting with the advice of Allen Dulles, appoints Wisner Director of the OPC.

Allen Dulles, DeWitt C. Poole, Spencer Phenix, and Frederic Dolbeare meet several times informally and discuss establishing a civilian organization to work with refugees and use their talents in communicating with their compatriots at home. The group on occasion consults with Peter Mero, who functions as a consultant to the CIA and the OPC, on the possibilities of shortwave broadcasting into Eastern Europe; with H. Gregory Thomas on the possibility of establishing shortwave transmitter bases on the Iberian Peninsula; and with Edward W. Barrett, who was the wartime director of the Voice of America. The purpose was to discuss the creation of an international propaganda operation.

1949

February   Kennan consults with Ambassador Joseph Grew regarding the building of a civilian organization to work with refugees. Grew also consults with DeWitt Poole.

March	Poole, on his own, leases office space in the Empire State Building in New York.
May 17	A national Committee for a Free Europe is incorporated under the laws of the State of New York. Allen Dulles assumes the presidency.
June 2	The Committee for a Free Europe is announced to the general public. Poole assumes the presidency and Grew becomes chairman. The word *National* is added to the title, making it the National Committee for a Free Europe.

NCFE establishes a committee on press and broadcasting that, in November, it converts to divisional status. It employs Robert Lang as consultant to advise in establishing a broadcast operation.

July 7	Board appoints a finance committee to give attention to fund raising.
November	Poole assigns the lease for space in the Empire State Building from himself to NCFE.
December	Lang and a New York lawyer, H. Struve Hensel, a wartime Navy Department assistant secretary, leave for Europe to check the possibility of leasing or obtaining free broadcast time for reaching into East European countries. They are discouraged by prospects, but see in RIAS an example they might follow: a government-owned station broadcasting full time into Eastern Europe.

The Air Force University and the Rockefeller Foundation jointly finance a Harvard University project to study the attitudes of Russian émigrés in the Munich area of West Germany.

1950

January	NCFE decides to work on a national fund-raising campaign and employs Abbott Washburn to serve as a consultant and plan such a project. Washburn and associates, working during the winter and spring, develop plans for a massive nationwide campaign to be capped by the installation of a "freedom bell" in the City Hall in West Berlin following a triumphant tour across the United States during the summer and fall.

Lang is instructed in February to go to Germany to take possession of a low-power shortwave transmitter that is being made available to NCFE by "friends."

NCFE decides in March to establish headquarters in Munich and negotiates for space for a headquarters building. Also obtains from the air force a former German air base at Lampertheim, West Germany, suitable for a transmitter base.

April 14	NSC issues NSC 68 calling for a non-military counter—offensive against the USSR embracing economic, political, and psychological warfare.

In the summer an American Institute for the Study of the USSR is established in Munich ostensibly independently but clearly with governmental funds. The institute operates in parallel with the Harvard project.

May 18   A contract is let for casting the Freedom Bell.

Summer   OPC personnel recruit Allen Grover of Time, Inc., Eugene Lyons, William H. Chamberlin, and others to serve on the board of the new organization to be created to deal with Soviet refugees in Western Europe. John F. B. Mitchell, Jr., is simultaneously recruited to draft articles of incorporation and bylaws for such an organization.

NCFE completes plans for a headquarters building in Munich and begins construction.

Broadcast division of NCFE begins recruiting personnel both in Munich and New York. Experienced American broadcast personnel are employed to train exiles in American techniques and to begin production of programs.

July 4   The broadcast division of NCFE, now known as Radio Free Europe, begins a broadcast schedule with a program beamed to Czechoslovakia from the Lampertheim base. Policy control over broadcast material becomes an issue of major concern in the NCFE organization. Tension grows within the board concerning whether to assign principal responsibility for policy to the broadcast division or to retain it within the corporate headquarters.

July 7   The Institute for the Study of the History and Culture of the Soviet Union is founded in Munich by the OPC.

September   Rear Admiral Hillenkoetter is replaced as director of CIA by General "Beetle" Smith, who starts at once to make plans for incorporation of Wisner's Office of Policy Coordination within the CIA. Since funding for NCFE had come from the OPC, this marks a change of responsibility from the OPC to the CIA.

1951

January 2   Allen Dulles becomes deputy director of the CIA with responsibility for the OPC and the Office of Special Operations, putting him in direct line of command over Wisner.

January 12   Informal meeting of prospective incorporators and directors of the American Committee for the Freedom of the Peoples of the USSR, Inc., an organization that would be formed under OPC or CIA aegis to perform a role with Soviet refugees similar to that performed by NCFE with East European refugees.

January 16   Lang presents architect drawings for a Munich building to the NCFE board. He is instructed to proceed.

Poole resigns presidency of NCFE and is succeeded by C. D. Jackson, publisher of *Fortune* magazine.

January 19	A meeting of the incorporators for the American Committee for the Freedom of the Peoples of the USSR approves the articles of incorporation and elects board members.
Late January	H. Gregory Thomas leaves for Lisbon to negotiate leases and licenses with the government of Portugal for a major transmitter base.
February 8	Eugene Lyons is elected president of Amcomlib.
	Free Europe establishes the Crusade for Freedom, Incorporated as a separate corporation. Lucius Clay is elected chairman and Abbott Washburn, vice chairman; Allen Dulles is one of the incorporators.
April 12	Thomas is back from Lisbon with permission to establish a transmitter base and licenses to broadcast.
May 3	RARET, Inc., is formally proclaimed in Portugal as the instrumentality to own and operate a transmitter base for NCFE there.
May 22	Amcomlib changes its name to the American Committee for the Liberation of the Peoples of Russia, Inc.
June	Amcomlib leases space for a production center on East 45th Street in New York and starts to employ personnel.
June 21	The émigré groups meet at Starnberg in West Germany and hope that the results of a shaky truce may hold the organization together.
	Wings number one and two of the Munich building for RFE are completed.
July 4	Broadcasting to Eastern Europe begins from Gloria. The transmitter used is the same 7½-kilowatt portable unit that started broadcasting from Lampertheim exactly a year earlier. It was moved from Lampertheim to Gloria.
August	RFE moves its German transmitter base from Lampertheim to Biblis.
	Balloons carrying materials prepared by refugees under the direction of the publications division of NCFE are launched from Regensburg, West Germany, toward Czechoslovakia.
	Representatives of a number of Soviet émigré groups representing both Russian and non-Russian nationalities meet in Stuttgart, Germany, to try to form a unified council of the emigration that would operate a radio station for Amcomlib. The possibility for unity seems doubtful.
October	RFE begins a full schedule of broadcasts to Hungary.
November	Émigré groups meet in Wiesbaden to carry on efforts toward unification. There is still little sign of progress.
December	RFE broadcasts a 50-kilowatt signal from Gloria.

1952

February 11	Eugene Lyons resigns presidency of Amcomlib and is succeeded by Admiral Alan G. Kirk. The committee decides to negotiate with the German government to establish and operate radio and transmitter facilities in Germany. They purchase the Lampertheim base from NCFE.
February	Wings three and four of the RFE building in Munich are completed.
March 1	C. D. Jackson resigns and is succeeded by Admiral Harold B. "Min" Miller.
March 21	Poole resigns from board.
April	Master Control is opened in Munich.
April 21	At its annual meeting, Amcomlib decides it must urgently tackle the problem of organizing a group to sponsor the station in Germany.
June	Forrest McCluney, who had been European director for Radio Free Europe and subsequently employed by Amcomlib, goes to Munich to supervise the creation and operation of a radio station production center in Munich.
August	Wings five and six of the RFE building are completed.
October 10	Admiral Kirk resigns as president of Amcomlib and is replaced by Admiral Leslie C. Stevens.
November 11	The new base at Gloria is dedicated.

1953

During the year, RFE is busy rounding out its program preparation and production staffs, training personnel, perfecting a news/information-gathering effort, and establishing a system for policy control. Its overall attitude toward its function, which was belligerent and pejorative during its formative stages, is now being gradually modified to a more thoughtful and objective approach.

January 29	Whitney Shepardson succeeds Admiral Miller as FE president.
March 1	Radio Liberation, the air arm of Amcomlib, goes on the air from Lampertheim. Ten minutes later, jamming starts from the Soviet Union.
March 5	Stalin dies, giving an opportunity to RL's radio staff to cover a major story and achieve an instant audience.
March 16	Amcomlib's name is changed to the American Committee for Liberation from Bolshevism, Inc.
March 23	A coordinating center is finally proclaimed. It is made up of four Great Russian groups and five nationalities. The radio station is now to be described as the "Radio Station of the Coordinating Center for the Anti-Bolshevik Struggle."
	Two small transmitters are now operating at Lampertheim.
April 23	Amcomlib staff level has reached 320, with 46 employees in New York and 274 in Munich. This marks a growth from 19 in New York and 4 in Munich a year earlier.

June 17	Riots in East Berlin test abilities of both RFE and RL at covering a fast-breaking story.
June	The Coordinating Center that was proclaimed on April 23 splits into two parts.
August 1	RL drops the "Coordinating Center" identification and abandons all hopes for creation of a coordinating center.
September 1	Amcomlib discontinues financial support for all political groups and adopts a new identification: "Your compatriots behind the border."

1954

March	RL announces that it is now broadcasting 6 to 7 hours daily in 11 languages.
March 24	Amcomlib board proposes that in lieu of creating a coordinating center it establish "a working alliance" or "an equal partnership" with émigré groups.
September	An RL employee, Leonid Karas, is found drowned in the Munich area under mysterious circumstances. It is assumed Karas is a victim of Soviet assassins. This is the first evidence of assassination efforts, but there had been threats, intimidations, and high-handed persuasion to RL staff members to return to the Soviet Union.
September 28 to October 31	CIA turns over to RFE's Polish service enough tapes of interviews with a former high-ranking official of the Polish Secret Police to constitute the bulk of 101 broadcasts. These broadcasts are transmitted in their entirety to Poland, and printed versions of them are sent into Poland by balloon. Other RFE services and RL services, as well, make use of the materials developed out of the tapes in broadcasts into their own audience areas.
October 6	Stevens resigns as Amcomlib president and is succeeded by Howland Sargeant, a former assistant secretary of state for public affairs.
November	Efforts to rely on the emigration as the operator of the radio station are abandoned once and for all.
	The second assassination occurs in Munich. Abo Fatalibey, the head of the Azerbaijan section of RL, is found dead as the result of an assassin's bullet. The assumption again is that Soviet agents were responsible.

1955

| May 1 | RL makes its first broadcast from Taipei beamed to eastern parts of Siberia and the Maritime Provinces of the Soviet Union. |
| | Government engineers begin to make propagation studies in Spain, looking for possible use of that country as a base for transmitter operations designed to reach the Soviet Union. |

June	Sargeant leaves for Spain to begin negotiations for a lease for a transmitter base and licenses to broadcast.
July	Franco approves Sargeant's request in principle.

1956

February	Soviet Premier Khrushchev speaks for 6 hours to the Soviet parliament, condemning the Stalin regime.
June 4	The Khrushchev speech is published verbatim in a number of American newspapers, including the *New York Times*. The CIA had succeeded, by judicious use of agents, in smuggling the full text out of the Soviet Union and decided in late May to release it to the press. Both RFE and RL make good use of it in preparing broadcasts for transmission to all of the target areas.
June 27–28	A series of riots occur in the city of Poznan in Poland. There is bloodshed and the rioters are put down by force.
Summer	The chief of engineering for RL, Colonel McGiffert, is sent to Spain to search the countryside for base sites suitable for RL transmissions.
September	The workers who were involved in the riots in Poznan on June 27 and 28 are tried and given only very light sentences, thus easing some of the pressure on the Polish government.
September 5	Amcomlib changes its name to Radio Liberation, Inc.
October 1	General Willis D. Crittenberger is named president of Free Europe Committee, replacing Whitney Shepardson.
October 19	Dramatic changes occur in the composition of the Polish government; the government's Politburo is disbanded. At the time of the meeting concerning disbandment, Khrushchev, Molotov, and Mikoyan, three of the top Russian leaders, arrive in Warsaw ostensibly to restore the Politburo with its strong pro-Russian orientation. A resolute stand by the Poles forces them to back down and return to Moscow with the mission a failure.
	RL follows events in Eastern Europe carefully and makes many broadcasts to the Soviet Union concerning these events. Some critics, however, believe they are tentative and ineffective.
October 23	Violent demonstrations break out in Budapest Hungary.
October 25	A full-scale revolution is in progress throughout Hungary. Russian tanks arrive on the scene to restore order. Fighting continues between the freedom fighters and the Russians.
November 4	The Hungarian freedom fighters seem to have won the battle. The Russians withdraw.
November 6	Russian tanks reappear and reenter the fight with considerable success.
	Eisenhower is reelected to U.S. presidency.
November 11	The revolution is apparently over except for scattered action in areas away from Budapest. Thousands of refugees are fleeing across the border into Austria.

November   Representatives of the Soviet Union violently attack RFE for having stirred up the revolution and encouraged freedom fighters to give their lives in a futile battle against the Soviet Union. A storm of criticism sweeps both Europe and the United States. RFE launches its own investigation and analysis to determine whether it had made any errors. The German government also launches an intensive investigation.

1957

January 25   The West German government announces results of its report on RFE coverage of Hungary's abortive revolution. It absolves RFE of blame for inciting revolution and gives it a clean bill of health. The RFE study finds some evidence of doubtful tactics but no overt evidence of the Radio's having encouraged the revolt.

Free Europe recognizes its first union, the German Union of Employees.

July 15   RL announces an agreement with the government of Spain for use of a base at the Playa de Pals. The property is purchased from the owner and turned over to the government of Spain, which in turn grants a license to broadcast from the site and a lease for use of the property.

1958

Construction is started at Pals.

RL issues a revised policy manual, pointing its staff toward promoting "liberalization" rather than "liberation."

October 3   Archibald A. Alexander is named president of Free Europe Inc., replacing Crittenberger.

1959

March 23   RL transmits its first programs from Pals over a hastily installed 100-kilowatt transmitter. A contract between the government of Spain and Amcomlib goes into effect for a duration of 12 years, until March 23, 1971.

RL begins referring to itself as the "freedom stations," abandoning its formerly harsher line.

September   Khrushchev makes his first trip to the United States and is covered intensively by RL, even though many members of the Russian service argue that coverage of the trip might give the Russian dictator too much publicity and prominence.

Free Europe, Inc., orginates the West European Advisory Committee to help it in maintaining friendly relations in Western Europe and to give it advice concerning West European attitudes.

The American Newspaper Guild is recognized by Free Europe.

The RFE news department is given additional responsibilities and additional authority to impose an objective attitude in its news reporting, but its research function is separated from it and established as an independent unit reporting to each of the broadcast desks.

1960

October   Khrushchev makes a second trip to the United States and is given even more coverage by RL. One of the events carried live into the Soviet Union is Khrushchev's UN speech, including the famous shoe-pounding episode and the follow-up by American personnel.

A 250-kilowatt transmitter begins operating from the Pals base in Spain.

The first signs appear of possible trouble on the Czechoslovak service of RFE. The long-time director of the desk, Dr. Firt, retires and is replaced by an unpopular member of the staff. Staff members begin a memo-writing campaign denouncing Firt's successor and asking for a change.

November   European director, Eric Hazelhoff, fires the 18 editors on the Czech desk he considers most responsible for the campaign of insubordination. Turmoil reigns in the Czechoslovak service and spreads throughout the organization.

December   As a result of vigorous action by both Free Europe headquarters in New York and the CIA, Hazelhoff and his two deputies are fired. Immediately thereafter, the 18 terminated editors return to their jobs, and the process of restoring harmony begins.

A third union, the Bavarian Journalists Association, is recognized.

1961

February   Retired Major General C. Rodney Smith, a vice president of the Free Europe staff in New York, is sent to Munich to restore order and continue bringing harmony to the turbulent organization. The chain of command is totally reorganized. The directorship of RFE is moved from New York to Munich, and Smith accepts the job. He gives more responsibility to each of the broadcast service directors and to the director of news.

June 8   John Richardson, Jr., succeeds Archibald Alexander as RFE president.

1962

The major 1962 event, the Cuban missile crisis, was reported extensively by both the RFE and RL services.

1963

November   The major story was the assassination of President Kennedy.

1964

January   The Radio Liberation Committee changes its name formally to the Radio Liberty Committee and changes the designation of its radio operation to Radio Liberty.

1967

John Richardson resigns and is replaced by William Durkee, who had been involved in CIA oversight of the Radios in the early 1950s.

February 14   *The New York Times* carries a news story reporting on an article scheduled to appear in the March issue of *Ramparts Magazine*. The article describes in some detail how the CIA furnished financial aid to the National Student Association.

February 15   A piece by Neil Sheehan in *The New York Times* follows up on the February 14 piece going into further detail and suggesting that the CIA financed not only the NSA, but a number of other organizations operating out of the United States in the international field.

There is one line in the Sheehan piece which points to involvement of RFE and RL. "It is believed the agency provides clandestine aid to anti-communist labor unions, publications, and radio and television stations."

The Sheehan piece also names the foundations that have been used for conduits to transfer funds to private agencies operating with government support.

A think piece by James Reston of *The New York Times* suggests that the revelation by *Ramparts* places in jeopardy CIA programs of aid to anti-Communist publications, radio and television stations, and labor unions. He further asserts that Presidents Eisenhower, Kennedy, and Johnson were knowledgeable about the matter and that Senators McCarthy and Fulbright had also been informed.

President Johnson instructs the CIA to close out aid to all student groups. He calls for review of aid to all other programs intended to combat Communist activities in private organizations. Eight Democratic congressmen ask the president to open an immediate investigation at the highest level.

February 21   An article in *The New York Times* describes the process of passing money through from dummy foundations to the organizations. It identifies the Hobby foundation as a principal conduit. This story also reports that on February 15 the president appointed a committee made up of Attorney General Katzenbach, HEW Secretary Gardiner, and CIA chief Helms to look into the charges and determine the legality and advisability of government financing of private organizations.

February 26   The Sunday *Washington Post* carries a lengthy piece on page one of the "Feature" section describing in detail how monies from the CIA were transferred to dummy foundations for being transferred in turn to various private organizations. Free Europe was named specifically as one of the organizations receiving funds in this manner. RL was totally missed.

March 13 CBS News carries a 1-hour documentary in prime time that argues that anyone who gave money to the Crusade for Freedom was financing a CIA activity.

March 9 The Katzenbach committee reports. With a literal interpretation of the report, funding to both Free Europe and the RL Committee could cut off immediately. Intervention, however, by Helms and Senator Ellender succeeds in giving the president a loophole that permits continued funding.

1968

Czechoslovakia becomes a major story in the world media as the harsh controls of previous administrations begin to thaw during the so-called Prague spring.

August Soviet tanks invade Czechoslovakia to reimpose harsh controls and oust the relatively liberal Dubcek government. A hard liner, Husak, is given the prime ministership.

1969

Jewish migration from the Soviet Union begins.

A staff-reduction program and severe cost reductions begin at both Free Europe and the RL Committee.

1970

January Riots and demonstrations break out again in Poland, principally at Gdansk. RFE Polish service gets word of the riots early by monitoring a Swedish radio station across the Baltic Sea from Gdansk and furnishes intensive coverage that is restrained, thoughtful, and as objective as possible. The government of Poland resigns and order is restored under an ostensibly more liberal regime. RFE is credited with playing an important role in restraining workers and avoiding more bloodshed.

1971

January 24 Senator Case of New Jersey releases to the press a speech he plans to deliver on the Senate floor the next day in which he specifically identifies Free Europe and the RL Committee as wards of the CIA and asks that financing of them be brought out into the open.

January 25 Case introduces a bill, S-18, in the Senate providing for overt financing through the secretary of state.

March 23 The lease at Playa de Pals in Spain is renewed by the Spanish government and the RL Committee for a 5-year term.

May 24 A working party composed of personnel from the Department of State and the CIA, having drafted a bill to create an organization to operate Free Europe and RL independently of overt government control, now attempts to persuade Case to introduce on the Senate floor their bill for an American Committee for Private International Communications.

June 8   The Senate Foreign Relations Committee meets and takes no action, but Senator Fulbright asks the GAO for a thorough report and analysis of both Free Europe and the RL Committee. He asks the Congressional Research Service of the Library of Congress to prepare similar reports.

July 21   Senate Foreign Relations Committee rejects the ACPIC bill but approves Senate bill S-18 and sends it on to the Senate floor.

July 30   The Senate passes S-18, but the House still has taken no action.

September 21   The House rejects the ACPIC bill.

September 30   The House proposes an amendment to S-18, creating a government commission and giving the commission interim supervisory authority over Free Europe and the RL Committee.

November 19   The House passes the bill as amended; no action can now be taken until there is a conference with Senate committee members and a compromise bill has been reported.

1972

January 16   The conference committee fails to take action. Funding under a continuing resolution will expire on February 22. Unless some bill is passed by that time, liquidation must proceed.

January 26   The conference committee again is deadlocked. Fulbright's position is described as "icy."

February 17   A critical Evans and Novak column irritates Fulbright further. Fulbright responds on the floor of the Senate with his strongest attack yet against the two corporations.

February 22   Funding finally expires and on the basis of an amendment that had been attached to the bill before it was passed the previous year, funding cannot be renewed or extended. Only new legislation will permit it to continue. Radios continue operating on dwindling reserves.

February 23   Conference committee again fails to find common ground.
Fifty senators, however, sign a resolution calling for continuation of both organizations.

March 22   After considerable behind-the-scenes negotiations, a compromise is approved and passed by both the House and Senate authorizing $36 million for fiscal year 1972.

The Congressional Research Service of the Library of Congress issues reports on the two Radios that are generally laudatory.

March 30   The president signs the appropriation bill for fiscal 1972. This will carry the Radios, however, only to June 30, 1972. A new appropriation will be necessary for the year starting July 1.

May 10   President Nixon announces his intention to appoint a commission to examine the whole question of financing for the two organizations. He asks the secretary of state to submit a bill guaranteeing support for FY 1973.

May 25	The GAO submits its analytical report, which is also quite laudatory.
June 5, 6, 7	The Senate Foreign Relations Committee holds hearings on S3045, hears Dr. Kurt Stikker from the Netherlands who has come to the United States as chairman of WEAC.
June 12	The Senate Committee reports out the bill without amendment.
June 16	The funding bill for FY 1973 passes the Senate.
August 7	The funding bill for FY 1973 passes the House.
August 10	The president announces the names of members of a commission he has appointed to study the long-term future of the Radios.
August 20	The president signs the bill into law.
October	Herman Van Roijen succeeds Stikker as chairman of WEAC.

1973

February 3	The commission appointed by the president and led by Milton Eisenhower reports to the White House and suggests the creation of the Board for International Broadcasting as the government's oversight agency.
Spring	Bills are introduced in both House and Senate to create a Board for International Broadcasting and appropriate $50 million for FY 1974.
June 12 and 23	The Senate Foreign Relations Committee holds hearings. Fulbright continues to be critical, but it is obvious now that his opposition is not enough to stop passage of a BIB bill.
October 19	The BIB bill is enacted into law.
November	The boards of Free Europe and RLC present to the OMB a plan for physical consolidation in Munich and further staff reductions.
November and December	The boards of both Free Europe and RL announce plans for (a) single management of the two corporations, (b) common support services, and (c) joint operating locations in New York and Munich. These three steps are in harmony with recommendations made in the GAO report delivered on May 25, 1972, and are also supported by the Eisenhower Commission. The plan, however, suggests maintaining the two separate corporations, as had been recommended by the Eisenhower commission.
December	Free Europe and the RL Committee begin negotiations with the German government for renovation of the English Garden site, adding 2000 square meters to the building to accommodate RL functions. The cost will be a little less than $1 million. Completion to be in October/November 1975; RL to move in immediately thereafter.

1974

Late April	All members of the five-man BIB have been appointed by the president.

April 30	BIB organizes, seeks office space, and begins to employ staff.
	Revolution in Portugal ousts the last remnants of the Salazar and successor governments and throws the country into a state of confusion, thus placing the lease for the Gloria property in jeopardy.
June	Three BIB directors visit Munich to prepare a report on recommendations for future.
July	The group of three directors reports on a consolidation plan that parallels the one prepared the previous November by Radio managements.
October	German authorities grant permission for renovation of the English Garden building.
November	The consolidation plan presented by the BIB directors is accepted by the full BIB and calls for a single management, consolidation of management and technical support, and a joint operating location.

1975

February 28	The three unions write formally to BIB chairman Abshire promising to use "every channel at their disposal to rectify" conditions at the two Radios.
April 30	The Portuguese lease formally expires, but is extended to October by the shaky government in power.
May 13	The presidents of the two corporations, Free Europe and the RL Committee, announce the necessity of terminating an additional 100 employees. This announcement comes on top of terminations that have succeeded in reducing the staff by between 400 and 500 since 1969.
May 20	A representative of the New York Newspaper Guild testifies before the House Appropriations Committee, supporting the Radio budget for 1976, but asking that special provisions be made to assist employees being terminated.
May 28	The Newspaper Guild writes to Abshire reporting that the unions have decided on "industrial action."
May 30	Unions post a message on the bulletin boards in Munich calling for a vote on industrial action to be taken June 2, 3, and 4.
June 3	Abshire writes to the Newspaper Guild explaining the BIB position.
June 2, 3, and 4	Ninety-three percent of union members vote for industrial action. The exact nature of the action is as yet undecided.
June 30	Durkee and Sargeant relinquish office as presidents of Free Europe and the RL Committee, respectively.
July 1	Sig Mickelson assumes both presidencies.
July 10	Industrial action takes place in the form of a "spontaneous demonstration" as the new president enters the English Garden building for a formal statement to the staff and a press conference. Following the industrial action, tension seems to subside, and, while there is by no means total employee/management peace, at the same time, there are no further strike votes taken and it is promised that

	there will be no further industrial action.
October 30	The Portuguese lease, according to strict interpretation, expires, but the government assures that no action will be taken to oust RFE or to suspend action. Renegotiation is promised after formal elections are held later in the spring of 1976.
November 20	Franco dies. This throws the whole question of renewal of the RL lease, due to expire March 23, into considerable doubt. Spanish government authorities have been reluctant to open any negotiations, and the Radios have to face the possibility that they could be ousted as of March 23 of the next year.

1976

February	Credentials for RFE and RL to cover the Winter Olympic Games in Innsbruck, Austria, are withdrawn after the opening of the Games by vote of the executive committee of the International Olympic Committee. There are protests from the BIB, the secretary of state, and from members of the Senate, but Radio personnel are cautioned by U.S. Olympic officials that letting politics enter into the matter might result in an adverse vote later regarding the Summer Games.
Late March	Negotiations begin for a renewal of the lease on the Gloria facility in Portugal. Parliamentary elections are scheduled for April.
April	RFE/RL management, deciding that it is impossible to continue the two separate corporations and that outright merger is an absolute necessity, proceeds to employ legal counsel to draw up the required papers.
July 2	David Binder of the *New York Times* publishes a leak from an early draft of the GAO report of 1976, suggesting that outrageous salaries are being paid to some American employees in Munich. Senators Pastore and Mansfield condemn the Radios for overpaying staff members and call the salaries "shocking and scandalous."
July	The question of granting credentials to RFE and RL personnel to cover the Summer Olympics in Montreal comes to a head at an IOC meeting in Montreal on July 14 just prior to the opening of the Games. RFE/RL wins by a 42 to 21 margin after a lengthy and vitriolic debate.
September 24	Abshire writes to Senator Sparkman, chairman of the Foreign Relations Committee, suggesting that the merger documents to be voted upon by the Free Europe and Radio Liberty Committee boards should spell out the role, duties, and obligations of corporate officers and directors and furnish an adequate definition of "fiduciary responsibility."
September 30	Sparkman replies, insisting that the corporate charter should acknowledge "accountability of corporate officers to the BIB."
October 1	Radio Liberty Committee, Inc. and Free Europe, Inc., cease to exist as such and are replaced by RFE/RL, Inc.
October 14	The directors of the new corporation meet to ratify the documents

and to elect directors and officers. Abshire addresses them, calling again for spelling out accountability.

October   A serious dispute breaks out between two elements of the Russian service in Munich. One element represents mostly the traditional Great Russians and is composed of long-time members of the staff; the other is made up of the newcomers, many of them Jewish, who have in the interim assumed positions of higher responsibility than their older compatriots. Management shakes up the leadership of the service and causes a near revolt. Staff members refer to the period of tension as the "October revolution of 1976."

1977

January   A Russian émigré scientist, Leonid Plyusch, is invited to appear before members of the RL staff in Munich. In the course of his controversial remarks, he mentions the Jewish migration, whereupon an Armenian cyberneticist suggests that Jews are the "entropy of Europe." The Armenian's statement is regarded as another evidence of anti-Semitism on the part of non-Jews on the staff and leads to a recurrence of the bitterness of the previous fall. Some Jewish staff members take legal action against non-Jewish members and there are countersuits.

April   The McGovern subcommittee of the Senate Foreign Relations Committee holds hearings on the FY 1978 budget. During the hearings, BIB staff executive director Walter Roberts spells out a new plan for assuring "accountability and fiduciary responsibility." He suggests that the private board be eliminated and the BIB assume both oversight and managerial functions. Senator Pell responds that if such a bill is introduced, he will support it.

Late April   The Pell amendment is introduced.

May 10   The corporate board urges Congress not to take action until important public policy questions are ironed out.

August   The Pell amendment is defeated by a Senate vote. The opposition is led by Senator Humphrey.

October   RFE/RL charter is amended to grant the BIB chairman *ex officio* status on all corporate committees and a veto on nominating committee choices. This also insures that he will be invited to all RFE/RL board meetings. This seems to ease the tension for the time being.

Under pressure from the BIB and its chairman, John Gronouski, the RFE/RL board votes to move its administrative headquarters from Washington, where they had been relocated in the fall of 1975, to Munich, where the RFE/RL president could take direct command of the operational facility, as well as the administrative office in Washington.

November/
December   RFE/RL staff plan for move of personnel and facilities to the Munich office.

1978

February   Move of most administrative functions to Munich is carried out. Alexander Buchan, executive vice president for European operations, is named acting chief operations officer. Mickelson assumes office as vice chairman and continues in charge of Washington office.

August   Glenn Ferguson assumes presidency and takes up residence in Munich.

1981

January   BIB staff member James Critchlow spends two weeks in Munich doing detailed report on the output of the Russian service of RL. Based on the evidence he is able to obtain, his report is highly critical and condemns the service for not maintaining tight enough policy control. The report is leaked to the press and becomes a *cause célèbre* in Washington.

Relationships between BIB staff and RFE/RL management continue to deteriorate.

February 21   A bomb, estimated in weight between 10 and 25 kilos, causes enormous damage to RFE headquarters building. Suspicion points to East Europeans or the Soviet Union for responsibility. Much of the money that had been budgeted for physical renovation and staff rejuvenation has to be expended on repairs to the building and improving security measures.

The Pell amendment is reintroduced in the Senate, and quickly obtains both subcommittee and committee support, and is passed by the full Senate.

1982

The Pell amendment is passed by the House of Representatives and signed by the president. The RFE/RL board resigns. James Buckley, former senator from New York and counselor of the State Department, assumes the RFE/RL presidency. Ferguson resigns. The BIB staff, under the chairmanship of Frank Shakespeare, takes over management of RFE/RL in addition to oversight.

Appendix

Presidents of Free Europe, Inc., and the Radio Liberty Committee

Free Europe

1949	Allen W. Dulles
1949–51	DeWitt C. Poole
1951–52	C.D. Jackson
1952–53	Adm. H.B. Miller
1953–56	Whitney Shepardson
1956–59	Gen. Willis D. Crittenberger
1959–61	Archibald A. Alexander
1961–67	John Richardson, Jr.
1967–75	William P. Durkee
1975–76	Sig Mickelson

Radio Liberty Committee

1951–52	Eugene Lyons
1952	Adm. Alan G. Kirk
1952–54	Adm. Leslie C. Stevens
1954–75	Howland H. Sargeant
1975–76	Sig Mickelson

RFE/RL, Inc.

1976–78	Sig Mickelson
1978	Alexander Buchan (Acting)
1978–82	Glenn W. Ferguson
1982–	James Buckley

Key Personnel in RFE/RL History

DAVID M. ABSHIRE	Assistant Secretary of State for Congressional Relations during hearings on future of the Radios; first chairman of BIB.
FRANK ALTSCHUL	New York investment banker, original member of Free Europe Board, and first head of RFE division of Free Europe.
EDWARD W. BARRETT	Member of Free Europe Corporation, 1949; member of the board, 1975–76, and RFE/RL board, 1976–82.
TOMAS PINTO BASTO	Member RARET board, 1951 to present.
MANUEL BIVAR	Portuguese broadcasting executive assigned as liaison to Free Europe 1951–74; RFE consultant, 1974 to the present.
THOMAS BRADEN	Director of International Organizations Division of the CIA with responsibility for Free Europe, 1951–54.
JAMES F. BROWN	Director of RFE, 1977 to present; previously, director of research.
GEN. LUCIUS D. CLAY	U.S. commander in Berlin, 1948; chairman, Crusade for Freedom; later, chairman of Free Europe, to 1975.
VICTORIA MONDITSCH DREVING (Vicky Semenova)	Member (since 1952), Russian service of RL.
ALLEN W. DULLES	One of organizers of Free Europe and first president, 1949; director of Central Intelligence, 1953–61.
WILLIAM P. DURKEE	Member of CIA international operations staff with responsibility for overseeing Free Europe, 1951–54; later, director RFE and president Free Europe, 1967–75.
EVDOKIM EVDOKIMOV	Staff member of RFE Bulgarian service; chairman of Munich unit of American Newspaper Guild.
PER FEDERSPIEL	Danish member of the West European Advisory Committee from its founding in 1959.

HARRY FISDELL	Executive vice president, American Newspaper Guild of New York.
LEWIS GALLANTIERE	Long-time policy advisor to Free Europe.
JOSEPH C. GREW	Former ambassador; one of the originators of Free Europe and first chairman of its board.
WILLIAM GRIFFITH	Policy advisor to director of RFE Europe in the 1950s.
JOHN GRONOUSKI	Chairman of BIB, 1977–81.
ALLEN GROVER	Vice president, Time, Inc., and one of the organizers of Amcomlib.
JOHN S. HAYES	Chairman, Radio Liberty committee early 1970s; chairman, RFE/RL, 1976–81.
ERIC HAZELHOFF	European director of RFE, 1957–60.
C. D. JACKSON	President of Free Europe, 1951–52.
GEORGE KENNAN	Policy advisor to secretary of state, 1948–49; proposed creating private citizen group to deal with refugee problem and encouraged creation of Free Europe and Amcomlib.
FOY KOHLER	Director of Voice of America early 1950s; member, BIB, 1974–77.
ROBERT E. LANG	First director of RFE, 1949–53.
ISAAC DON LEVINE	Early director of Amcomlib; worked on behalf of committee trying to organize refugees in Europe.
FRANKLIN A. LINDSAY	Senior officer at OPC assigned responsibility for organizing Amcomlib.
EUGENE LYONS	First president of Amcomlib, 1951–52.
DOUGLAS MANSHIP	Director of RFE/RL, 1975–82; chairman, 1981–82.
ERNESTO MARRERO	Spanish Ministry of Communications executive assigned as liaison to Amcomlib.
GENE MATER	News director of RFE, 1961–65.
VLADIMIR MATUSEVITCH	Staff member of Russian service, Radio Liberty; managing editor, 1974–76.

STEVEN Y. McGIFFERT	Long-time chief engineer for Amcomlib, designed broadcast facilities and supervised construction.
CORD MEYER	CIA officer responsible for overseeing Radio, 1954–71.
JOHN F.B. MITCHELL, JR.	New York attorney who drafted Amcomlib articles of incorporation.
FORREST McCLUNEY	First European manager for RFE, later for RL.
JAN NOWAK	Long-time head of RFE Polish broadcast service, retired 1975.
DeWITT C. POOLE	One of the organizers of the Free Europe Committee; president, 1949–51.
WALTER ROBERTS	Executive director of BIB, 1975 to present.
FRANCIS F. RONALDS, JR.	Long-time RL executive serving as news director, program director, and executive director.
CAPT. TOMAS ROSA	Portuguese military officer assigned to RFE liaison following 1974 revolution.
HOWLAND SARGEANT	President Amcomlib and Radio Liberty Committee, 1954–75.
C. RODNEY SMITH	Director of RFE, 1961–67.
DIRK STIKKER	Chairman of West European Advisory Committee during Fulbright committee hearings.
H. GREGORY THOMAS	One of the organizers of Free Europe Committee, director (to 1975), and successful negotiator for property and broadcast rights in Portugal.
HERMAN VAN ROIJEN	Chairman, West European Advisory Committee, 1973–76.
RALPH WALTER	Free Europe employee from 1951 to 1982 serving as policy advisor, director RFE, and executive vice-president of RFE/RL.

ABBOTT WASHBURN

Director of Crusade for Freedom, 1950–52; member of BIB, 1974–75.

FRANK WISNER

Director of Office of Policy Coordination (1948–50) during founding of both Amcomlib and Free Europe as OPC venture; later, senior CIA officer with line responsibility for Radios.

Index